The
Epistles
Literally

A Literal Translation of the Greek

First Edition

By Edward Kurath

The Epistles Literally

Copyright © 2020 by Edward Kurath
Published by: Divinely Designed
24326 Winder Place, Golden, Colorado 80403
www.divinelydesigned.com

ISBN 978-0-9764551-7-2

First printing April 2020

Printed in the United States of America

Table of Contents

Introduction

Welcome to a fresh look at the Epistles.

There are TWO aspects to our salvation:

1. The one-time event when we made Jesus our Lord. With this we also will go to heaven when we die.

2. The provision of the lifelong, ongoing daily forgiving of our sins, and the resulting transformation into the image of Jesus. When we forgive, God guarantees that He will forgive us (Matthew 6:14).

Most English translations bury the second aspect of our salvation, which is the most important part of Christianity. No other religion has the ability to provide forgiveness of our sins.

In the Epistles, the second aspect appears in 190 verses, whereas the first aspect only appears in 19 verses. Obviously the writers of the Epistles thought that the second aspect is very important.

This is a literal translation of the Greek. You will see that this means the translation is sometimes not smooth English, but accuracy is much more important than ease of reading. If you are interested in knowing what the writers really meant, then this is the translation that will give you the whole truth.

There are 137 verses in the Epistles that are especially important in bringing out the second aspect of salvation. Those verses are listed below.

If you would like more details and commentary on all the Epistles, that is available in my book, "Transformation In The Epistles." If you would like more details and commentary on only the 137 key verses, that is available in my book, "The Whole Truth Will Set You Free."

Introduction

I pray that you will be greatly blessed as you see the whole truth in these highly anointed Epistles.

List of Key Verses:
The verses in bold are especially crucial.

Romans: 5:18, 8:5, 8:6, 8:7, 8:28, 10:10, 10:11, 11:27, **12:2,** 13:9.
1 Corinthians: 3:11, 7:19, 11:32, 12:25, 16:13.
2 Corinthians: 1:9, 1:22, 5:15, **5:17**, 5:18, 6:9.
Galatians: 3:5, 3:11, 3:14, 3:22, 5:14, 5:23, 5:24.
Ephesians: 2:10, 2:16, 3:12, 3:17, 4:20, 4:24, 6:6, 6:17
Philippians: 1:10, 2:3, 2:6, 2:10, 2:11, 2:12, 2:13, 3:9.
Colossians: 1:6, 1:13, 1:14, 2:12, **2:13**, 3:9, 3:10, 3:23.
1 Thessalonians: 2:19, 3:13, 5:23.
2 Thessalonians: 2:16, 3:7.
1 Timothy: 1:6, 6:13, 6:14.
2 Timothy: 1:7, 1:10, **3:16.**
Titus: 1:8.
Hebrews: 1:3, 1:14, 2:3-4, 3:11, 4:3, 4:5, 4:11, 4:14, **6:1-2**, 6:12, 6:18, 8:8, 8:9, 9:8, 9:11, 9:14, 10:9, 10:19, 10:22, 10:26, 10:34, 10:38, 11:6, **12:14-15**, 12:26, 13:7, 13:8, 13:22.
James: 2:13, 4:4, 4:10, 5:8.
1 Peter: 1:15, 1:17, 2:21, 2:24, 2:25, 3:16, 4:7, 4:17, 5:6.
2 Peter: 1:3, 1:4, 1:6, 1:16, 2:21, 3:2.
1 John: 1:6, 2:3, 2:6, 2:17, 2:28, 3:6, 3:7, 3:8, 3:9, 3:10, 3:11, 3:22, 3:23, 3:24, 4:11, 4:16, 4:21, 5:3, 5:4, 5:20.
2 John: 1:4, 1:5, 1:6, 1:7.

Introduction To Romans

Romans was without a doubt written by the Apostle Paul. It is probably the most comprehensive discussion of the Christian faith that was delivered directly to him by Jesus Christ. He did not learn about the faith from other people, and he did not learn it over time. The truth was delivered directly through revelation from the risen Jesus Christ.

> *For I neither received it from man, nor was I taught it, but it came through the revelation of Jesus Christ* (Galatians 1:12).

It would appear that his reason for writing the letter was to give the church in Rome a complete picture of the Christian faith.

At the time he wrote this epistle, he had not yet been to the church in Rome. In his other letters he had previously personally spent time establishing each of those other churches to which the epistle was addressed, so he personally knew they had already been properly taught the principles of the faith. Therefore in those other letters he only had to address specific problems which that particular church was encountering.

Since the miracle of sanctification (the forgiveness of our sins) is the heart of Christianity, in writing a complete picture of the Christian faith to the Romans, one would expect Paul to put a lot of emphasis on sanctification. You will see that he did!

1:1 Paul, a servant of Jesus Christ, called to be an apostle, having been (passive) set apart for the Good News of God,

1:2 which He promised before through His prophets in the Holy Scriptures,

1:3 concerning His Son, the One becoming out of the seed of David according to the flesh,

1:4 the One being decreed (passive) Who was declared to be the Son of God in power, according to the Spirit of holiness, out of the resurrection from the dead, Jesus Christ our Lord,

1:5 through whom we received grace and apostleship, into obedience of faith in all the nations, over His name's sake;

1:6 in whom you all also being (PI), the called ones of Jesus Christ;

1:7 to all who are continuously being in Rome, beloved of God, called saints: grace to you and peace from God our Father and the Lord Jesus Christ.

1:8 First, I am thanking (PI) my God through Jesus Christ over all of you, that your faith is being proclaimed (passive) (PI) in the whole world.

1:9 For God being (PI) my witness, whom I am serving (PI) in my spirit in the Good News of His Son, how unceasingly I am making (PI) mention of you all

1:10 always in my prayers, continuously requesting, if by any means now at last I may be prospered in the will of God to come to you.

1:11 For I am longing (PI) to see you all, that I may impart to you all some spiritual gift, to the end that you all may be established;

1:12 but this is being (PI), to be consoled (passive) in you all, each of us by the other's faith, both yours and mine.

1:13 Now I am not desiring (PI) to have you all to continuously be unaware, brothers, that I often planned to come to you all, and was hindered so far, that I might have some fruit in you all also, even as in the rest of the Gentiles.

1:14 I am being (PI) a debtor both to Greeks and to foreigners, both to the wise and to the foolish.

1:15 So, as much as is in me, I am eager to preach the Good News to you all also, the ones in Rome.

1:16 For I am not being ashamed (PI) of the Good

News of Christ, for it now is being (PI) the power of God into salvation to the one continuously believing; for the Jew first, and also for the Greek.

1:17 For in it is being revealed (PI) (passive) God's righteousness out of faith into faith. As it has been written (passive), "But the righteous shall live out of faith."

1:18 For the wrath of God is being revealed (PI) (passive) from heaven against all ungodliness and unrighteousness of men, continuously suppressing the truth in unrighteousness,

1:19 because that which is known of God being (PI) revealed in them, for God revealed it to them.

1:20 For the things that cannot be seen with the physical eyes of Him since the creation of the world are continuously being clearly seen (passive), being perceived (PI) through the things that are made, that is, His eternal power and divinity; into them to continuously be without excuse.

1:21 Because, knowing God, they didn't glorify (him) as God, neither gave thanks, but were made (passive) vain in their reasoning, and their senseless heart was darkened (passive).

1:22 Continuously professing themselves to continuously be wise, they were made (passive) fools,

1:23 and traded the glory of the incorruptible God in the likeness of an image of corruptible man, and of birds, and four-footed animals, and creeping things.

1:24 Therefore also God gave them up in the lusts of their hearts into uncleanness, to continuously dishonor their bodies in themselves,

1:25 who exchanged the truth of God in a lie, and worshiped and served the creature rather than the Creator, Who is being (PI) blessed forever. Amen.

1:26 For this reason, God gave them up into vile passions. For their women changed the natural function into that which is against nature.

1:27 Likewise also the men, leaving the natural function of the woman, were burned (passive) in their lust toward one another, men continuously doing what is inappropriate with men, and continuously receiving in themselves the due penalty of their error.

1:28 And even as they refused to continuously have God in their knowledge, God gave them up into a reprobate mind, to continuously do those things continuously being not fitting;
1:29 having been filled (passive) with all unrighteousness, sexual immorality, wickedness, covetousness, malice; full of envy, murder, strife, deceit, evil habits, secret slanderers,
1:30 backbiters, hateful to God, insolent, haughty, boastful, inventors of evil things, disobedient to parents,
1:31 without understanding, covenant breakers, without natural affection, unforgiving, unmerciful;
1:32 who, knowing the ordinance of God, that those continuously practicing such things are being (PI) worthy of death, not only are doing (PI) the same, but also are approving (PI) of those continuously practicing them.
2:1 Therefore you all are being (PI) without excuse, O man, the one continuously judging. For in that which you are judging (PI) another, you are condemning (PI) yourself. For the one continuously judging is practicing (PI) the same things.

2:2 and we know that the judgment of God is being (PI) according to truth against those continuously practicing such things.
2:3 But are you thinking (PI) this, O man who is continuously judging those continuously practicing such things, and are continuously doing the same, that you will escape the judgment of God?
2:4 Or are you despising (PI) the riches of His goodness, forbearance, and patience, not continuously knowing that the goodness of God is leading (PI) you to repentance?
2:5 But according to your hardness and unrepentant heart you are treasuring up (PI) to yourself wrath in the day of wrath, and of revelation of the righteous judgment of God;
2.6 who "will pay back to everyone according to their works:"
2:7 Indeed, to those who according to patience of well-doing are seeking (PI) glory, honor, and incorruptibility, eternal life;
2:8 but to those out of self-seeking, and indeed continuously not persuaded to the truth, but are continuously persuaded to unrighteousness, wrath and indignation,

2:9 oppression and anguish, on every soul of man continuously working out evil, both to the Jew first, and also to the Greek.

2:10 But glory, honor, and peace go to every man continuously working good, of the Jew first, and also of the Greek.

2:11 For there is being (PI) no partiality with God.

2:12 For as many as sinned without law will also perish without the (NT) law. As many as have sinned in the (OT) law will be judged (passive) by the (OT) law.

2:13 For it isn't the hearers of the (NT) law who are righteous ones before God, but the doers of the (NT) law will be declared righteous (passive).

2:14 (for when Gentiles not continuously having the (OT) law may be continuously doing by nature the things of the (OT) law, these, continuously not having the (OT) law, are being (PI) a law to themselves,

2:15 any one showing the work of the (NT) law written in their hearts, their conscience continuously testifying of them, and their deliberations among themselves continuously accusing or else continuously excusing

2:16 in the day when God will judge the secrets of men, according to my Good News, through Jesus Christ.

2:17 Behold, you being called (PI) (passive) a Jew, and resting (PI) in the (OT) law, and boasting (PI) in God,

2:18 and knowing (PI) His will, and distinguishing (PI) the things continuously being different, being continuously instructed (passive) out of the (OT) law,

2:19 and are confident that you yourself to continuously be a guide of the blind, a light of the ones in darkness,

2:20 a corrector of the foolish, a teacher of babies, continuously having in the (OT) law the form of knowledge and of the truth.

2:21 You therefore continuously teaching another, are you not teaching (PI) yourself? The one continuously proclaiming that a man is not to be continuously stealing, are you stealing (PI)?

2:22 The one continuously saying a man not to continuously commit adultery, are you committing adultery (PI)? You, the one

continuously abhoring idols, are you robbing (PI) temples?
2:23 You who is boasting (PI) in the (OT) law, through your transgression of the (OT) law are you dishonoring (PI) God?
2:24 For "the name of God is being blasphemed (passive) in the Gentiles because of you all," just as it has been written (passive).
2:25 For circumcision indeed is profiting (PI) , if you may be continuously a doer of the (OT) law, but if you may continuously be a transgressor of the (OT) law, your circumcision has become uncircumcision.
2:26 If therefore the uncircumcised (Gentile) may continuously keep the ordinances of the (OT) law, won't his uncircumcision be accounted (passive) as circumcision?
2:27 And won't the uncircumcision (who) out of (his) natural disposition (is) continuously fulfilling the (OT) law judge you, who by the letter (the (OT) law) and circumcision are a transgressor of the (OT) law?
2:28 For he is not a Jew who is being (PI) one outwardly, neither (is that) circumcision which is apparent in the flesh;

2:29 but (he is) a Jew who continuously is one not in outward appearance (physical circumcision), and circumcision (is that) of the heart, in the spirit not to the letter; whose praise is not out of men, but out of God.
3:1 Then what advantage does the Jew have? Or what is the profit of circumcision?
3:2 Much in every way! For indeed first of all, they were entrusted (passive) with the oracles of God.
3:3 For what if some were without faith? Will their lack of faith nullify the faithfulness of God?
3:4 Let it not begin to be. But let God continuously be true, but every man a liar. As it has been written (passive), "That you might be justified in your words, and might prevail when you continuously come in being judged (passive)."
3:5 And if our unrighteousness is presenting (PI) as worthy of the righteousness of God, what will we say? Is God unrighteous continuously inflicting wrath? I am speaking (PI) like men do.
3:6 May it never be! For then how will God judge the world?

3:7 For if the truth of God in my lie abounded to His glory, why am I also still being judged (passive) (PI) as a sinner?

3:8 Why not (as we being slanderously reported (passive) (PI), and as some are affirming (PI) us to be continuously saying), "We may do evil, that good may come?" Whose judgment is being (PI) just.

3:9 What then? Are we being better (PI) than they? No, in no way. For we previously warned both Jews and Greeks, all to continuously be under sin.

3:10 As it was written (passive), "There is being (PI) no one righteous; no, not one.

3:11 There is existing (PI) no one continuously understanding. There is being (PI) no one continuously seeking God.

3:12 They all turned aside. They together were made unprofitable (passive). There exists (PI) no one continuously doing good. No, there exists (PI) not so much as one."

3:13 "Their throat is a tomb having been opened (passive). With their tongues they defraud." "The poison of vipers is under their lips;"

3:14 "whose mouth is being full (PI) of cursing and bitterness."

3:15 "Their feet are eager to shed blood.

3:16 Destruction and misery are in their ways.

3:17 The way of peace, they haven't known."

3:18 "There is being (PI) no fear of God before their eyes."

3:19 And we know that whatever things the (OT) law is saying (PI), it is speaking (PI) to those in the (OT) law, that every mouth may be closed (passive), and all the world may be brought under the judgment of God.

3:20 Because out of the works of the (OT) law, no flesh will be declared righteous (passive) in His sight. For through the (OT) law (is) the knowledge of sin.

3:21 But now apart from the (OT) law, the righteousness of God has been revealed (passive), continuously being testified (passive) by the (OT) law and the prophets;

3:22 and the righteousness of God (is) through faith of Jesus Christ into all and on all the ones continuously believing. For there is being (PI) no difference,

3:23 for all have sinned, and are having been made to fall

short (passive) (PI) of the glory of God;

3:24 being continuously declared righteous (passive) freely in His grace through the redemption in Christ Jesus;

3:25 whom God set forth to be an atoning sacrifice, through faith in His blood, for a demonstration of His righteousness through the passing over of sins having been done before;

3:26 in God's forbearance to demonstrate His righteousness in this present time; that He is to continuously be just, and the One continuously justifying the ones out of faith of Jesus.

3:27 Where then is the boasting? It is excluded. By what kind of law? Of works? No, but through the (NT) law of faith.

3:28 We are reckoning (PI) therefore a man is to continuously be declared righteous (passive) to faith apart from the works of the (OT) law.

3:29 Or is God the God of Jews only? Isn't He the God of Gentiles also? Yes, of Gentiles also,

3:30 since indeed there is one God Who will declare righteous the circumcised out of faith, and the uncircumcised by means of the faith.

3:31 Are we then nullifying (PI) the (OT) law through faith? May it never be! But we are establishing (PI) the (OT) law.

4:1 What then will we say that Abraham, our forefather according to the flesh to have found?

4:2 For if Abraham was justified (passive) by works, he is having (PI) something to boast about, but not toward God.

4:3 For what is the Scripture saying (PI)? "But Abraham believed God, and it was accounted (passive) to him into righteousness."

4:4 And to him continuously working, the reward is not being counted (PI) as grace, but as something owed.

4:5 And not to the one continuously working, but (to the one) continuously believing on the One continuously declaring righteous the ungodly, his faith is being accounted (PI) into righteousness.

4:6 Even as David also is pronouncing (PI) blessing of the man to whom God is counting (PI) righteousness apart from works,

4:7 "Blessed are they whose iniquities were forgiven (passive), whose sins were covered (passive).

4:8 Blessed is the man to whom the Lord will by no means charge with sin."

4:9 Is this blessing then on the circumcised, or also on the uncircumcised? For we are saying (PI) that the faith was accounted (passive) to Abraham into righteousness.

4:10 How then was it accounted (passive)? Continuously being in circumcision, or in uncircumcision? Not in circumcision, but in uncircumcision.

4:11 And he received the sign of circumcision, a seal of the righteousness of the faith in the uncircumcision, for him to continuously be the father of all the ones continuously believing through uncircumcision into righteousness to also be accounted (passive) to them.

4:12 And he is the father of circumcision to those who not only are of the circumcision, but also to the ones continuously walking in the footprints of faith in the uncircumcision of Abraham, the father of us.

4:13 For the promise to Abraham or to his seed to continuously be heir of the world wasn't through the (OT) law, but through the righteousness of faith.

4:14 For if the heirs (are) the ones of the (OT) law, faith has been and continues to be made void (passive) and the promise has been made (passive) of no effect.

4:15 For the (OT) law is working (PI) wrath, for where there is being (PI) no (OT) law, neither (is there) wrongdoing.

4:16 Because of this it is of faith, that (it may be) according to grace, to the end the promise to continuously be relied upon to all the seed, not only to the one of the (OT) law (the Jews), but also to the one of the faith of Abraham (the Gentiles), who is being (PI) the father of us all.

4:17 As it has been written (passive), "I have made you a father of many nations" in the presence of God whom he believed: the One continuously giving life to the dead, and continuously calling the things that are not continuously being as continuously being.

4:18 Who against hope believed in hope, into him to become the father of many nations, according to that having been spoken (passive), "So will your seed be."

4:19 And not being weakened to faith, he didn't consider his own body, already having been made impotent (passive), (he continuously being about a hundred years old), and the deadness of Sarah's womb.

4:20 Yet, he was not separated from (passive) the promise of God to unbelief, but was made strong (passive) to faith, giving glory to God,

4:21 and being fully persuaded (passive) that what He (God) had promised, He is also being (PI) able to perform.

4:22 And therefore "it was accounted (passive) to him (Abraham) into righteousness."

4:23 Yet it was not written (passive) because of him only that it was accounted (passive) to him,

4:24 but also on account of us, to whom it is being about (PI) to be continuously accounted (passive), to the ones continuously believing on the One rousing Jesus, our Lord, from the dead,

4:25 Who was delivered up on account of our trespasses, and was raised (passive) on account of our justification.

5:1 Being therefore declared righteous (passive) out of faith, we are having (PI) peace toward God through our Lord Jesus Christ;

5:2 through whom also we have access to faith into this grace in which we stood and continue to stand. We are rejoicing (PI) on hope of the glory of God.

5:3 And not only this, but we also are rejoicing (PI) in our sufferings, knowing that suffering is working (PI) perseverance;

5:4 and perseverance, proven character and proven character, hope:

5:5 and hope is not disappointing (PI) us, because the love of God has been poured out (passive) in our hearts through the Holy Spirit being given (passive) to us.

5:6 For while we were continuously still being yet weak, at the appointed time Christ died for the ungodly.

5:7 For one will hardly die for a righteous man, for a virtuous man perhaps someone would even be daring (PI) to die.

5:8 And God is commending (PI) His own love toward us,

that while we were still continuously being sinners, Christ died for the sake of us.

5:9 Much more then, having been declared righteous (passive) in His blood, (been born again) we will be saved (passive) from God's wrath through Him (through the process of sanctification).

5:10 For if, continuously being enemies, being reconciled (passive) to God through the death of His Son, much more, being reconciled (passive), we will be saved (passive) in His life.

5:11 And not only (so), but also we are continuously rejoicing in God through our Lord Jesus Christ, through Whom now we have received the reconciliation.

5:12 Because of this, as sin entered into the world through one man, and through the sin the death; and so death passed through into all men, on all which sinned.

5:13 For until the (OT) law, sin was in the world; but sin is not being charged (PI) (passive), (when) there is continuously not existing a law.

5:14 But the death reigned from Adam until Moses, and upon those not sinning on the likeness of Adam's disobedience, who is being (PI) a pattern of the One being about to continuously come.

5:15 But the free gift isn't like the trespass. For if by the trespass of the one (Adam) the many died, much more (profusely) the grace of God, and the free gift in the grace of the One man, Jesus Christ into the many.

5:16 And the free gift is not as through one man sinning: for indeed the result of judgment came by one to condemnatory judgment, but the free gift out of many trespasses into acquittal.

5:17 For if by the trespass of the one, death reigned through the one; much more will those continuously receiving the abundance of grace and of the free gift of righteousness will reign in life through the One, Jesus Christ.

5:18 So then as through one trespass, all men received condemnatory judgment, thus also through one result of being justified (by God), into all men (came) justification of life.

5:19 For as through the one man's disobedience many were made (passive) sinners, so also through the obedience of the One, many will be made (passive) righteous.

5:20 And the (OT) law came in besides, that the trespass might abound; but where sin abounded, grace abounded more exceedingly;

5:21 that even as sin reigned in death, thus also grace may reign through righteousness into eternal life through Jesus Christ our Lord.

6:1 What shall we say then? Shall we remain in sin that the grace may abound?

6:2 May it never be! We who died to sin, how will we still live in it?

6:3 Or are you all not knowing (PI) that all we who were baptized (passive) into Christ Jesus were baptized (passive) into His death?

6:4 We being buried (passive) therefore with Him through baptism to the death, that just like Christ was raised (passive) out of the dead through the glory of the Father, and thus we also might live our lives in newness of life.

6:5 For if we have become united with Him to the likeness of His death, but now we will also be of His resurrection;

6:6 continuously knowing this, that our old man was crucified (passive) (with Him), that the body of the sin may be done away with (passive), no longer to be continuously enslaving us to the sin.

6:7 For the one who has died has been caused to be declared righteous and thus freed (passive) from sin.

6:8 And if we died with Christ, we are believing (PI) that we will also live with Him;

6:9 knowing that Christ, having been raised (passive) out of the dead, is dying (PI) no more. Death no more is having (PI) dominion over Him!

6:10 For the One Who died, died to sin one time; yet He is living (PI), He is living (PI) to God.

6:11 Thus also be reckoning inwardly (PI) yourselves indeed to continuously be dead to the sin, and continuously living to God in Christ Jesus our Lord.

6:12 Therefore don't be having (PI) sin reign in your mortal body, to continuously obey it in the strong desire of it.

6:13 Neither you all be presenting (PI) your members to the sin as instruments of unrighteousness, but present yourselves to God, as continuously living out of the dead, and your members as instruments of righteousness to God.

6:14 For sin will not have dominion over you all. For you all are not continuously being under (OT) law, but under grace.

6:15 What then? Shall we sin, because we are not being (PI) under (OT) law, but under grace? May it never be!

6:16 Don't you all know that to what (neuter) you all are presenting (PI) yourselves as servants to obedience, servants you all are being (PI) to what (neuter) you all are obeying (PI); whether of sin into death, or of obedience into righteousness?

6:17 But thanks be to God, that, whereas you were bondservants of sin, yet you all obeyed from the heart to that form of teaching to which you all were given (passive).

6:18 And being made free (passive) from sin, you all were enslaved (passive) to righteousness.

6:19 I am speaking (PI) in human terms because of the weakness of your flesh, for even as you all presented your members as servants to uncleanness and to wickedness upon wickedness, so now present your members as servants to righteousness into sanctification.

6:20 For when you all were servants of the sin, you were free in regard to the righteousness.

6:21 What fruit then did you have at that time in the things of which you all are now being ashamed (PI)? For the end of those things (is) death.

6:22 And now, being made free (passive) from the sin, and being enslaved (passive) to God, you all are having (PI) your fruit into sanctification, but the result eternal life.

6:23 For the wages of sin is death, and the free gift of God (is) eternal life in Christ Jesus our Lord.

7:1 Or are you all not knowing (PI), brothers (for I am speaking (PI) to men continuously knowing the (OT) law), that the (OT) law is being lord (PI) over a man for as long as he is living (PI)?

7:2 For the woman that has a husband is bound (passive) by (OT) law to the husband while he is continuously living, but if the husband dies, she is discharged (passive) from the (OT) law of the husband.

7:3 So then if, while the husband is continuously living, she is joined to another man, she would be called an adulteress. But if the husband dies, she is being (PI) free from the (OT) law, so that she is not to continuously be an adulteress, though she is joined to another man.

7:4 So that in the same way, my brothers, you all also were made dead (passive) to the (OT) law through the body of Christ, into you all beginning to become (joined) to a different One, to the One being raised (passive) out of the dead ones, that we may bring forth fruit to God.

7:5 For when we were in the flesh, the sinful passions which were through the (OT) law, worked in our members to bring forth fruit to death.

7:6 But now we have been discharged (passive) from the death of (OT) law in which we were held (passive); accordingly us to continuously be slaves in newness of the spirit, and not in oldness of the letter.

7:7 What shall we say then? Is the (OT) law sin? Never make it so! But I wouldn't have known sin, except through the (OT) law. For I wouldn't have known coveting, unless the (OT) law had said, "You shall not covet."

7:8 But sin, finding occasion through the commandment, produced in me all kinds of strong desire. For apart from the (OT) law, sin is dead.

7:9 But I once lived apart from the (OT) law, but when the commandment came, sin revived, but I died.

7:10 And to me the commandment, which was found (passive) for life, this (I found to be) for death;

7:11 for sin, taking occasion through the commandment, deceived me, and through it killed me.

7:12 Thus the (OT) law indeed is holy, and the commandment holy, and righteous, and good.

7:13 Did then that which is good become death to me? Never make it so! But sin, that it might be made to be appearing (passive) to be sin, by continuously working death to me through the good; that through the commandment sin might become exceeding sinful.

7:14 For we know that the (OT) law is being (PI) spiritual, but I am being (PI) fleshly, having been sold as slave (passive) under sin.

7:15 For what I am doing (PI) I am not understanding (PI). For what I am willing (PI) to do I am not practicing (PI); but that which I am hating (PI), this is what I am doing (PI).

7:16 But if I am doing (PI) what I am not willing (PI) to do, I am agreeing (PI) to the (OT) law (that it is) good.

7:17 But now it is no longer I that is doing (PI) it, but sin which is continuously dwelling in me.

7:18 For I have known and now know this good behavior is not dwelling (PI) in me (this is being (PI) in my flesh). For to continuously be willing is being present (PI) to me; but to continuously be effecting the good I am not finding (PI).

7:19 For not the good behavior which I am willing (PI) I am doing (PI), but this evil which I am not willing (PI) I am practicing (PI).

7:20 But if what I am not willing (PI), that I am doing (PI), it is no more I that am doing (PI) it, but sin continuously dwelling in me.

7:21 Consequently I am finding (PI) (in regard) to the (OT) law, me to be continuously willing to continuously do the good; but for this reason to me the evil is being present (PI).

7:22 For I am delighting (PI) in God's (OT) law according to the inward man,

7:23 but I am seeing (PI) a different law in my members, continuously warring against the law of my conscious mind, and continuously bringing me into captivity to the law of sin continuously being in my members.

7:24 What a wretched man I am! Who will rescue me out of the body of this death?

7:25 I am thanking (PI) God through Jesus Christ, our Lord! Consequently then with the conscious thought, I myself am serving (PI) God's (OT) law, but with the flesh, the law of sin.

8:1 There is therefore now no condemnation to those in Christ Jesus, not continuously living their life according to the flesh, but according to the Spirit.

8:2 For the (NT) law of the Spirit of life in Christ Jesus freed me from the law of sin and of death.

8:3 For the impotence of the (OT) law in which it was weak through the flesh, God, His own Son having sent in the likeness of sinful flesh and on account of sin, condemned sin in the flesh;

8:4 that the just effect of the (OT) law might be fulfilled (passive) in us, the ones not continuously living their lives according to the flesh, but according to the Spirit.

8:5 For the ones continuously being according to the flesh, are being devoted to (PI) the things of the flesh, but the ones (continuously being according to the Spirit, (are being devoted to (PI)) the things of the Spirit.

8:6 For the bent of the flesh (is) death, but the bent of the Spirit (is) life and peace;

8:7 because the bent of the flesh (is) hostile towards God; for it is not being subject (PI) (passive) to God's law, for neither is it being able (PI).

8:8 But those continuously being in the flesh are not being able (PI) to please God.

8:9 But you all are not being (PI) in the flesh but in the Spirit, if it is so that the Spirit of God is dwelling (PI) in you all. But if any man is not having (PI) the Spirit of Christ, this one is not being (PI) of Him.

8:10 But if Christ (is) in you, the body indeed (is) dead because of sin, but the spirit (is) alive through righteousness.

8:11 But if the Spirit of the One raising up Jesus from the dead is dwelling (PI) in you all, the One raising Christ Jesus from the dead will also give life to your mortal bodies through His Spirit continuously dwelling in you all.

8:12 So then, brothers, debtors we are being (PI), not to the flesh, to continuously live according to the flesh.

8:13 For if you all are living (PI) according to the flesh, you all are being about (PI) to continuously die; but if to the Spirit you all are putting to death (PI) the practices of the body, you will live.

8:14 For as many as are being led (PI) (passive) by the Spirit of God, these are being (PI) sons of God.

8:15 For you all didn't receive the spirit of bondage again into fear, but you all received the Spirit of adoption, in which we are crying (PI), "Abba! Father!"

8:16 The Spirit Himself is testifying (PI) with our spirit that we are being (PI) children of God;

8:17 And if children, then heirs; heirs indeed of God, yet joint heirs of Christ; if indeed we are suffering together (PI) with Him, that we may also be glorified (passive) with Him.

8:18 For I am considering (PI) that the sufferings of this present time (are) not worthy (to be compared) with the glory continuously being about to be revealed (passive) into us.

8:19 For the eager expectation of the creation is waiting (PI) for the revealing of the sons of God.

8:20 For the creation was being subjected (passive) to vanity, not of its own will, but because of the One subjecting (it) in hope,

8:21 that also the creation itself will be delivered (passive) from the bondage of corruption into the liberty of the glory of the children of God.

8:22 For we know that the whole creation is groaning (PI) and is travailing (PI) in pain together until now.

8:23 Yet not only so, but ourselves also, continuously having the first fruits of the Spirit, and we ourselves are groaning (PI) in ourselves, continuously waiting for adoption, the redemption of our body.

8:24 For we were saved (passive) in hope, but hope continuously being seen (passive) is not being (PI) hope. For why is anyone hoping (PI) for what he is seeing (PI)?

8:25 But if we are not seeing that which we are hoping for, we are waiting with patience.

8:26 But also in the same way, the Spirit is helping (PI) our weaknesses, for what we should pray according to what is being necessary (PI) we don't know. But the Spirit Itself is making intercession (PI) over us to groanings which can't be expressed in words.

8:27 But the One continuously searching the hearts knows what (is) the result of the mindset of the Spirit, because He is making intercession (PI) for the saints according to God.

8:28 But we know that to the ones continuously loving God all is working together (PI) into good into the ones continuously being called ones according to purpose.

8:29 That whom He foreknew, He also predestined to be having the form of the likeness of His Son, to continuously be into Him, the firstborn in many brethren.

8:30 But whom He predestined, those He also called. And whom He called, those He also declared righteous. And whom He declared righteous, those He also glorified.

8:31 What then shall we say about these things? If God (is) for us, who (is) against us?

8:32 Surely He Who didn't spare His own Son, but delivered Him up for us all, how would He not also with Him grant all things to us?

8:33 Who shall bring a charge against God's chosen ones? God (is) the One continuously declaring righteous.

8:34 Who is the one continuously condemning? It is Christ Who died, but rather, also being raised (passive) (from the dead), Who also is being (PI) in the right hand of God, Who also is making intercession (PI) for the sake of us.

8:35 Who shall separate us from the love of Christ? Oppression, or anguish, or persecution, or famine, or nakedness, or peril, or sword?

8:36 Even as it has been written (passive), "That on account of You we are being killed (PI) (passive) all day long. We were accounted (passive) as sheep of slaughter."

8:37 But, in all these things, we are being more than conquerors through the One loving us.

8:38 For I have been and continue to be persuaded (passive), that neither death, nor life, nor angels, nor principalities, nor powers, nor things being present, nor things continuously being ready to come about,

8:39 nor height, nor depth, nor any other created thing, will be able to separate us from the love of God, in Christ Jesus our Lord.

9:1 I am telling (PI) the truth in Christ. I am not lying (PI), my conscience continuously testifying with me in the Holy Spirit,

9:2 that to me is being (PI) great sorrow and unceasing pain in my heart.

9:3 For I could wish that I myself to continuously be accursed from Christ for my brothers' sake, my relatives according to the flesh,

9:4 who are being (PI) Israelites; whose is the adoption, and the glory, and the covenants, and the giving of the (OT) law, and the service, and the promises;

9:5 of whom are the fathers, and out of whom is Christ as concerning the flesh, the One continuously being over all, God, blessed forever. Amen.

9:6 But it is not as though the word of God has come to nothing. For not all the ones out of Israel, are Israel.

9:7 Neither, because they are being (PI) Abraham's seed, are they all children. But, "In Isaac will your seed be called."

9:8 That is, it is not being (PI) the children of the flesh (natural descendants of Abraham) who are children of God, but the children of the promise He is accounting (PI) as a seed.

9:9 For this is a word of promise, "At the appointed time I will come, and Sarah will have a son."

9:10 Yet not only so, but also Rebecca having conceived by one, by our father Isaac.

9:11 For being not yet born (passive), neither having done anything good or bad, that the purpose of God according to election may continuously stand, not of works, but out of the One continuously calling.

9:12 it was said (passive) to her, "The elder will serve the younger."

9:13 Even as it has been written (passive), "Jacob I loved, but Esau I hated."

9:14 What shall we say then? Is there unrighteousness with God? May this not come to pass!

9:15 For He is saying (PI) to Moses, "I will have mercy on whom ever I may continuously have mercy, and I will have compassion on whom ever I may continuously have compassion."

9:16 So then it is not of the one continuously willing, nor of the one continuously exerting strenuous effort, but of God continuously being merciful.

9:17 For the Scripture is saying (PI) to Pharaoh, "For this very purpose I caused you to be raised up, so that I might show in you my power, and so that My name might be being proclaimed (passive) in all the earth."

9:18 So then, He is having mercy (PI) on whom He is desiring (PI), but He is hardening (PI) whom He is desiring (PI).

9:19 You will say then to me, "Why is He still finding fault (PI)? For who withstands His will?"

9:20 But indeed, O man, who are you being (PI), the one continuously replying against God? The thing formed will not declare to the One forming, "Why did You make me like this?"

9:21 Or is not the potter having (PI) a right over the clay, from the same lump to make one part a vessel for honor, and another for dishonor?

9:22 Namely if God, continuously willing to show His wrath, and to make His power known, endured in much patience vessels of wrath having been made (passive) for destruction,

9:23 and that He might make known the riches of His glory on vessels of mercy, which He prepared beforehand for glory,

9:24 us, whom He also called, not from the Jews only, but also from the Gentiles.

9:25 As He is saying (PI) also in Hosea, "I will call them 'My people,' which were not My people; and her having been 'beloved' (passive), who was not having been beloved (passive)."

9:26 And "It will be that in the place where it was said (passive) to them, 'You are not My people,' There they will be called (passive) 'sons of the continuously living God.'"

9:27 But Isaiah is crying (PI) concerning Israel, "If the number of the children of Israel may continuously be as the sand of the sea, the remnant will be saved (passive);

9:28 For His word He is continuously fulfilling entirely and continuously decreeing in righteousness, that His word having been decreed, will the Lord execute upon the land."

9:29 And as Isaiah has said before, "If the Lord of angelic hosts had not left us a seed, we would have become like Sodom, and would have been made (passive) like Gomorrah."

9:30 What shall we say then? That the Gentiles, not continuously pursuing after righteousness, attained to righteousness, but the righteousness out of faith;

9:31 but Israel, continuously pursuing a (OT) law of righteousness, didn't attain the (NT) law of righteousness.

9:32 Why? Because they didn't seek out of faith, but as out of works of the (OT) law. For they stumbled over the stumbling stone;

9:33 even as it has been written (passive), "Behold, I am laying (PI) in Zion a stumbling stone and a rock of a trap; and every one continuously believing on Him will not be put to shame (passive)."

10:1 Brothers, indeed the desire of my heart and my prayer to God is being (PI) for Israel, that they may be saved.

10:2 For I am testifying (PI) to them that they are having (PI) a zeal for God, but not according to knowledge.

10:3 For continuously being ignorant of God's righteousness, and continuously seeking to establish their own righteousness, they were not being subject (passive) to the righteousness of God.

10:4 For Christ is the fulfillment of the (NT) law into righteousness to everyone continuously believing.

10:5 For Moses is writing (PI) about the righteousness of the (OT) law, "That the one doing them will definitely live in them."

10:6 But the righteousness which is of faith is saying this, "You may not say in your heart, 'Who will ascend into heaven?' (that being (PI), to bring Christ down);

10:7 or, 'Who will descend into the abyss?' (that being (PI), to bring Christ up from the dead.)"

10:8 But what is it saying (PI)? "The word is being (PI) near you, in your mouth, and in your heart;" that being (PI),

the word of faith, which we are preaching (PI):

10:9 that if you may confess in your mouth the Lord Jesus, and may believe in your heart that God raised Him from the dead, you will definitely be saved.

10:10 For to the heart, it is being believed (PI) (passive) into righteousness; but to the mouth it is being confessed (PI) (passive) into salvation.

10:11 For the Scripture is saying (PI), "The one continuously believing on Him will not be put to shame (passive)."

10:12 For there is being (PI) no distinction between Jew and Greek; for the same Lord of all is continuously being rich to all the ones continuously calling Him.

10:13 For every one who may ever call upon the name of the Lord will definitely be saved.

10:14 Then how will they call for aid into Whom they have not believed? But how will they believe of whom they have not heard? But how will they hear apart from one continuously proclaiming?

10:15 But how will they proclaim if they are not sent forth? As it has been written (passive): "How beautiful are the feet of the ones continuously preaching peace, the ones continuously preaching the good things!" 10:16 But not all obeyed the good news. For Isaiah is saying (PI), "Lord, who believed in hearing of us?" 10:17 So faith comes out of hearing, but hearing through the word of God. 10:18 But I am saying (PI), did they not hear? Yes, most certainly, "Their sound went out into all the earth, their words to the ends of the inhabited world." 10:19 But I am asking (PI), didn't Israel know? First Moses is saying (PI), "I will provoke you all to jealousy with that which is no nation, on a nation void of understanding I will make you all angry." 10:20 But Isaiah is being very bold (PI), and saying (PI), "I was found (passive) by those not continuously seeking Me. I was revealed to those not continuously inquiring after Me." 10:21 But as to Israel He is saying (PI), "All day long I stretched out My hands to a people continuously disobeying and continuously opposing." 11:1 Then I am not saying (PI) God cast away His people. May it never be! For I also am being (PI) an Israelite, a descendant of Abraham, of the tribe of Benjamin. 11:2 God didn't cast away His people, whom He foreknew. Or don't you know what the Scripture is saying (PI) in Elijah? As he is pleading (PI) with God against Israel, continuously saying: 11:3 "Lord, they have killed Your prophets, and they have broken down Your altars; and I alone am left (passive), and they are seeking (PI) my life." 11:4 But what is the answer God is saying (PI) to him? "I have reserved for Myself seven thousand men, who have not bowed the knee to Baal." 11:5 Even so then also in this present time a remnant according to the election of grace has come into existence. 11:6 But if by grace, then it is no longer of works; otherwise grace is coming to be (PI) no longer grace. But if it is of works, it is no longer being (PI) grace; otherwise work is no longer being (PI) work. 11:7 What then? That which Israel is seeking (PI) for, this it didn't obtain, but the chosen ones obtained it, but the rest were hardened (passive).

11:8 According as it has been written (passive), "God gave them a spirit of stupor, eyes not to continuously see, and ears not to continuously hear, to this very day."

11:9 And David is saying (PI), "Let (passive) their table be made into a snare and into a cause of destruction, and into a trap, and into a retribution to them.

11:10 Let their eyes be darkened (passive), to not be continuously seeing, and bow down their back always."

11:11 Then I am asking (PI), did they not stumble that they might fall? May it never be! But to their fall salvation (has come) to the Gentiles, to provoke them to jealousy.

11:12 But if their fall (is) the riches of the world, and their loss the riches of the Gentiles; how much more their fullness?

11:13 For I am speaking (PI) to you all, to the Gentiles. In as much as I indeed am being (PI) an apostle to Gentiles, I am glorifying (PI) my ministry;

11:14 if by any means I may provoke to jealousy those who are my flesh, and may save some of them.

11:15 For if the rejection of them (is) the reconciling of the world, what would their acceptance be, if not life from the dead?

11:16 But if the first fruit (is) holy, also the lump. And if the root (is) holy, so are the branches.

11:17 But if some of the branches were broken off (passive), but you, continuously being a wild olive, were grafted in (passive) in them, and you became partaker with them of the root and of the richness of the olive tree;

11:18 don't continuously boast over the branches. But if you are boasting (PI), it is not you who are supporting (PI) the root, but the root (supports) you.

11:19 You will say then, "The branches were broken off (passive), that I might be grafted in."

11:20 True; to (their) unbelief they were broken off (passive), but you stand by your faith. Don't continuously be conceited, but continuously fear;

11:21 for if God didn't spare the natural branches, lest perhaps neither might He spare you (singular).

11:22 See then the goodness and severity of God. Indeed toward the ones falling,

severity; but on you, goodness, if you continue in His goodness; otherwise you also will be cut off (passive).
11:23 But they also, if they don't remain in their unbelief, will be grafted in (passive), for God is being (PI) able to graft them in again.
11:24 For if you were cut out (passive) of that which is by nature a wild olive tree, and were grafted (passive) contrary to nature into a good olive tree, how much more the ones (which are) the natural branches, shall be grafted (passive) into their own olive tree?
11:25 For I am not desiring (PI) you all to continuously be ignorant, brothers, of this mystery, so that you may not continuously be wise in yourselves, that a partial hardening has come to Israel, until the fullness of the Gentiles may come in,
11:26 and thus all Israel will be saved (passive). Even as it has been written (passive), "There will come out of Zion the One continuously rescuing, and He will turn away ungodliness from Jacob.
11:27 And this is My covenant to them, when I may take away their sins."

11:28 Indeed according to the Good News, they are enemies for the sake of you all. But concerning the election, they are beloved because of the fathers (plural).
11:29 For the gifts and the calling of God (are) irrevocable.
11:30 For as you all (Gentiles) also in time past were unbelieving to God, but now were shown mercy (passive) to the wilfull unbelief of these ones (Israel),
11:31 Also thus these (Isreal) now were unbelieving to the piety of you all (Gentiles), that they (Israel) may also receive mercy (passive).
11:32 For God has included together all into unbelief, that He might have mercy on all.
11:33 Oh the depth of the riches both of the wisdom and the knowledge of God! How unsearchable His judgments, and untraceable His ways!
11:34 "For who knew the understanding of the Lord? Or who became His counselor?"
11:35 "Or who has first given to Him, and it will be repaid (passive) to Him again?"
11:36 That out of Him, and through Him, and into Him, (are) all things. To Him be the glory for ever! Amen.

12:1 Therefore I am urging (PI) you all, brothers, through the mercies of God, to present your bodies a continuously living sacrifice, holy, well pleasing to God, which is your reasonable service.

12:2 And you all don't continuously conform yourselves to this world, but you all be continuously being transformed (passive) to the renewing of the mode of thinking of you all, into prove you all to continuously be fit and proper. What (is) the will of God? The good and well-pleasing and completely morally mature.

12:3 For I am saying (PI) through the grace having been given (passive) to me, to every man continuously being in you all, not to continuously think something as being important beyond what is right and proper (PI) to continuously think, but to continuously think soberly, to each as God distributed the measure of faith.

12:4 For even as we are having (PI) many members in one body, but all the members are not having (PI) the same function,

12:5 so we, who are many, we are being (PI) one body in Christ, but individually members one of another.

12:6 But continuously having gifts differing according to the grace having been given (passive) to us, if prophecy, according to the proportion of faith;

12:7 or service, in service; or the one continuously teaching, in the teaching;

12:8 or the one continuously exhorting, in the exhorting; the one continuously giving, in liberality; the one continuously leading, in diligence; the one continuously being merciful, in cheerfulness.

12:9 Love (is) you all continuously abhoring that which is evil, you all continuously clinging to that which is good.

12:10 Love into one another in brotherly love, in mutual respect continuously taking the lead of each other.

12:11 not lagging in diligence; you all continuously being fervent in spirit; you all continuously serving the Lord;

12:12 you all continuously rejoicing in hope; you all continuously enduring in troubles; you all continuously being steadfast in prayer;

12:13 you all continuously contributing to the needs of the saints; you all continuously pressing hard after hospitality.

12:14 You all continuously bless the ones continuously persecuting you all, you all continuously bless and you all continuously do not curse.

12:15 To continuously rejoice with the ones continuously rejoicing. To continuously weep with those continuously weeping.

12:16 You all continuously being of the same opinion toward one another, not continuously being of the high opinion, but continuously being led away to the humble, not continuously coming to be wise of yourselves as the source.

12:17 Continuously rendering no one evil in place of evil. Continuously taking thought (of) the good in the sight of all men.

12:18 If it is possible, as much as it is up to you all, continuously being at peace with all men.

12:19 Not continuously avenging yourselves, beloved, but give place to (God's) wrath. For it has been written (passive), "Vengeance belongs to Me; I will avenge, the Lord is saying (PI)."

12:20 Therefore "If your enemy may be continuously hungry, continuously feed him. If he may continuously be thirsty, continuously give him a drink; for in continuously doing so, you will heap coals of fire on his head."

12:21 Don't be continuously overcome (passive) of the evil, but continuously overcome the evil in the good.

13:1 Let every soul continuously be in subjection to the authorities continuously being higher, for there is being (PI) no authority except from God, and those who continuously exist are being (PI) having been ordained (passive) by God.

13:2 Therefore the one continuously resisting the authority, has withstood the ordinance of God; and those having withstood will receive to themselves judgment.

13:3 For rulers are not being (PI) a terror of the good works, but of the evil. But are you willing (PI) to continuously not fear the authority? Continuously do the good, and you will have praise from the same,

13:4 for he is being (PI) a servant of God to you for good. But if you may continuously do that which is evil, continuously be afraid, for he isn't bearing (PI) the sword in vain; for he is being (PI) a servant of God, an avenger for wrath to the one continuously practicing evil.

13:5 Therefore you need to continuously be in subjection, not only because of the wrath, but also through the conscience.

13:6 For this reason you also are paying (PI) taxes, for they are being (PI) servants of God's service, attending continually on this very thing.

13:7 Give therefore to everyone what you owe: taxes to whom taxes are due; customs to whom customs; respect to whom respect; honor to whom honor.

13:8 Continuously owe no one anything, except to continuously love one another; for the one continuously loving another has fulfilled the (NT) law.

13:9 For the "You will not commit adultery," "You will not murder," "You will not steal," "You will not give false testimony," "You will not covet," and whatever other principle there is, is being summed up (PI) (passive) in the saying, "You will love your neighbor as yourself."

13:10 Love is doing (PI) no evil to the neighbor. Love therefore (is) the fulfillment of the (NT) law.

13:11 And this you all having perceived the time, now is the hour for us to be roused (passive) out of sleep, for now our salvation (is) nearer to us than when we (first) believed.

13:12 The night is far gone, and the day is near. Therefore throw off the works of darkness, and put on the armor of light.

13:13 Live your lives properly, as in the day; not in reveling and drunkenness, not in sexual promiscuity and lustful acts, and not in strife and jealousy.

13:14 But you all put on the Lord Jesus Christ, and of the flesh, continuously be making no provision, into its strong impure desires.

14:1 But you all continuously accept one continuously being weak in faith, not for searching out and pronouncing judgment of their opinions.

14:2 Indeed, one is believing (PI) to eat all (things), but he who is weak is eating (PI) vegetables.

14:3 Don't continuously let him continuously eating despise the one continuously not eating, and don't let the one continuously not eating judge the one continuously eating, for God took him to Himself.

14:4 Who are you being (PI), the one continuously judging another's servant? To his own lord he is standing (PI) or is falling (PI). Yes, he will be made to stand (passive), for God is being (PI) able to make him stand.

14:5 One man is judging (PI) one day as more important. Another is judging (PI) every day (alike). Let each man continuously be fully assured (passive) in his own mind.

14:6 The one continuously observing the day is observing (it) (PI) to the Lord; and the one not continuously observing the day, to the Lord he is not observing (it) (PI). The one continuously eating is eating (PI), to the Lord, for he is thanking (PI) God. And the one not continuously eating, to the Lord he is not eating (PI), and is thanking (PI) God.

14:7 For none of us is living (PI) to himself, and none is dying (PI) to himself.

14:8 For if we may continuously live, we are living (PI) to the Lord. Or if we may be dying, we are dying (PI) to the Lord. If therefore we may continuously live or may continuously die, we are being (PI) the Lord's.

14:9 For to this end Christ died, rose, and lived again, that He might be Lord of both the dead and the continuously living ones.

14:10 But you, why are you judging (PI) your brother? Or you again, why are you despising (PI) your brother? For we will all stand before the judgment seat of Christ.

14:11 For it has been written (passive), "'As I am living (PI),' the Lord is saying (PI), 'to Me every knee will bow. Every tongue will confess to God.'"

14:12 So then each one of us will give account of himself to God.

14:13 Therefore by no means may we continuously judge one another anymore, but judge this rather, no man to continuously put a stumbling block in his brother's way, or an occasion for falling.

14:14 I have known, and have been persuaded (passive) in the Lord Jesus, that nothing (is) unclean of itself; except that to the one continuously considering anything to be unclean, to him it continuously (is) to be unclean.

14:15 But if because of food your brother is being grieved (PI) (passive), you are no longer walking (PI) in love. Don't continuously destroy with your food him for whom Christ died.

14:16 Then don't continuously let your good be slandered (passive),

14:17 for the Kingdom of God is not being (PI) the act of eating and the act of drinking, but righteousness, and peace, and joy in the Holy Spirit.

14:18 For the one continuously serving to Christ in these things (is) well-pleasing to God and men, proved in the furnace of adversity.

14:19 So then, we may continuously pursue the (things) of peace, and the (things) of the building up of one another.

14:20 Don't continuously overthrow God's work for the sake of food. All things indeed (are) clean, however it is evil to the man through (whom) continuously eating (creates a) stumbling block.

14:21 (It is) the good to not eat meat, nor drink wine, nor (do anything) in which your brother is stumbling (PI), or is being caused to be led astray (PI) (passive), or is being weakened (PI).

14:22 Are you having (PI) faith? Continuously have it to yourself in the presence of God. Happy is the one not continuously judging himself in that which he is regarding as fit and proper (PI).

14:23 But the one continuously doubting if ever he eats, he has been condemned and continues to be condemned (passive), because (it is) not out of faith; but whatever is not of faith is being (PI) sin.

Verses 14:24 through 14:26 are not in what is called the Majority Greek Text, so I will not include them here. This brings up the issue of which Greek text is the original one, and that question is beyond the scope of this translation.

15:1 Now we who are strong are owing (PI) to continuously bear the weaknesses of the weak, and not to be continuously pleasing ourselves.

15:2 For each one of us continuously please his neighbor for the good, toward building him up.

15:3 For even Christ didn't please Himself. But, as it has been written (passive), "The reproaches of the ones continuously reproaching You fell on Me."

15:4 For whatever things were written (passive) before were written (passive) for our learning, that through patience and encouragement of the Scriptures we may continuously have hope.

15:5 Now the God of patience and of encouragement grant you all to continuously be of the same opinion in one another according to Christ Jesus,

15:6 that with one accord you all in one mouth may continuously glorify the God and Father of our Lord Jesus Christ.

15:7 Therefore you all continuously receive to yourselves one another, even as Christ also took us to Himself, to the glory of God.

15:8 Now I am saying (PI) Christ to have become a servant of the circumcision for the truth of God, to confirm the promises given of the fathers,

15:9 and the Gentiles to glorify God for His mercy. As it has been written (passive), "Because of this, I will give praise to You in the Gentiles, and to Your name I will sing."

15:10 Again He is saying (PI), "Be gladdened (passive), you Gentiles, with His people."

15:11 And again, "Continuously Praise the Lord, all you Gentiles! And praise Him all the peoples."

15:12 And again, Isaiah is saying (PI), "There will be the root of Jesse, and the One continuously rising to continuously rule the Gentiles; on Him the Gentiles will hope."

15:13 But the God of hope fill all of you of all joy and of peace, to continuously believe toward the purpose (that) you all to continuously superabound in hope, in the power of the Holy Spirit.

15:14 But I myself have also been persuaded (passive) about you all, my brothers, that you yourselves also are being having been filled (passive) of goodness, are being (PI) having been filled (passive) of all knowledge, also continuously being able to continuously admonish one another.

15:15 But I wrote the more boldly to you all, brothers, in part, as continuously reminding you all, because of the grace having been given (passive) to me by God,

15:16 that me to continuously be a minister of Christ Jesus to the Gentiles, continuously serving as a priest of the Good News of God, that the offering up of the Gentiles might come to be acceptable, having been sanctified (passive) in the Holy Spirit.

15:17 I am having (PI), therefore, my boasting in Christ Jesus in things pertaining to God.

15:18 For I will not dare to continuously speak of any things except those of which Christ worked through me, into the obedience of the Gentiles, in word and deed,

15:19 in the power of signs and wonders, in the power of God's Spirit; so that I, from Jerusalem, and around as far as to Illyricum, the Good News of Christ to have supplied fully;

15:20 but, thus continuously aspiring to continuously bring the Good News, not where Christ has been named (passive), that I may not continuously build on another's foundation.

15:21 But, as it has been written (passive), "To whom it was not spoken of (passive) concerning Him, they will see; and (they) who have not heard will understand."

15:22 Therefore also I was hindered (passive) much from to be coming to you all,

15:23 but now, no longer continuously having any place in these regions, but continuously having longing to come to you all from many years,

15:24 If ever I may be continuously going to Spain, I will come to you all. For I am hoping (PI), continuously passing through, to see you all, and to be sent forward by you all, if of you all first I be somewhat filled (passive).

15:25 But now I am going (PI) to Jerusalem, continuously serving the saints.

15:26 For Macedonia and Achaia were well pleased to make some contribution for the poor of the saints in Jerusalem.

15:27 For it has been their good pleasure, and they are being (PI) their debtors. For if the Gentiles participated in their (the Jews') spiritual things, they (the Gentiles) are owing (PI) also to minister to them in fleshly things.

15:28 Then on finishing this, and sealing to them this fruit,

I will go on by way of you all to Spain.

15:29 But I know that, in continuously coming to you all, I will come in the fullness of the blessing of the Good News of Christ.

15:30 Yet I am begging (PI) you all, brothers, through our Lord Jesus Christ, and through the love of the Spirit, to strive together with me in your prayers to God over me,

15:31 that I may be delivered (passive) from the ones continuously being unbelieving in Judea, and that my service into Jerusalem may be becoming well received to the saints;

15:32 that I may come to you all in joy through the will of God, and I will be refreshed together with you all.

15:33 Now the God of peace be with you all. Amen.

16:1 Yet I am commending (PI) to you all Phoebe, our sister, continuously being a servant of the assembly in Cenchreae,

16:2 that you receive her in the Lord, in a way worthy of the saints, and that you assist her in whatever matter she may continuously need from you all, for she herself also has been a helper of many, and of my own self.

16:3 Greet Priscilla and Aquila, my fellow workers in Christ Jesus,

16:4 who for my soul, laid down their own necks; to whom not only I am thanking (PI), but also all the assemblies of the Gentiles.

16:5 Greet the assembly that is in their house. Greet Epaenetus, my beloved, who is being (PI) the first fruits of Achaia to Christ.

16:6 Greet Mary, who labored much for us.

16:7 Greet Andronicus and Junia, my relatives and my fellow prisoners, who are being (PI) notable in the apostles, who also were in Christ before me.

16:8 Greet Amplias, my beloved in the Lord.

16:9 Greet Urbanus, our fellow worker in Christ, and Stachys, my beloved.

16:10 Greet Apelles, the approved in Christ. Greet those who are of the (household) of Aristobulus.

16:11 Greet Herodion, my kinsman. Greet them of the (household) of Narcissus, the ones continuously being in the Lord.

16:12 Greet Tryphaena and Tryphosa, who continuously labor in the Lord. Greet

Persis, the beloved, who labored much in the Lord.

16:13 Greet Rufus, the chosen in the Lord, and his mother and mine.

16:14 Greet Asyncritus, Phlegon, Hermes, Patrobas, Hermas, and the brothers together with them.

16:15 Greet Philologus and Julia, Nereus and his sister, and Olympas, and all the saints together with them.

16:16 Greet one another in a holy kiss. The assemblies of Christ are greeting (PI) you all.

16:17 Now I am begging (PI) you all, brothers, to continuously look out for those who are causing the divisions and occasions of stumbling, contrary to the doctrine which you all learned, are continuously causing, and you all turn away from them.

16:18 For such ones (are) not serving (PI) our Lord, Jesus Christ, but their own belly; and by their smooth and flattering speech, they are deceiving (PI) the hearts of the innocent.

16:19 For your obedience has become known to all. I am rejoicing (PI) therefore over you all. But I am desiring (PI) you all to continuously be wise indeed, into the good, but innocent into the evil.

16:20 And the God of peace will crush Satan under your feet in swiftness. The grace of our Lord Jesus Christ (be) with you all.

16:21 Timothy, my fellow worker, is greeting (PI) you all, as do Lucius, Jason, and Sosipater, my relatives.

16:22 I, Tertius, the one writing the letter, is greeting (PI) you all in the Lord.

16:23 Gaius, my host and host of the whole assembly, is greeting (PI) you all. Erastus, the treasurer of the city, is greeting (PI) you all, as does Quartus, the brother.

16:24 The grace of our Lord Jesus Christ (be) with you all! Amen.

Verses 16:25 through 16:27 are not in the World English Bible because it is based upon a different Greek source document. The Greek for these verses is the "Majority Text."

16:25 Now to the One continuously being able to establish you all according to my gospel, and the preaching of Jesus Christ according to the revelation of the mystery

having been kept secret (passive) in time past,
16:26 but now having been made manifest (passive), and of prophetic writings according to the command of the eternal God having been made known (passive) to obedience of faith to all the nations.

16:27 To the only wise God (be) the glory through Jesus Christ forever. Amen.

Written (passive) to the Romans from Corinth through Phoebe the servant of the church in Cenchrea.

Introduction To 1 Corinthians

This letter was written by the Apostle Paul, and there is little dispute about this. He knew the Corinthians well, because he lived and taught among them for a year and a half, establishing the foundation of their faith. Since he had personally taught them and ministered to them, he knew they were familiar with the "Good News" that Jesus came to take away our sins. He left them in AD 51 to continue his evangelistic journeys.

He heard of practices going on in the church in Corinth that disturbed him, which was the impetus for writing this letter in about AD 55. It is a strongly worded letter, and much of it addresses specific issues, and his advice about them. A bit later, he somewhat regretted the harshness of this letter, and 2 Corinthians is much more conciliatory.

The issue of transformation into the image of Jesus is addressed in the first four chapters. Then he launches into the specific issues with which he is concerned. His discussion of these issues constitutes the middle chapters, from Verse 5:1 through 11:34. This emphasis on behavior is unusual in Paul's writings. We can with confidence assume he was not advocating rule keeping, because he knows full well that trying to keep the law is deadly. See Verse 15:56. In other letters he speaks against trying to keep the law in strong language. Usually his emphasis is on the importance of transformation of a person's character through the sacrifice of Jesus Christ, with their behavior only being addressed as a consequence and result of that transformation.

Therefore, Paul's directions to the Corinthians are a description of their "bad fruit." He wants them to recognize the "bad fruit," but he would never expect them to make changes through will power, as that would be contrary to his theology. In many places in this epistle Paul refers to the "Good News." The "Good News" is that Jesus came to provide the way for our sins to be taken away. This then produces a "good root" which will produce "good fruit," which is the behavior he is advocating.

Chapter 13, which is often referred to as "The Love Chapter," will likely surprise you. That chapter is actually focused on the necessity for us to be transformed into the image of Jesus, and then love is the "good fruit" from that transformation. If the "good root" of Jesus has not implanted God's kind of love in a person, then they will not continuously display the "good fruit" that Paul lists. The presence of God's kind of love in a person is a significant example of the "good fruit" of which he speaks so emphatically in this epistle.

1:1 Paul, called an apostle of Jesus Christ through the will of God, and our brother Sosthenes, 1:2 to the assembly of God, the one continuously being in Corinth, to the ones having been sanctified (passive) in Christ Jesus, called saints, together with all the ones continuously calling on the name of our Lord Jesus Christ in every place, both theirs and ours:

1:3 Grace to you and peace from God our Father and the Lord Jesus Christ.

1:4 I am always being thankful (PI) to my God concerning you all, based upon the grace of God being given (passive) you all in Christ Jesus;

1:5 that in everything you all were enriched (passive) in Him, in all speech and all knowledge;

1:6 even as the testimony of Christ was confirmed (passive) in you all:

1:7 so that you all come not to continuously be made behind (passive) in any gift; continuously waiting for the revelation of our Lord Jesus Christ;

1:8 Who will also confirm you all until the end, blameless in the day of our Lord Jesus Christ.

1:9 God (is) faithful, through whom you all were called (passive) into the fellowship of His Son, Jesus Christ, our Lord.

1:10 But I am begging (PI) you all, brothers, through the name of our Lord, Jesus Christ, that you all may continuously speak the same thing; and that there may continuously be no divisions in you all, but you all may continuously be being perfected (passive) together in the same mind and in the same opinion.

1:11 For it has been reported to me concerning you all, my brothers, by those who are from Chloe's household, that there are being (PI) contentions in you all.

1:12 And I am meaning (PI) this, that each one of you all is saying (PI), "I indeed am being of Paul," "But I am being (PI) of Apollos," "But I of Cephas," but "I of Christ."

1:13 Has Christ been divided (passive)? Paul was not crucified for you all. Or were you all baptized into the name of Paul?

1:14 I am thanking (PI) God that I baptized none of you all, if not Crispus and Gaius,

1:15 so that no one may say that I baptized you into my own name.

1:16 And I also baptized the household of Stephanas; besides, I don't know if I baptized any other.

1:17 For Christ sent me not to continuously baptize, but to continuously preach the Good News--not in wisdom of words, that the cross of Christ may not be made void (passive).

1:18 For the word of the cross indeed is being (PI) foolishness to the ones continuously perishing, but to us, the ones continuously being saved (passive) it is being (PI) to us the power of God.

1:19 For it was written (passive), "I will destroy the wisdom of the wise, and I will make void the comprehension of the intelligent."

1:20 Where is the wise one? Where is the scribe? Where is the reasoner of this world? Hasn't God made foolish the wisdom of this world?

1:21 For in as much as that in the wisdom of God, the world through its wisdom didn't know God, God delighted through the foolishness of the preaching to save the ones continuously believing.

1:22 And inasmuch as Jews are asking (PI) for a sign, and Greeks are seeking (PI) after wisdom,

1:23 but we are preaching (PI) Christ having been crucified (passive); indeed a snare to Jews, and foolishness to Greeks,

1:24 but to the called ones, both Jews and Greeks, Christ (is) the power of God and the wisdom of God.

1:25 That the foolishness of God is being (PI) wiser than (that) of men, and the weakness of God is being (PI) stronger than (the strength) of men.

1:26 For you are seeing (PI) your calling, brothers, that not many people wise according to the flesh, not many people powerful, and not many people noble;

1:27 but God chose the foolish things (plural noun) of the world that He may continuously put to shame the wise people. And God chose the weak things (plural noun) of the world, that He may continuously put to shame the strong things (plural noun);

1:28 and God chose the ignoble things (plural noun) of the world, and the things continuously being despised (passive), and the things continuously not existing, that He may bring to nothing the things continuously existing:

1:29 so that no flesh may boast in the sight of Him.

1:30 But out of Him (genitive), you all are existing (PI) in Christ Jesus, Who was beginning to become to us wisdom from of God (genitive), and also righteousness, and sanctification, and redemption:

1:31 that, according as it was written (passive), "The one continuously boasting, let him continuously boast in the Lord."

2:1 And coming to you all, brothers, I didn't come with excellence of speech or of wisdom, continuously proclaiming to you all the testimony of God.

2:2 For I determined not to know of anything in you all, except Jesus Christ, and Him having been crucified (passive).

2:3 And I became unto you all in weakness, in fear, and in much trembling.

2:4 And my speech and my preaching were not in persuasive words of human wisdom, but in demonstration of the Spirit and of power,

2:5 that your faith may not continuously be in the wisdom of men, but in the power of God.

2:6 But we are speaking (PI) wisdom in the ones completely blameless, but a wisdom not of this world, nor of the rulers of this world, who are continuously being done away with (passive).

2:7 But we are speaking (PI) God's wisdom in a mystery, the (wisdom) that has been hidden (passive), which God foreordained before the ages, into our glory,

2:8 which none of the rulers of this world has known. For had they known it, they wouldn't have ever crucified the Lord of glory.

2:9 But as it was written (passive), "Things which an eye didn't see, and an ear didn't hear, and didn't enter into the heart of man, which God has prepared to the ones continuously loving Him."

2:10 But to us, God revealed (them) through His Spirit. For the Spirit is searching (PI) all, even the depths of God.

2:11 For who of men has perceived the (things) of a man, if not the spirit of the man in him? Thus also, no one knows the (things) of God, if not the Spirit of God.

2:12 But we received, not the spirit of the world, but the Spirit out of God, that we may know the (things) being graciously given to us by God.

2:13 Which (things) also we are speaking (PI), not in taught words of human wisdom, but in words taught of the Holy Spirit, continuously comparing spiritual things to spiritual things.

2:14 But the natural man is not receiving (PI) the (things) of God's Spirit, for it is being (PI) foolishness to him, and he is not being able (PI) to know, that is being discerned (PI) spiritually.

2:15 But the spiritual one indeed is discerning (PI) all (things), but he himself is being judged (PI) (passive) by no one.

2:16 "For who knew the mind of the Lord? Who will instruct Him?" But we are having (PI) the mind of Christ.

3:1 And brothers, I couldn't speak to you all as to spiritual, but as to fleshly, as to babies in Christ.

3:2 I fed you milk, and not solid food; for you weren't yet able. Indeed, not even now are you all being able (PI),

3:3 for you all are still being (PI) fleshly. For where jealousy, strife, and factions (are) in you all, aren't you all being (PI) fleshly, and aren't you all living your lives (PI) in the ways of men?

3:4 For when one may continuously say, "I am being

(PI) of Paul," but another, "I of Apollos," are you all not being (PI) fleshly?

3:5 Who then is Paul being (PI), and who Apollos, but than servants through whom you believed; and to each as the Lord gave?

3:6 I planted. Apollos watered. But God makes it grow up.

3:7 So that neither the one continuously planting is being (PI) anything, nor the one continuously watering, but God continuously making it grow up.

3:8 But the one continuously planting and the one continuously watering are being (PI) one, but each will receive his own reward according to his own labor.

3:9 For we are being God's fellow workers. You all are being (PI) the farm of God, the building of God.

3:10 According to the grace of God being given (passive) to me, as a wise foreman I laid a foundation, but another is building (PI) on it. But let him continuously consider how he is building on it (PI).

3:11 For no one is being able (PI) to lay a foundation besides the one continuously being laid, which is Jesus Christ.

3:12 But if anyone is building (PI) on this foundation gold, silver, costly stones, wood, hay, or stubble;

3:13 the work of each man will be revealed. For the Day shall make it evident, because it is continuously being revealed (PI) (passive) in fire; and the fire will test what sort of work each man's work is being (PI).

3:14 If any man's work is remaining which he built on it, he will receive a reward.

3:15 If any man's work is burned (passive), he will be made to suffer loss (passive), but he himself will be saved (passive), but as through fire.

3:16 Don't you all know that you all are being (PI) the temple of God, and that God's Spirit is living (PI) in you all?

3:17 If anyone is destroying (PI) the temple of God, God will destroy this one; for God's temple is being (PI) holy, which you all are now being (PI).

3:18 Let no one continuously deceive himself. If anyone in you all is thinking (PI) himself to be wise in you all in this world, let him become a fool, that he may become wise.

3:19 For the wisdom of this world is being (PI) foolishness with God. For it has been written (passive), "He is continuously grasping the wise in their craftiness."

3:20 And again, "The Lord is knowing (PI) the reasoning of the wise, that they are being (PI) in vain."

3:21 So that no one continuously boast in men. For all things are being (PI) yours,

3:22 whether Paul, or Apollos, or Cephas, or the world, or life, or death, or things being present, or things continuously coming. All is being (PI) yours,

3:23 and you all are Christ's, and Christ is God's.

4:1 So let a man continuously think of us as servants of Christ, and stewards of the mysteries of God.

4:2 But, moreover, it is required (PI) (passive) in stewards, that any be found (passive) faithful.

4:3 But to me it is being (PI) a very small thing that I may be judged (passive) by you all, or of man night and day. But I am not judging (PI) my own self.

4:4 For I am aware of nothing to myself. Yet I have not been justified (passive) in this, but the One continuously judging (PI) me is being (PI) the Lord.

4:5 Thus you all continuously do not judge anything before the time, until ever the Lord may come, Who also shall bring to light the hidden things of darkness, and reveal the counsels of the hearts. And then the praise from God will come to each.

4:6 But these things, brothers, I have in a figure into myself and Apollos for your sakes, that in us you may learn not above what has been written (passive) to continuously be of an opinion that no one (who is) over one may continuously be puffed up (passive) against the different one.

4:7 For who is making a distinction (PI)? And what are you having (PI) which you didn't receive? But if also you did receive it, why are you boasting (PI) as not receiving it?

4:8 You all are being having been filled (PI) (passive). You all have already become rich. You all have come to reign without us. And I surely wish that you did reign, that we also may reign to you all.

4:9 For, I am thinking (PI) that our God has displayed us, the apostles, last as an exhibit appointed to death, that we were become a spectacle to the world, and to angels, and to men.

4:10 We are fools through Christ, but you all are the wise in Christ. We are weak, but you all are strong. You all have honor, but we have dishonor.

4:11 Even to this present hour we are being hungry (PI), and we may continuously thirst, are being naked (PI), are being beaten (PI) (passive), and are having no certain dwelling place (PI).

4:12 And we are toiling (PI), continuously working to our own hands. Continuously being reviled (passive), we are blessing (PI). Continuously being persecuted, we are enduring (PI).

4:13 Continuously being defamed (passive), we are entreating (PI). We are become as the filth of the world, the scum of all things, until now.

4:14 I am not writing (PI) these things to be continuously shaming you all, but I am admonishing (PI) you all as my beloved children.

4:15 For though you may continuously have ten thousand tutors in Christ, but not many fathers. For in Christ Jesus, I became your father through the Good News.

4:16 I am begging (PI) you all therefore, continuously be becoming imitators of me.

4:17 Because of this I have sent Timothy to you all, who is being (PI) my beloved and faithful in the Lord, who will remind you all of my ways in Christ, even as I am teaching (PI) everywhere in every assembly.

4:18 Now some are being puffed up (passive), as though I were not continuously coming to you all.

4:19 But I will come to you all shortly, if the Lord may be willing. And I will know, not the word of the ones having been puffed up (passive), but the power.

4:20 For the Kingdom of God is not in word, but in power.

4:21 What are you all wanting (PI)? May I come to you all in a rod, or in love and to a spirit of gentleness?

5:1 It is actually being reported (PI) (passive) that there is sexual immorality in you all, and such sexual immorality as is not even being named (PI) (passive) in the Gentiles, that one to continuously have his father's wife.

5:2 You all are being (PI) having been puffed up (passive), and didn't rather mourn, that the one doing this deed might be removed (passive) from among you all.

5:3 For I most certainly, as continuously being absent to body but continuously being present to spirit, have already, as though continuously being present, judged him who has done this thing.

5:4 In the name of our Lord Jesus Christ, you all being gathered together (passive), and of my spirit, with the power of our Lord Jesus Christ,

5:5 to deliver such a one to Satan into the destruction of the flesh, that the spirit may be being saved (passive) in the day of the Lord Jesus.

5:6 Your boasting is not good. Don't you all know that a little yeast is leavening (PI) the whole lump?

5:7 You all then purge out the old yeast, that you all may continuously be a new lump, even as you all are now being (PI) unleavened. For indeed Christ, our Passover, was sacrificed (passive) for the sake of us.

5:8 So that we may continuously keep the feast, not in old yeast, neither in the yeast of malice and wickedness, but in the unleavened bread of sincerity and of truth.

5:9 I wrote to you all in the letter to not continuously keep company with sexual sinners;

5:10 And not entirely meaning with the sexual sinners of this world, or to the covetous, or extortioners, or idolaters; or else you all are obligated (PI) to come out of the world.

5:11 But now I wrote to you all not to continuously associate if ever anyone continuously being named (passive) a brother who may be a sexual sinner, or covetous, or an idolater, or a slanderer, or a drunkard, or an extortioner. Not even to continuously eat with such a person.

5:12 For what to me to continuously judge also the ones not within? Aren't you all judging (PI) those who are within?

5:13 But those who are outside, God judges. And you all put away the wicked man out from yourselves.

6:1 Is any of you all, continuously having a matter toward the neighbor, being bold (PI) to continuously be being judged (passive) on of the unrighteous, and not on of the saints?

6:2 Don't you all know that the saints will judge the world? And if in you all the world is being judged (PI), are you all being (PI) unworthy to judge the smallest matters?

6:3 Don't you all know that we will judge angels? Not surely life's affairs?

6:4 Indeed then, if ever you all may continuously have tribunals pertaining to this life, the ones being contemptible (passive), these you all are seating (PI) in the assembly?

6:5 I am saying (PI) this to move you all toward shame. Is there existing (PI) not even one wise man in you all who will be able to judge between his brothers?

6:6 But brother is being sued (PI) (passive) with brother, and that on unbelievers!

6:7 Therefore it is indeed altogether being (PI) a defect in you all, that you all are having (PI) lawsuits among yourselves. Why not rather be being wronged (PI) (passive)? Why not rather be being defrauded (PI) (passive)?

6:8 But you all are doing wrong (PI), and are defrauding (PI), and these things to brothers.

6:9 Or don't you all know that the unrighteous will not inherit the Kingdom of God? Don't continuously be deceived (passive). Neither the sexually immoral, nor idolaters, nor adulterers, nor male prostitutes, nor homosexuals,

6:10 nor thieves, nor covetous, nor drunkards, nor slanderers, nor extortioners, will inherit the Kingdom of God.

6:11 And these were some of you all, but you all were washed. But you all were sanctified (passive). But you all were justified (passive) in the name of the Lord Jesus, and in the Spirit of our God.

6:12 "All things are being lawful (PI) to me," but not all things are being expedient (PI). "All things are being lawful (PI) to me," but I will not be brought under the power (passive) by anything.

6:13 "Foods to the belly, and the belly to foods," but God will also bring to nothing both it and them. But the body is not to sexual immorality, but to the Lord; and the Lord to the body.

6:14 But God also raised up the Lord, and will also raise us up through His power.

6:15 Don't you all know that your bodies are being (PI) members of Christ? Shall I then be taking away the members of Christ, and may I make them members of a prostitute? May that not begin to become!

6:16 Or don't you all know that the one continuously being joined (passive) to a prostitute is being (PI) one body? For, "The two," he is saying (PI), "will be into one flesh."

6:17 But the one continuously being joined (passive) to the Lord is being (PI) one spirit.

6:18 Continuously flee sexual immorality! "Every sin which ever a man may do is being (PI) outside the body," but the one continuously committing sexual immorality is sinning (PI) into his own body.

6:19 Or don't you all know that your body (is) a temple of the Holy Spirit being (PI) in you all, Which you all are having (PI) from God? You all are not being (PI) of yourselves,

6:20 for you all were bought (passive) of a price. You all therefore by all means glorify God in your body and in your spirit, which is being (PI) of God.

7:1 But concerning the things about which you all wrote to me: it is good for a man not to be continuously touching a woman.

7:2 But, because of sexual immoralities, let each man continuously have his own wife, and let each woman continuously have her own husband.

7:3 Let the husband be continuously rendering to his wife the affection continuously being owed (passive) her, but likewise also the wife to her husband.

7:4 The wife isn't having authority (PI) of her own body, but the husband. But likewise also the husband isn't having authority (PI) of his own body, but the wife.

7:5 Don't continuously deprive one another, unless it is by consent toward a season, that you all may continuously give yourselves to fasting and to prayer, and may continuously be together again, that Satan may not continuously tempt you all because of your want of power to regulate your appetites.

7:6 But this I am saying (PI) by way of concession, not of commandment.

7:7 For I am wishing (PI) all men to continuously be also as me. But each man is having (PI) his own gift out of God, one indeed in this manner, but one indeed in another manner.

7:8 But I am saying (PI) to the unmarried and to the widows, it is being (PI) good to them if they may remain even as I am.

7:9 But if they are not having the ability to be continent (PI), let them marry. For it is being (PI) better to marry than to continuously be burned (passive).

7:10 But to the ones having married, I am commanding (PI)--not I, but the Lord--that the wife not to be separated (passive) from her husband

7:11 (but if she is separated (passive), let her continuously remain unmarried, or to be reconciled (passive) to her husband), and that the husband not to continuously leave his wife.

7:12 But to the rest I am saying (PI)--not the Lord--, if any brother is having (PI) an unbelieving wife, and she is being content (PI) to continuously live with him, let him not continuously leave her.

7:13 The woman who is having (PI) an unbelieving husband, and he is being content (PI) to continuously live with her, let her not continuously leave him.

7:14 For the unbelieving husband has been sanctified (passive) in the wife, and the unbelieving wife has been sanctified (passive) in the husband. Since otherwise your children would be being (PI) unclean, but now are being (PI) holy.

7:15 But if the unbeliever is departing (PI), let them be continuously separated (passive). The brother or the sister has not been enslaved in such cases, but God has called us in peace.

7:16 For how do you know, wife, if you will save your husband? Or how do you know, husband, if you will save your wife?

7:17 If (you will not save your spouse), the Lord has divided to each man, as God has called each, so let him be continuously walking. And thus I am prescribing (PI) in all the assemblies.

7:18 Was anyone called (passive) having been circumcised (passive)? Let him not be becoming uncircumcised. Has anyone been called in uncircumcision? Let him not be being continuously circumcised (passive).

7:19 Circumcision is being (PI) nothing, and uncircumcision is

being (PI) nothing, but the keeping of the precepts of God.
7:20 Let each man continuously stay in the calling in which he was called (passive).
7:21 Were you called (passive) a bondservant? Don't continuously let that bother to you, but if also you are being able (PI) to become free, rather use it.
7:22 For the one being called (passive) in the Lord (being) a bondservant is being (PI) the Lord's free man. Likewise also the one free is being (PI) Christ's bondservant.
7:23 You all were bought (passive) of a price. Don't continuously become bondservants of men.
7:24 Brothers, let each man, in which he was called (passive), continuously stay in this with God.
7:25 But concerning virgins, I am having (PI) no commandment from the Lord, but I am giving (PI) my judgment as one having obtained mercy (passive) by the Lord to continuously be trustworthy.
7:26 I am thinking (PI) then it is good to continuously be ready, because of the distress that is on us, that it is good for a man to continuously be as he now is.
7:27 Have you been bound (passive) to a wife? Don't continuously seek to be freed. Have you been freed (passive) from a wife? Don't continuously seek a wife.
7:28 But if also you may marry, you have not sinned. And if the virgin may marry, she has not sinned. Yet such will have oppression to the flesh, but I am sparing (PI) you all.
7:29 But I am saying (PI) this, brothers: that the time having been wrapped up (passive), from now on is being (PI) that both the ones continuously having wives may continuously be as not continuously having;
7:30 and the ones continuously weeping as not continuously weeping; and the ones continuously rejoicing as not continuously rejoicing; and the ones continuously buying as those not continuously possessing;
7:31 and the ones continuously using this world, as not continuously using it immoderately. For the mode of this world is passing away (PI).
7:32 But I am desiring (PI) to have you all to continuously be free from cares. The unmarried is being concerned (PI) about the things of the Lord, how he will please the Lord;
7:33 but the one marrying is being concerned (PI) about the things of the world, how he will please his wife.
7:34 A difference has been made (passive) between the wife and the virgin. The unmarried is caring (PI) about the things of

the Lord, that she may continuously be holy to body and to spirit. But the one marrying is caring (PI) about the things of the world--how she will please her husband.

7:35 But this I am saying (PI) in respect to continuously being expedient of you all; not that I may ensnare you all, but toward the appropriate, and constant attention to the Lord without distraction.

7:36 But if any man to continuously be behaving inappropriately on his virgin, as is being customary (PI), if she may continuously be past the flower of her age, and if thus it ought (PI) to continuously begin to be, let him continuously do what he is desiring (PI). He is not sinning (PI). Let them be marrying.

7:37 But he who stands steadfast in his heart, continuously having no necessity, but is having (PI) power over his own inclination and has decided in his heart to continuously keep his own virgin, is doing (PI) well.

7:38 So then both the one continuously giving in marriage is doing (PI) well, but the one not continuously giving in marriage is doing (PI) better.

7:39 A wife is bound (passive) to (OT) law during the time her husband is living (PI); but if the husband may be made dead (passive), she is being (PI) free to be married (passive) to whoever she is desiring (PI), only in the Lord.

7:40 But she is being (PI) happier if she may remain (as she is), according to my judgment, and I am thinking (PI) I also am to continuously have God's Spirit.

8:1 But concerning idol sacrifices: We know that we all are having (PI) knowledge. Knowledge is puffing up (PI), but love is building up (PI).

8:2 But if anyone is thinking (PI) to perceive anything, he has not yet known as it is being necessary (PI) to know.

8:3 But if anyone is loving (PI) God, this one has been known by Him.

8:4 Therefore concerning the eating of idol sacrifices, we know that an idol (is) nothing in the world, and that there is no other God if not one.

8:5 For though there are being (PI) things continuously being called (passive) "gods," whether in the heavens or on earth; as there are being (PI) many "gods" and many "lords;"

8:6 yet to us (there is) one God, the Father, of whom (are) all things, and we into Him; and one Lord, Jesus Christ, through Whom (are) all things, and we through Him.

8:7 But the knowledge isn't in all men. But some, to consciousness of the idol until now, are eating (PI) as of an idol sacrifice, and their conscience, continuously

being weak, is being defiled (PI)
(passive).

8:8 But food will not be
commending (PI) us to God. For
neither, if we may eat, we are
abounding (PI); neither if we
may not eat, are we being made
to lack (PI) (passive).

8:9 But continuously be careful
that by no means does this
liberty of yours may become a
stumbling block to the ones
continuously being weak.

8:10 For if a man may see you
the one continuously having
knowledge continuously sitting
in an idol's temple, won't the
conscience of him continuously
being weak, be emboldened
(passive) into to continuously eat
the idol sacrifices?

8:11 And the brother
continuously being weak will
perish on your knowledge,
because of whom Christ died.

8:12 But thus, continuously
sinning into the brothers, and
continuously wounding, their
conscience continuously being
weak, you are sinning (PI) into
Christ.

8:13 Therefore, if food is causing
(PI) my brother to stumble, I
may eat no meat forevermore,
that I may not cause my brother
to stumble.

9:1 Am I not being (PI) an
apostle? Am I not being (PI)
free? Haven't I seen Jesus
Christ, our Lord? Aren't you all
being (PI) my work in the Lord?

9:2 If to others I am not being
(PI) an apostle, but surely I am
being (PI) to you all; for you all
are being (PI) the seal of my
apostleship in the Lord.

9:3 My defense to the ones
continuously examining me is
being (PI) this.

9:4 Are we having (PI) no right
to eat and to drink?

9:5 Are we having (PI) no right
to continuously take along a
sister, a wife, even as the other
apostles, and the brothers of the
Lord, and Cephas?

9:6 Or have only Barnabas and I
not having (PI) a right to not
continuously work?

9:7 Who is being a soldier (PI) to
supply his own rations? Who is
planting (PI) a vineyard, and is
not eating (PI) out of its fruit? Or
who is providing for (PI) a flock,
and out of milk of the flock is
not eating (PI)?

9:8 Am I not speaking (PI) these
things according to the ways of
men? Or is not the (OT) law also
saying (PI) the same thing?

9:9 For it has been written
(passive) in the (OT) law of
Moses, "You shall not muzzle an
ox continuously threshing out the
grain." It is not of the oxen that
is being of interest (PI) to God.

9:10 or for our sake, he assuredly
is saying (PI), "For our sake it
was written (passive) that the one
continuously plowing is owing
(PI) to continuously plow on
hope, and the one continuously

threshing, of hope to continuously partake on hope."

9:11 If we sowed to you all spiritual things, is it a great thing if we reap of you all fleshly things?

9:12 If others are partaking (PI) of this right of you all, not we more? Nevertheless we did not use this right, but we are forbearing (PI) all things, that we may cause no hindrance to the Good News of Christ.

9:13 Don't you all know that those continuously working the sacred things are eating (PI) out of the temple, and the ones continuously attending to the altar are having their portion (PI) to the altar?

9:14 Thus also the Lord ordained to the ones continuously announcing the Good News to continuously live out of the Good News.

9:15 But I used none of these things, I don't write these things that it may be done so in my case; for I would rather to die, than that anyone may make my boasting void.

9:16 For if I may continuously preach the Good News, boast is not being (PI) to me; for necessity is lying heavily (PI) to me; but it is being (PI) woe to me if I may not continuously preach the Good News.

9:17 For if I am doing (PI) this of my own will, I am having (PI) wages. But if not of my own will, I have a stewardship entrusted (passive) (to me).

9:18 What then is being (PI) my wage? That in continuously preaching the Good News, I may present the Good News of Christ without charge, so as not to abuse my authority in the Good News.

9:19 For continuously being free out of all, I brought myself under bondage to all, that I might gain the more.

9:20 And to the Jews I became as a Jew, that I might gain Jews; to those under the (OT) law, as though I were under the (OT) law, that I might gain those who are under the (OT) law;

9:21 to those without (OT) law, as without law (not continuously being without law to God, but under law to Christ), that I might win those without (OT) law.

9:22 To the weak I became as weak, that I might gain the weak. I have become all to all men, that I may by all means save some.

9:23 But I am doing (PI) this for the sake of the Good News, that I may be a joint partaker of it.

9:24 Don't you all know that the ones continuously racing in a stadium, indeed all are racing (PI), but one is getting (PI) the prize? Thus continuously run, that you all may win.

9:25 But every man continuously contending is controlling himself (PI) in all things. Those indeed then may receive a corruptible crown, but we an incorruptible.

9:26 I therefore am running like that, as not uncertainly. I am fighting like that, as not continuously beating the air,

9:27 but I am beating (PI) my body and bringing (PI) it into submission, lest somehow to others preaching, I myself might be rejected.

10:1 But I am not willing (PI) you all to continuously be ignorant, brothers, that our fathers were all under the cloud, and all passed through the sea;

10:2 and were all baptized into Moses in the cloud and in the sea;

10:3 and all ate the same spiritual food;

10:4 and all drank the same spiritual drink. For they drank out of a spiritual Rock continuously following (them), but the Rock was Christ.

10:5 But not in most of them, God was well pleased, for they were overthrown (passive) in the wilderness.

10:6 But these things were our examples, into us not to continuously be lusters after evil things, as they also lusted.

10:7 Neither continuously be idolaters, as some of them. As it has been written (passive), "The people to eat and to drink, and rose up to continuously play."

10:8 Neither may we continuously commit sexual immorality, as some of them committed prostitution, and in one day twenty-three thousand fell.

10:9 Neither may we continuously test the Christ, as some of them tested, and perished by the serpents.

10:10 Neither continuously grumble, as some of them also grumbled, and perished by the destroyer.

10:11 But all these things happened to them as examples, but it was written (passive) toward our admonition, into whom the ends of the ages came.

10:12 So that the one continuously supposing to stand continuously beware that he may not fall.

10:13 No temptation has taken you all if not common to man. But the faithful God, Who will not allow you all to be tempted (passive) above which you all are being able (PI), but will with the temptation also to continuously enable you all of the way of escape to endure it.

10:14 Therefore, my beloved, continuously flee from idolatry.

10:15 I am speaking (PI) as to wise men. You all judge what I am saying (PI).

10:16 The cup of blessing which we are blessing (PI), is it not being (PI) the fellowship of the blood of Christ? Is (PI) the bread which we are breaking (PI), is it not being (PI) the fellowship of the body of Christ?

10:17 That we are being (PI) one bread and one body; for we all are partaking (PI) of the one loaf of bread.

10:18 Continuously consider Israel according to the flesh: are not (PI) the ones continuously eating the sacrifices participants of the altar?

10:19 What am I saying (PI) then? An idol is being (PI) anything, or that an idol sacrifice is being (PI) anything?

10:20 But I say that the things which the Gentiles are sacrificing (PI), they are sacrificing (PI) to demons, not to God, but I am not desiring (PI) that you all to continuously begin to become participants of demons.

10:21 You all are not being able (PI) both to continuously drink the cup of the Lord and the cup of demons. You are not being able (PI) both to continuously partake of the table of the Lord, and of the table of demons.

10:22 Or are we provoking to jealousy (PI) the Lord? We are not continuously being stronger than He!

10:23 "All things are being lawful (PI) for me," but not all things are being profitable (PI). "All things are being lawful (PI) for me," but not all things are building up (PI).

10:24 No one continuously seek of himself, but each one of the other one.

10:25 Everything continuously being sold (passive) in the butcher shop, continuously eat,

continuously asking no question for the sake of conscience,

10:26 for "the earth is the Lord's, and the filling of her."

10:27 But if one of the unbelievers is inviting (PI) you all (to a meal), and you are being inclined (PI) to continuously go, continuously eat whatever is continuously being placed (passive) before you all, continuously asking no questions for the sake of conscience.

10:28 But if anyone may say to you all, "This is being (PI) an idol sacrifice," don't be eating it for the sake of the one talking, and the conscience. For "the earth is the Lord's, the fullness of her."

10:29 But conscience, I am saying (PI), not your own, but the other's. For why is my liberty being judged (PI) (passive) of the other's conscience?

10:30 But if I am partaking (PI) with thankfulness, why am I being denounced (PI) (passive) for that for which I am giving thanks (PI)?

10:31 Whether therefore you are eating (PI), or are drinking (PI), or whatever you are doing (PI), continuously do all into the glory of God.

10:32 Continuously begin to become no occasions for stumbling, and to Jews, and to Greeks, and to the assembly of God;

10:33 even as I also am pleasing (PI) all in all things, not continuously seeking my own benefit, but what is continuously advantageous of the many, that they may be saved (passive).

11:1 Be continuously becoming followers of me, even as I also am of Christ.

11:2 But I am praising (PI) you all, brothers, that you all have remembered me and continue to remember me in all things, and holding firm (PI) the teachings, even as I delivered them to you all.

11:3 But I am desiring (PI) you all to know that the head of every man is being (PI) Christ, but the head of the woman (is) the man, but the head of Christ the God.

11:4 Every man continuously praying or continuously prophesying, continuously having his head down, is dishonoring (PI) his head.

11:5 But every woman continuously praying or continuously prophesying with her head uncovered is dishonoring (PI) her head. For it is being (PI) one and the same thing as to having been shaved (passive).

11:6 For if a woman is not being covered (PI) (passive), let her also be shorn. But if (it is) shameful to the woman to be shorn or to continuously be shaved (passive), let her continuously be covered (passive).

11:7 For a man indeed is being obligated (PI) not to have his head continuously covered (passive), continuously being the image and glory of God, but the woman is being (PI) the glory of the man.

11:8 For man is not being out of woman, but woman out of man;

11:9 for also neither was man created (passive) because of the woman, but woman because of the man.

11:10 For this cause the woman is being obligated (PI) to continuously have authority over her head, because of the angels.

11:11 However, neither is the man independent of the woman, nor the woman independent of the man, in the Lord.

11:12 For as woman out of man, so the man also through a woman; but all out of God.

11:13 You all judge in yourselves. Is it being (PI) continuously appropriate that a woman to continuously pray to God uncovered?

11:14 Or is even nature itself teaching (PI) you all that if a man may continuously have long hair, it is being (PI) dishonoring to him?

11:15 But if a woman may continuously have long hair, it is being (PI) a glory to her, seeing that her hair has been given (passive) to her instead of clothing.

11:16 But if any man is seeming (PI) to continuously be contentious, we are having (PI) no such custom, neither do God's assemblies.

11:17 But continuously declaring this, I am not praising (PI), that you all are coming together (PI) not into the better but into the worse.

11:18 For first of all, of continuously coming together in the assembly, I am hearing (PI) divisions to continuously exist in you all, and I am partly believing (PI) it.

11:19 For heresies must be (PI) in you all, that the approved ones to continuously be revealed in you all.

11:20 Then the continuous coming together of you all on the same place, it is not being (PI) the Lord's supper to be eaten.

11:21 For each one is taking before (PI) another his own supper in to be eating, and one is being hungry (PI), but another is being drunken (PI).

11:22 For aren't you all having (PI) houses to continuously eat and to continuously drink in? Or are you all despising (PI) God's assembly, and putting (PI) them to shame who are not continuously having? What may I tell you all? May I praise you all? In this I am not praising (PI) you all.

11:23 For I received from the Lord that which also I delivered to you all, that the Lord Jesus in the night to which He was betrayed (passive) took bread.

11:24 When giving thanks, He broke it, and said, "Take, eat. This is being (PI) My body, continuously being broken (passive) for you all. Continuously do this into the memory of Me."

11:25 In the same way also the cup, after supper, continuously saying, "This cup is being (PI) the new covenant in My blood. Continuously do this, as often as you may continuously drink, into the memory of Me."

11:26 For as often as you may continuously eat this bread and may continuously drink this cup, you are proclaiming (PI) the Lord's death until of certain circumstances He may come.

11:27 So that whoever may continuously eat this bread or may continuously drink the Lord's cup in a way unworthy of the Lord will be guilty of the body and the blood of the Lord.

11:28 But let a man continuously examine himself, and thus let him continuously eat out of the bread, and continuously drink out of the cup.

11:29 For the one continuously eating and continuously drinking in an unworthy way is eating (PI) and is drinking (PI) judgment to himself, if he is not continuously discerning the Lord's body.

11:30 For this cause many in you all (are) weak and sickly, and a considerable number are being made to sleep (PI) (passive).

11:31 For if we had been continuously discerning ourselves, we wouldn't ever be judged (passive).

11:32 But when we are continuously being judged (passive), we are being instructed (PI) (passive) by the Lord, that we may not be condemned (passive) together with the world.

11:33 Therefore, my brothers, when continuously coming together into to eat, continuously wait for one another.

11:34 But if anyone is being hungry (PI), let him continuously eat in home, that when you all continuously may come together, not into judgment. But the rest I will set in order as ever I may come.

12:1 But concerning of the spiritual things, brothers, I am not wanting (PI) you all to continuously be ignorant.

12:2 You all know that when you all were heathen, you were continuously being led away (passive) toward those mute idols, as ever you all were led (passive).

12:3 Therefore I am making known (PI) to you all that no man continuously speaking in God's Spirit is saying (PI), "Jesus (is) accursed." And no one is being able (PI) to say, "Lord Jesus," if not in the Holy Spirit.

12:4 But there are being (PI) various apportionments of gifts, but the same Spirit.

12:5 There are being (PI) various apportionments of ministry, and the same Lord.

12:6 And there are being (PI) various kinds of workings, but it is being (PI) the same God, the One continuously acting all things in all.

12:7 But to each one is being given (PI) (passive) the manifestation of the Spirit toward continuously benefiting (all).

12:8 For to one indeed is being given (PI) (passive) through the Spirit the word of wisdom, but to another the word of knowledge, according to the same Spirit;

12:9 but to another faith, in the same Spirit; but to another gifts of healings, in the same Spirit;

12:10 but to another workings of powerful deeds; but to another prophecy; but to another discerning of spirits; but to another different kinds of languages; but to another the interpretation of languages.

12:11 But the one and the same Spirit is working (PI) all of these, continuously distributing to each one separately as He is desiring (PI).

12:12 For even as the body is being (PI) one, and is having (PI) many members, but all the members of the body, continuously being many, are being (PI) one body; thus also the Christ.

12:13 For also in one Spirit we were all baptized (passive) into one body, whether Jews or Greeks, whether bond or free; and all are made to imbibe (passive) in one Spirit.

12:14 For also the body is not being (PI) one member, but many.

12:15 If the foot may say, "Seeing that I am not being (PI) the hand, I am being (PI) out of the body," it is not thus being (PI) out of the body.

12:16 And if the ear may say, "Seeing that I am (PI) not being the eye, I am being (PI) out of the body," it is not being (PI) out of the body.

12:17 If the whole body (were) an eye, where (would be) the hearing? If the whole were hearing, where (would be) the smelling?

12:18 But now God has set the members, each one of them, in the body, just as He desired.

12:19 But if they were all one member, where would the body (be)?

12:20 But now indeed many members, but one body.

12:21 But the eye is not being able (PI) to tell the hand, "I am having (PI) no need of you," or again the head to the feet, "I am having (PI) no need of you."

12:22 But, much rather, the members of the body continuously seeming to continuously be inherently weaker, are being (PI) necessary.

12:23 And which we are thinking (PI) to continuously be less honorable of the body, to these we are bestowing (PI) more abundant honor; and our unpresentable parts having (PI) more abundant comeliness;

12:24 but the presentable parts having (PI) no such need. But God composed the body together, giving more abundant honor to the one continuously being made to be inferior (passive),

12:25 that there continuously may be no division in the body, but that the members continuously may have the same care for one another.

12:26 And when one member is suffering (PI), all the members are suffering together with it (PI). Or one member is being honored (PI) (passive), all the members are rejoicing with it (PI).

12:27 But you all are being(PI) the body of Christ, and members, parts out of the whole.

12:28 God also indeed has set some in the assembly: first apostles, second prophets, third teachers, then powers, then gifts of healings, helps, governments, various kinds of languages.

12:29 All are not apostles. All are not prophets. All are not teachers. All are not powerful.

12:30 All are not having (PI) gifts of healings. All are not speaking (PI) with various languages. All are not interpreting (PI).

12:31 But continuously earnestly desire the best gifts. And still, I am showing (PI) to you all a most excellent way.

13:1 If ever I may continuously speak to the languages of men and of angels, but I am not continuously having love, I have become a continuously sounding brass, or a continuously clanging cymbal.

13:2 If I may continuously have prophecy, and may have known all mysteries and all knowledge; and if ever I may continuously have all faith, so as to continuously remove mountains, but I may continuously not have love, I am being (PI) nothing.

13:3 If I may dole out all the things I continuously possess to feed the poor, and if I may give my body to be burned (passive), but may not continuously have love, I am being benefited (PI) (passive) not the least.

13:4 Love is being patient (PI) and is being kind (PI); love is not being envious (PI). Love is not bragging (PI), is not being made proud (PI) (passive),

13:5 is not being inappropriate (PI), is not seeking (PI) its own way, is not being provoked (PI) (passive), is not taking account (PI) (of) evil;

13:6 is not rejoicing (PI) at unrighteousness, but is rejoicing (PI) to the truth;

13:7 bearing (PI) all things, believing (PI) all things, hoping (PI) all things, enduring (PI) all things.

13:8 Love is never failing (PI). But whether prophecies, they will be done away with (passive). Or various languages, they will cease. Or knowledge, it will be done away with (passive).

13:9 For we are knowing (PI) imperfectly, and we are prophesying (PI) imperfectly,

13:10 but when the maturity may come, then the imperfect will be done away with (passive).

13:11 When I was a child, I spoke as a child, I continuously had the mindset of as a child, I reckoned as a child. But when I became a man, I put away childish things.

13:12 For now we are seeing (PI) as by a mirror in an enigma, but then face toward face. Now I am knowing (PI) of part, but then I will know fully, even as I was also fully known (passive).

13:13 But now faith, hope, and love are remaining (PI) --these three. But love (is) the greatest of these.

14:1 Continuously pursue love, but continuously earnestly pursue spiritual gifts, but especially that you all may continuously prophesy.

14:2 For the one continuously speaking to an (unknown) language is speaking (PI) not to men, but to God; for no one is understanding (PI); but to the

Spirit he is speaking (PI) mysteries.

14:3 The one continuously prophesying is speaking (PI) edification, exhortation, and consolation to men.

14:4 The one continuously speaking to an (unknown) language is edifying (PI) himself, but the one continuously prophesying is edifying (PI) the assembly.

14:5 But I am desiring (PI) you all to continuously speak to (unknown) languages, but rather that you all may continuously prophesy. For greater is the one continuously prophesying than the one continuously speaking to unknown languages, unless he may continuously interpret, that the assembly may receive edification.

14:6 But now, brothers, if I may come to you all continuously speaking to (unknown) languages, what would I profit you all, unless I may speak to you all either in revelation, or in knowledge, or in prophesy, or in teaching?

14:7 Likewise, things without souls, continuously giving a voice, whether pipe or harp, if they may not give a distinction to the sounds, how will it be known (passive) the continuously being fluted (passive), or the continuously being harped (passive)?

14:8 For if the trumpet may give an uncertain sound, who will prepare himself unto war?

14:9 Thus also if ever you all may not (be) giving intelligible expression through the tongue, how will it be known (passive) what is continuously being spoken? For you all will be continuously speaking into the air.

14:10 If it may be, there are being (PI) so many kinds of sounds in the world, and none is without meaning,

14:11 then if ever I may not know the import of the sound, I will be a foreigner to the one continuously speaking, and the one continuously speaking a foreigner in the presence of me.

14:12 Thus also you all, since you all are being (PI) zealots of spiritual things, continuously seek that you all may continuously abound toward the building up of the assembly.

14:13 Therefore let the one continuously speaking to an (unknown) language continuously pray that he may continuously interpret.

14:14 For if I may continuously pray to an (unknown) language, my spirit is praying (PI), but my understanding is being (PI) unfruitful.

14:15 What is it being (PI) then? I will pray to the spirit, but I will pray to the understanding also. I will sing to the spirit, but I will sing to the understanding also.

14:16 Otherwise if you may bless to the spirit, how will the one continuously filling the place of the unlearned say the "Amen" on your giving of thanks, seeing he did not know what you are saying (PI)?

14:17 For you most certainly are giving thanks (PI) well, but the other person is not being built up (PI) (passive).

14:18 I am thanking (PI) to my God, I am continuously speaking to (unknown) languages more than all of you all.

14:19 However in the assembly I am desiring (PI) to speak five words by means of my understanding, that I might instruct others also, than ten thousand words in an (unknown) language.

14:20 Brothers, don't continuously be children to the thoughts, yet to evil continuously be babies, but to thoughts continuously be becoming mature.

14:21 In the (OT) law it was written (passive), "That in different languages, and in different lips I will speak to this people. And neither thus will they hear of me, the Lord is saying (PI)."

14:22 So that the (different) languages are being (PI) for a sign, not to the ones continuously believing, but to the unbelieving; but the prophesy is (a sign), not to the unbelieving, but to the ones continuously believing.

14:23 If therefore the whole assembly may be assembled on the same place and all may continuously speak to languages, but unlearned or unbelieving people may come in, won't they say that you all are being crazy (PI)?

14:24 But if all may continuously prophesy, but someone unbelieving or unlearned may come in, he is being reproved (PI) (passive) by all, and he is being judged (PI) (passive) by all.

14:25 And thus the secrets of his heart are beginning to become (PI) apparent. And thus falling on his face he will worship to God, continuously declaring that God is being (PI) in you all indeed.

14:26 Then what is it being (PI), brothers? When you may continuously come together, each one of you all is having (PI) a psalm, is having (PI) a teaching, is having (PI) another language, is having (PI) a revelation, is having (PI) an interpretation. Let all things (be done) toward edification.

14:27 If any man is speaking (PI) to another language, (let it be) according to two, or at the most three, and in part; and let one continuously interpret.

14:28 But if there may continuously be no interpreter, let him continuously keep silent in the assembly, but let him continuously speak to himself, and to God.

14:29 But the prophets, let them continuously speak, two or three, and let the others continuously discern.

14:30 But if (a revelation) may be made (passive) to another continuously sitting by, let the first continuously keep silent.

14:31 For you all are being able (PI) to continuously prophesy one by one, that all may continuously learn, and all may be continuously exhorted (passive).

14:32 And the spirits of the prophets are being subjected (PI) (passive) to the prophets,

14:33 for God is not being (PI) the god of confusion, but of peace. As in all the assemblies of the saints,

14:34 let your wives continuously keep silent in the assemblies, for it has not been permitted (passive) to them to continuously speak; but to continuously be in subjection, even as the (OT) law also is saying (PI).

14:35 But if they are desiring (PI) to learn anything, let them continuously ask their own husbands in home, for it is being (PI) shameful to a woman to continuously speak in the assembly.

14:36 Or was it from you all that the word of God went out? Or did it come into you all only?

14:37 If any man is thinking (PI) himself to continuously be a prophet, or spiritual, let him continuously recognize (the things) which I am writing (PI) to you all, that they are being (PI) the precepts of the Lord.

14:38 But if anyone is being ignorant (PI), let him continuously be ignorant.

14:39 Therefore, brothers, continuously desire earnestly to continuously prophesy, and don't continuously forbid to continuously speak to languages.

14:40 Continuously let all things be done decently and according to order.

15:1 But I am declaring(PI) to you all, brothers, the Good News which I preached to you all, which also you all received, in which you also stand,

15:2 through which also you all are being saved (PI) (passive), if you all are holding firmly (PI) to what word I preached to you all-- unless you all believed in vain.

15:3 For I delivered to you all in the first (things) that which I also received: that Christ died for our sins according to the Scriptures,

15:4 And that He was buried (passive), and that He was raised (passive) to the third day according to the Scriptures,

15:5 and that He was seen (passive) to Cephas, then to the twelve.

15:6 Then He was seen (passive) to over five hundred brothers at once, out of whom the majority are remaining (PI) until now, but some also were put to sleep (passive).

15:7 Then He was seen (passive) to James, then to all the apostles,

15:8 but last of all, as to the child born prematurely, He was seen (passive) to me also.

15:9 For I am being (PI) the least of the apostles, who is not being (PI) worthy to continuously be called (passive) an apostle, because I persecuted the assembly of God.

15:10 But to the grace of God I am being (PI) what I am being (PI), and His grace into me was not become futile, but I worked more than all of them; not I, but the grace of God with me.

15:11 Whether then I or those, thus we are preaching (PI), and thus you all believed.

15:12 But if Christ is being preached (PI) (passive), that He has been raised (passive) out of the dead, how are any in you all saying (PI) that there is being (PI) no resurrection of the dead?

15:13 But if there is being (PI) no resurrection of the dead, neither has Christ been raised (passive).

15:14 But if Christ has not been raised (passive), then our preaching is in vain, also the faith of you all (is in vain).

15:15 But we are being found (PI) (passive) false witnesses of God, because we testified about God that He raised up the Christ, whom He didn't raise up, if it is

so that the dead are not being raised (PI) (passive).

15:16 For if the dead aren't being raised (PI) (passive), neither has Christ been raised (passive).

15:17 But if Christ has not been raised (passive), vain (is) the faith of you all; you all are still being (PI) in your sins.

15:18 Then also the ones being put to sleep (passive) in Christ have perished.

15:19 If only in this life we are (PI) having hope in Christ, we are being (PI) of all men most pitiable.

15:20 But now Christ has been raised (passive) out of the dead. He became the first fruits of those having been put to sleep (passive).

15:21 For since death (came) through man, the resurrection of the dead also came through man.

15:22 For even as in Adam all are dying (PI), so also in Christ all will be made alive (passive).

15:23 But each in his own assigned order: Christ the first fruits, then those who are Christ's in His presence.

15:24 Then the end comes, when He may deliver up the Kingdom to God, and the Father; when He may abolish all rule and all authority and power.

15:25 For it is being necessary (PI) for Him to continuously reign until ever He may put all His enemies under His feet.

15:26 The last enemy being abolished (PI) (passive) is death.

15:27 For, "He subjected all things under His feet." But when He may say, "All things have been subjected (passive)," it is evident that (means) outside of the One subjecting all things to Him.

15:28 But when all things may have been subjected (passive) to the one subjecting to Him, then the Son will also Himself be subjected (passive) to the One subjecting all things to Him, that God may continuously be the all in all.

15:29 Or else what will they do, the ones continuously being baptized (passive) for the sake of the dead? If the dead are not being raised (PI) (passive) at all, why then are they being baptized (PI) (passive) for the sake of the dead?

15:30 Why are we also standing in jeopardy (PI) every hour?

15:31 I am dying (PI) daily. I affirm your boasting which I am having (PI) in Christ Jesus our Lord.

15:32 If I fought with wild animals in Ephesus in respect to man, what benefit to me? If the dead are not being raised (PI) (passive), "May we eat and may we drink, for tomorrow we are dying (PI)."

15:33 Don't continuously be deceived (passive)! "Evil conversations are corrupting (PI) good morals."

15:34 Wake up righteously, and don't continuously sin, for some are having (PI) ignorance of God. I am saying (PI) this toward your shame.

15:35 But someone will say, "How are the dead being raised (PI) (passive)?" but, "With what kind of body are they coming (PI)?"

15:36 You foolish one, (that) which you yourself are sowing (PI) is not being made alive (PI) (passive) if it may not die.

15:37 And which you are sowing, (PI) not the body that shall be coming to be, but you are sowing (PI) a bare grain, maybe of wheat, or of some of the rest.

15:38 But God is giving (PI) a body to him, even as He wills, and to each of the seeds the body of its own.

15:39 Not all flesh is the same flesh, but indeed (there is) flesh of men, but another flesh of animals, but another of fish, but another of birds.

15:40 And celestial bodies, and terrestrial bodies; but the glory of the celestial differs from that of the terrestrial.

15:41 Another glory of the sun, and another glory of the moon, and another glory of the stars; for one star is differing (PI) of another star in glory.

15:42 Thus also the resurrection of the dead. It is being sown (PI) (passive) in corruption; it is being raised (PI) (passive) in incorruption.

15:43 It is being sown (PI) (passive) in dishonor; it is being raised (PI) (passive) in glory. It is being sown (PI) (passive) in weakness; it is being raised (PI) (passive) in power.
15:44 It is being sown (PI) (passive) a natural body; it is being raised (PI) (passive) a spiritual body. There is being (PI) a natural body and there is being (PI) a spiritual body.
15:45 Thus also it was written (passive), "The first man, Adam, became into a continuously living soul." The last Adam (became) into a continuously life-giving spirit.
15:46 But the spiritual isn't first, but the natural, then the spiritual.
15:47 The first earthly man out of the earth. The second man the Lord out of heaven.
15:48 As is the one made of dust, such are those who are also made of dust; and as is the heavenly one, such also the ones heavenly.
15:49 And we bore the image of those made of dust, we will definitely also bear the image of the heavenly.
15:50 But I am saying (PI) this, brothers, that flesh and blood are not being able (PI) to inherit the Kingdom of God; neither corruption is inheriting (PI) incorruption.
15:51 Behold, I am telling you all a mystery. Indeed we will not all be made to sleep (passive), but we definitely will all be changed (passive),

15:52 in a moment, in the twinkling of an eye, in the last trumpet. For the trumpet will sound, and the dead will be raised (passive) incorruptible, and we will be changed (passive).
15:53 For it is being necessary (PI) this corruptible to put on incorruption, and this mortal to put on immortality.
15:54 But when this corruptible may put on incorruption, and this mortal may put on immortality, then the saying having been written (passive) will begin to become: "Death was swallowed up (passive) into victory."
15:55 "Death, where is your sting? Hades, where is your victory?"
15:56 But the sting of death (is) sin, but the power of sin (is) the (OT) law.
15:57 But thanks be to God, the One continuously giving to us the victory through our Lord Jesus Christ.
15:58 So that, my beloved brothers, be continuously becoming steadfast, immovable, always abounding in the work of the Lord, always having been aware that your labor is not being (PI) in vain in the Lord.
16:1 But about the collection into the saints, as I prescribed to the assemblies of Galatia, thus you all do likewise.
16:2 According to the first day of Sabbaths, each one of you all, nearby to himself continuously

lay aside, placing in store for the future, which ever he may continuously have been prospered (passive), that no collections may continuously be made when I may come.

16:3 But when I may arrive, whom if ever you all may approve, through these I will be sending letters to carry your gracious gift into Jerusalem.

16:4 But if it continuously may be appropriate of me to continuously go also, they will go with me.

16:5 But I will come unto you all when I may have passed through Macedonia, for I am passing through (PI) Macedonia.

16:6 But unto you all, perchance I will stay, or also wintering, that you all may send me wherever I may continuously go.

16:7 For I am not wishing (PI) to see you all now in passing through, but I am hoping (PI) to stay some time unto you all, if the Lord may continuously permit.

16:8 But I will stay in Ephesus until Pentecost,

16:9 for a great and effective door has opened to me, and there are many continuously opposing.

16:10 But if Timothy may come, continuously see that he may be unto you all without fear, for he is working (PI) the work of the Lord, as I also do.

16:11 Then no one may despise him. But you all set him forward in peace, that he may come unto me; for I am expecting (PI) him with the brothers.

16:12 But concerning Apollos, the brother, I strongly urged him that he may come to you all with the brothers; and it undoubtedly was not his desire that he may come now; but he will come when he may have an opportunity.

16:13 Continuously watch! Continuously stand firm in the faith! Continuously be courageous! Continuously be made strong (passive)!

16:14 In all your things, continuously begin to become in love.

16:15 But I am begging (PI) you all, brothers (you know the house of Stephanas, that it is being (PI) the first fruits of the Achaia, and that they have set themselves into service to the saints),

16:16 that you all also may continuously be subjected (passive) to such, and to everyone continuously cooperating together with us and continuously toiling.

16:17 But I am rejoicing (PI) on the coming of Stephanas, and Fortunatus, and Achaicus; that the want of you all these (men) supplied.

16:18 For they refreshed my spirit and yours. You all continuously recognize then those who are like that.

16:19 The assemblies of Asia are greeting (PI) you all. Aquila and Priscilla are greeting (PI) you all much in the Lord, together with the assembly that is in their house.

16:20 All the brothers are greeting (PI) you all. Greet one another in a holy kiss.

16:21 This greeting to my hand of Paul.

16:22 If any man is not loving (PI) the Lord Jesus Christ, let him continuously be accursed. Come, Lord!

16:23 The grace of the Lord Jesus Christ (be) with you all.

16:24 My love with all of you in Christ Jesus. Amen.

Was first written (passive) from Philippi unto Corinthians through Stephanas and Fortunatus and Achaicus and Timothy.

Introduction To 2 Corinthians

There is little dispute that 2 Corinthians was written by the Apostle Paul. There are some theologians that question whether Chapters 10-13 were part of the original letter. But it was accepted by the church as being authentic by the mid second century.

It is interesting that as I translated 2 Corinthians, I realized that I was connecting with a real person who lived long ago. It was very touching. In this letter he was very real about his struggles and problems. He is a real person, like us. If you will read this letter with this in mind, I think you will experience the same thing.

This letter was written to the Corinthians a bit after 1 Corinthians. Estimates are about a year and a half later.

This letter is less theological than most of his other letters, which means that there is less teaching about the forgiveness of sins by Jesus (sanctification). It is there, but it is less central. After all, he had previously spent a year and a half with them, teaching them, mentoring them, fellowshipping with them, living with them; so they would already be knowledgeable about how to be sanctified.

Paul recognized that 1 Corinthians was a bit harsh. 2 Corinthians is much more conciliatory, and yet he still does some correcting. One central theme is that there were other people coming into the church who were presenting themselves as apostles who should be followed, but who were not preaching the same Good News as Paul had. Apparently, some of the Corinthians were giving these newcomers more respect and credibility than they were giving to Paul. Paul was setting them straight about his calling and anointing and message.

1:1 Paul, an apostle of Christ Jesus through the will of God, and Timothy our brother, to the assembly of God, the one continuously being in Corinth, with all the saints, the ones continuously being in the whole of Achaia:

1:2 Grace to you all and peace from God our Father and the Lord Jesus Christ.

1:3 Blessed (be) the God and Father of our Lord Jesus Christ, the Father of mercies and God of all comfort;

1:4 the One continuously comforting us upon all our affliction, toward to continuously enable us to continuously comfort those in all affliction, through the comfort which we ourselves are being comforted (PI) (passive) by God.

1:5 Seeing that as the sufferings of Christ are superabounding (PI) into us, our comfort also is superabounding (PI) through Christ.

1:6 But if we are being afflicted (PI) (passive) over the comfort of you all, and salvation continuously working in endurance of the same sufferings which we also are suffering (PI).

1:7 Whether we are being comforted (PI) for the sake of the comfort of you all, and salvation, also our hope is confirmed because of you all, us being aware that even as you all are (PI) of the suffering, thus also of the comfort.

1:8 For we are not desiring (PI) to have you all continuously uninformed, brothers, concerning our affliction beginning to be to us in Asia, that we were weighed down (passive) exceedingly, beyond our power, so that to be despaired (passive) and to continuously live.

1:9 But we have had the sentence of death within ourselves, that we continuously may not be having trust on ourselves, but upon God the One continuously rousing the dead,

1:10 Who delivered us out of so great a death, and rescuing (PI) us, toward whom we have set our hope that He will also still deliver us;

1:11 you all also continuously helping together on our behalf to the supplication; that out of many persons, the gracious gift toward us, through many He may be thanked (passive) for the sake of us.

1:12 For our boasting is being (PI) this: the testimony of our conscience, that in purity and sincerity of God, not in fleshly wisdom but in the grace of God we were turned upside down (passive) in the world, but more superabundantly toward you all.

1:13 For we are writing (PI) no other things to you all, but what you all are reading (PI) or also acknowledging (PI), but I am hoping (PI) that even you all will acknowledge to the end;

1:14 as also you all acknowledged us in part, that we are (PI) boasting of you all, even as you all also of us, in the day of our Lord Jesus.

1:15 And to this confidence, I was determined to come first unto you all, that you all may continuously have a second grace;

1:16 and through you all to pass into Macedonia, and again from Macedonia to come unto you all, and to be sent forward (passive) by you into Judea.

1:17 This I therefore was thus continuously determining with myself, did I then use lightness? Or the things I am determining within myself (PI), am I determining within myself (PI) according to the flesh, that it continuously may be with me the "Yes, yes" and the "No, no?"

1:18 But as God is faithful, that our word toward you all was not "Yes and no."

1:19 For the Son of God, Jesus Christ, Who being preached (passive) among you all through us, through me, and Silvanus, and Timothy, was not "Yes and no," but has become in Him "Yes."

1:20 For how great (are the) promises of God, in Him the "Yes." Also in Him is the "Amen," to God unto glory through us.

1:21 But the One continuously establishing us with you all into Christ, and God, the One anointing us;

1:22 the One also sealing us, and giving us the down payment of the Spirit in our hearts.

1:23 But I am calling upon (PI) God, the witness over my soul, that I didn't come into Corinth continuously sparing you all,

1:24 Not that we are being lord (PI) of your faith, but we are being (PI) fellow workers of you all, of your joy. For you all stand firm to faith.

2:1 But I determined this to myself, not to come unto you all again in sorrow.

2:2 For if I am making you all sorry (PI), and who is (PI) the one continuously gladdening me if not the one continuously being sorrowed (passive) by means of me?

2.3 And I wrote this very thing to you all, that I may not continuously be having sorrow coming from whom I ought to continuously be rejoicing; having confidence toward you all, that the joy to me being (PI) of all of you.

2:4 For out of much affliction and anguish of heart I wrote to you all through many tears, not that you all may be made sorry (passive), but that you may know the love that I am having (PI) so abundantly into you all.

2:5 But if any (one) has caused sorrow, he has not made me sorry, but to some degree (that I may not continuously press too heavily) you all.

2:6 Sufficient this punishment to such (a one) by the many;

2:7 so that on the contrary you all rather to forgive him and to comfort him, lest by any means such (a one) should be swallowed up (passive) to excessive sorrow.

2:8 Therefore I am begging (PI) you all to confirm love toward him.

2:9 For toward this I also wrote, that I may know the proof of you all, if into all (things) you all are being (PI) obedient.

2:10 But to whom you all are forgiving (PI) anything, I also. For if I have forgiven anything, to whom I have forgiven because of you all in the presence of Christ,

2:11 that we may not be being taken advantage of (passive) by Satan; for we are not being ignorant (PI) of his schemes.

2:12 Now on coming into Troas unto the Good News of Christ, and of a door having been opened (passive) to me in the Lord,

2:13 I had no relief to my spirit, to not find Titus, my brother, but taking my leave to them, I went out into Macedonia.

2:14 But thanks be to God, the One always continuously giving us triumph in Christ, and continuously revealing through us the sweet aroma of the knowledge of Him in every place.

2:15 That we are being (PI) a sweet aroma of Christ to God, in the ones continuously being saved (passive), and in the ones continuously perishing.

2:16 Indeed, to the one a stench of death into death; but to the other a sweet aroma of life into life. And who is sufficient unto these (things)?

2:17 For we are being (PI) not as so many, continuously peddling the word of God. But as out of sincerity, but as out of God, in the sight of God, we are speaking (PI) in Christ.

3:1 Are we beginning (PI) again to continuously commend ourselves? Or are we not needing (PI), as some, letters of commendation unto you all or out of you all letters of commendation?

3:2 You all are being (PI) our letter, having been written (passive) in our hearts, continuously being known (passive) and continuously being read (passive) by all men;

3:3 continuously being revealed (passive) that you all are being (PI) a letter of Christ, being served (passive) by us, having been inscribed not to ink, but to the Spirit of the continuously living God; not in tablets of stone, but in tablets that are hearts of flesh.

3:4 But such confidence we are having (PI) through Christ unto God;

3:5 not that we are being (PI) sufficient from ourselves as the source, to account anything as out of ourselves; but our sufficiency (is) out of God;

3:6 Who also made us sufficient servants of a new covenant; not of the letter, but of the Spirit. For the letter is killing (PI), but the Spirit is giving life (PI).

3:7 But if the service of death, in letters having been engraved (passive) in stones, came to be in glory, so that the sons of Israel not to continuously have power to look steadfastly into the face of Moses because of the glory of his face; the one continuously being made to be done away (passive):

3:8 how shall not rather the ministry of the Spirit shall be in glory?

3:9 For if the ministry of condemnation (has) glory, much rather the ministry of righteousness is exceeding (PI) in glory.

3:10 For also the (ministry) having been glorified (passive) had not yet been glorified in this respect, on account of the continuously exceeding of glory.

3:11 For if that continuously having been done away with (passive) (is) of glory, rather to much (more) that continuously remaining (is) in glory.

3:12 Continuously having therefore such a hope, we are using (PI) great boldness,

3:13 and not even as Moses, who put a veil on his face toward the sons of Israel to not look steadfastly on the end of (that) continuously being done away with (passive).

3:14 But their minds were hardened (passive), for until the day on the reading of the old covenant the same veil is remaining (PI), not continuously being uncovered, which in Christ is being done away with (PI) (passive).

3:15 But to this day, if ever Moses is being read (PI) (passive), a veil is now lying (PI) on their heart.

3:16 But whenever one may turn back toward the Lord, the veil is now being taken away (PI) (passive).

3:17 But the Lord is being (PI) the Spirit, and also where the Spirit of the Lord (is), freedom (is) there.

3:18 But we all, having our face unveiled (passive), continuously mirroring the glory of the Lord, are being transformed (PI) (passive) into the same image from glory into glory, even as of the Spirit of the Lord.

4:1 Because of this, we are continuously having this ministry, even as we were shown mercy (passive), we are not being despondent (PI).

4:2 But we have renounced the hidden things of shame, not continuously walking in craftiness, nor continuously handling the word of God deceitfully; but to the manifestation of the truth continuously commending ourselves toward every man's conscience in the sight of God.
4:3 But if also our Good News is having been covered (passive), it is now (PI) having been covered (passive) in the ones continuously perishing;
4:4 in whom the god of this world blinded the understanding of the unbelieving, in order to not shine to them the illumination of the Good News of the glory of Christ, Who is being (PI) the image of God.
4:5 For we are not preaching (PI) ourselves, but Christ Jesus the Lord, also ourselves your servants through Jesus;
4:6 that God, the One having said "To shine light out of darkness," Who has shone in our hearts, for the purpose of illumination of the knowledge of the glory of God in the face of Jesus Christ.
4:7 But we are having (PI) this treasure in clay vessels, that the exceeding greatness of the power may continuously be of God, and not out of us.
4:8 Continuously being afflicted (passive) in all, but not continuously being crushed (passive); continuously being perplexed (passive), but not continuously despairing;
4:9 continuously being pursued (passive), but not continuously being forsaken (passive); continuously being cast down (passive), but not continuously perishing;
4:10 always continuously carrying in the body the putting to death of the Lord Jesus, that the life of Jesus may also be revealed (passive) in our body.
4:11 For ever we, the ones continuously living are being given up (PI) (passive) into death through Jesus, that the life also of Jesus may be revealed (passive) in our mortal flesh.
4:12 So then indeed death is now working (PI) in us, but life in you all.
4:13 But we, continuously having the same spirit of faith, according to that which was having been written (passive), "I believed, therefore I spoke." We also are believing (PI), and therefore also we are speaking (PI);
4:14 knowing that the One raising the Lord Jesus will also raise us through Jesus, and will definitely present us with you all.
4:15 For all (things are) because of you all, that the grace, being more than enough through the many, the thanksgiving may abound richly into the glory of God.
4:16 Therefore we are not being despondent (PI), but even if our

outward man is now being decayed (PI) (passive), but our inward man is now being renewed (PI) (passive) day by day.

4:17 For our momentary light affliction, is producing (PI) to us exceedingly into the highest possible degree an eternal weight of glory;

4:18 while we are not continuously contemplating the (things) continuously being seen (passive), but the (things) not continuously being seen (passive). For the (things) continuously being seen (passive) are temporary, but the (things) continuously not being seen (passive) are eternal.

5:1 For we know that if the earthly house of our tent may be dissolved (passive), we are having (PI) a building out of God, a house not made with hands, eternal, in the heavens.

5:2 For also in this we are groaning (PI), continuously longing to be clothed (with) our habitation out of heaven

5:3 if indeed also being clothed we will not be found (passive) naked.

5:4 For indeed we continuously being in this tent are groaning (PI), continuously being burdened (passive); on which we are not willing (PI) to be unclothed, but to be clothed, that the mortal may be swallowed up (passive) by life.

5:5 But God (is) the One making us into this very thing, also giving to us the down payment of the Spirit.

5:6 Always continuously having confidence and knowing that continuously being at home in the body, we are being absent (PI) from the Lord;

5:7 for we are walking (PI) through faith, not through sight.

5:8 But we are being courageous, (PI) and we are being well-pleased (PI) rather to be absent out of the body, and to be at home unto the Lord.

5:9 Therefore also we are making it our aim (PI), whether continuously being at home or continuously being absent, to continuously be well pleasing to Him.

5:10 For it is being necessary (PI) that we all be revealed (passive) before the judgment seat of Christ; that each one may receive through the body, in reference to which he has done, whether good or evil.

5:11 Knowing therefore the fear of the Lord, we are persuading (PI) men, but we are made manifest (passive) to God; but I also am hoping (PI) to have been made manifest (passive) in your consciences.

5:12 For we are not commending (PI) ourselves to you again, but continuously giving to you all opportunity of boast on account of us, that you all may continuously have toward the

ones continuously boasting in appearance, and not to heart.
5:13 For if we were beside ourselves to God, we are being sober minded (PI) to you all.
5:14 For the love of Christ is constraining (PI) us; because judging this, that One died for all, therefore all died.
5:15 And He died for all, that the ones continuously living no longer may continuously live to themselves, but to Him dying for their sakes and being raised (passive).
5:16 So that we know no one according to the flesh. But if even we have known Christ according to flesh, but now we are knowing (PI) Him no more.
5:17 So that if any new creation in Christ, the old passed away. Lo and behold, the all new has begun to be.
5:18 But all out of God, the One reconciling us to Himself through Jesus Christ, and giving to us the ministry of reconciliation;
5:19 how that God was in Christ continuously reconciling the world to Himself, not continuously imputing to them their trespasses, and committing in us the word of reconciliation.
5:20 We are then being ambassadors (PI) on behalf of Christ, as of God continuously entreating through us: we are begging (PI) you all on behalf of Christ, be reconciled (passive) to God.

5:21 For the One knowing no sin He made sin on our behalf; so that in Him we may continuously become the righteousness of God.
6:1 But continuously working together, we are entreating (PI) you all not to receive the grace of God into empty hands,
6:2 for He is saying (PI), "To an acceptable time I listened to you, and in a day of salvation I helped you." Lo and behold, now the acceptable time. Lo and behold, now the day of salvation.
6:3 Continuously giving no occasion to stumble in anything, that the ministry may not be blamed (passive),
6:4 but in everything continuously commending ourselves, as servants of God, in great endurance, in afflictions, in hardships, in distresses,
6:5 in beatings, in imprisonments, in riots, in labors, in watchings, in fastings;
6:6 in pureness, in knowledge, in patience, in kindness, in the Holy Spirit, in sincere love,
6:7 in the word of truth, in the power of God; through the implements of righteousness of the right hand and of the left,
6:8 through glory and dishonor, through evil report and good report; as deceivers, and true;
6:9 continuously being unknown (passive), and continuously being well known (passive); as continuously dying, and lo and behold, we are living (PI); as

continuously being disciplined (passive), and not continuously being killed (passive);

6:10 continuously being sorrowed (passive), yet always continuously rejoicing; as poor, yet continuously enriching many; as continuously having nothing, and continuously possessing all.

6:11 Our mouth has been open to you all, Corinthians. Our heart has been enlarged (passive).

6:12 You all are not restricted (PI) (passive) in expressing yourselves in us, but you all are restricted (PI) (passive) in your own inward affections.

6:13 But the same recompense I am speaking (PI) as to my children, you all also be delivered from straits (passive).

6:14 Don't continuously begin to become continuously being unequally yoked to unbelievers, for what fellowship to righteousness and iniquity? Or what fellowship to light with respect to darkness?

6:15 But what agreement to Christ toward Belial? Or what portion to a believer with an unbeliever?

6:16 But what agreement to a temple of God with idols? For you all continuously are a temple of the living God. Even as God said that "I will dwell in them; and I will live among them, and I will be their God, and they will be people to Me."

6:17 Therefore, "'Come out of the midst of them, and be being separated (passive),' the Lord is saying (PI). 'Continuously touch no unclean thing. And I will receive you all.

6:18 And I will be to you all into Father. And you all will be to me into sons and daughters,' the Lord Almighty is saying (PI)."

7:1 Continuously having therefore these promises, beloved, we may cleanse ourselves from all defilement of flesh and spirit, continuously perfecting holiness in the fear of God.

7:2 Receive us. We wronged no one. We corrupted no one. We took advantage of no one.

7:3 I am saying (PI) this not toward condemnation, for I have said before, that you all are being (PI) in our hearts into die together and to continuously live together.

7:4 Great boldness to me toward you all. Great boasting to me over you all. I have been filled (passive) to comfort. I am overflowing (PI) to joy on all our affliction.

7:5 For even of coming of us into Macedonia, our flesh had no relief, but being continuously afflicted (passive) in everything. Outside, fightings. Inside, fears.

7:6 Nevertheless God, the One continuously comforting the lowly, God comforted us in the coming of Titus;

7:7 But not only in his coming, but also in the comfort to which he was comforted (passive) over you all, continuously telling us of your longing, your mourning, and your zeal for me; so that I to rejoice more.

7:8 That if I ever made you all sorry in my letter, I am not regretting (PI) it, if even I did regret it. For I am seeing (PI) that my letter made you sorry, that if even for a while.

7:9 I am now rejoicing (PI), not that you were made sorry (passive), but that you were made sorry (passive) into repentance. For you were made sorry (passive) according to God, that you might suffer loss (passive) out of us in nothing.

7:10 For the sorrow according to God to repentance into salvation, is producing (PI) no regret. But the sorrow of the world is producing (PI) death.

7:11 For lo and behold, this same thing, you all to be made angry (passive) according to God, how much it produces to you all diligence, but indignation, but fear, but longing, but zeal, but execution of right! In everything you all demonstrated yourselves to continuously be pure in the matter.

7:12 If consequently I even wrote to you all, not on account of the one doing the hurting, neither on account of the one being hurt (passive), but that our earnest care toward you all to be revealed (passive) in the sight of God.

7:13 Through this we have been comforted (passive) on your comfort. But we rejoiced the more exceedingly on the joy of Titus, that his spirit has been refreshed (passive) from you all.

7:14 That if in anything I have boasted to him on your behalf, I was not disappointed (passive). But as we spoke all things to you all in truth, also our boasting toward Titus was beginning to become truth.

7:15 And his affection more abundantly into you all, is now (PI) him having continuously remembered all of your obedience, as with fear and trembling you received him.

7:16 I am rejoicing (PI) that in everything I am having confidence (PI) in you all.

8:1 But, brothers, we are making known (PI) to you all the grace of God having been given in the assemblies of Macedonia;

8:2 that in much proof of affliction the abundance of their joy and their deep poverty abounded into the riches of their liberality.

8:3 That according to their power, I am testifying (PI), and beyond their power, (they gave) of their own accord,

8:4 continuously begging of us with much entreaty to receive the grace and the fellowship of the ministry into the saints to receive us.

8:5 And not as we had hoped, but first they gave their own

selves to the Lord, and to us through the will of God.

8:6 Into to entreat us, Titus, that as he made a beginning before, so also he may complete into you all this grace.

8:7 But even as you all are abounding (PI) in everything, to faith, and to utterance, and to knowledge, and to all earnestness, and the love out of you all in us, that you all also may continuously abound in this grace.

8:8 I am speaking (PI) not according to command, but through the earnestness of others, continuously testing the sincerity of your love.

8:9 For you all are knowing the grace of our Lord Jesus Christ, that, continuously being rich, for your sakes He became poor, that of that One to poverty, you all may become rich.

8:10 I am giving (PI) a judgment in this: for this is being expedient (PI) for you all, who already started from a year ago, not only to do, but also to continuously be willing.

8:11 But now also complete the doing, so that even as the readiness of to continuously be willing, thus also to complete out of (you) to continuously have (it) in mind.

8:12 For if the readiness is lying before (PI), (it is) acceptable according to what you may continuously be having, not according to what you aren't having (PI).

8:13 For this is not that ease to others but affliction to you all, but out of equality. In the present time your superabundance into the lack of others.

8:14 that also the superabundance of others be becoming into your lack, so that there may be becoming equality.

8:15 As it has been written (passive), "He with much had no surplus, and he with little had no lack."

8:16 But thanks be to God, the One continuously imparting, the same earnest care for you all in the heart of Titus.

8:17 That indeed he accepted our exhortation, but himself continuously being very earnest, he went out to you all of his own accord.

8:18 But we have sent together with him the brother whose praise (is) in the Good News through all the assemblies.

8:19 But not only so, but also the one being appointed (passive) by the assemblies, a fellow traveler of us together with this grace, which is continuously being served (passive) by us, toward the glory of the same Lord, and readiness of you all.

8:20 Continuously avoiding this, no man may blame us in this bountiful giving continuously being administered (passive) by us.

8:21 Continuously providing the honorable (things), not only in the sight of the Lord, but also in the sight of men.

8:22 But we have sent to them our brother, whom we many times proved continuously being diligent in many things, but now much more diligent, to great confidence into you all.

8:23 Whether for the sake of Titus, my partner and fellow worker into you all, our brothers, they are the apostles of the assemblies, the glory of Christ.

8:24 Then show the proof of your love, and of our boasting over you all into them, shown into the presence of the assemblies.

9:1 For indeed concerning the ministering into the saints, it is now (PI) unnecessary to me to continuously be writing to you all,

9:2 for I know your readiness, of which I am boasting (PI) on your behalf to Macedonians, that Achaia has been prepared (passive) for a year past, and the zeal out of you all has stirred up many.

9:3 But I sent the brothers that our boasting on your behalf may not be being made in vain (passive) in this respect, that, just as I said, you all may continuously be having been prepared (passive),

9:4 Lest somehow, if ever the Macedonians may be coming together with me, and may be finding you all unprepared, we may be disgraced (passive), that we may not continuously lay before you all in this ground of confidence of this boasting.

9:5 I thought it necessary therefore to entreat the brothers that they may go before into you all, and may arrange ahead of time the generous gift promised before (passive) of you all, this to be ready as a generosity, and not even as greed.

9:6 But this: the one continuously sowing sparingly will also reap sparingly. The one continuously sowing on bountifully will also reap on bountifully.

9:7 Each man (give) according as he is determining (PI) to his heart; not out of grief, or out of compulsion; for God is loving (PI) a cheerful giver.

9:8 But the able God to lavish all grace into you, that you all, always continuously having all sufficiency in everything, you all may continuously superabound into every good work.

9:9 As it has been written (passive), "He scattered abroad, He gave to the poor. His righteousness is remaining (PI) forever."

9:10 But the One continuously supplying seed to the one continuously sowing and bread into food, may supply and may multiply your seed, and may increase the fruits of your righteousness;

9:11 in everything you all continuously being enriched into all liberality, which is working (PI) through us thanksgiving to God.

9:12 That the service of this ministry not only is now (PI) continuously replenishing the lack of the saints, but also is continuously superabounding through many givings of thanks to God;

9:13 through the proof of the service, this is continuously glorifying God on the obedience of your confession into the Good News of Christ, and to the liberality of your contribution into them and into all;

9:14 And their prayer for you all, continuously longing for you all by reason of the continuously exceeding grace of God on you all.

9:15 But thanks to God on His unspeakable gift!

10:1 But I Paul, myself, am entreating (PI) you all through the humility and gentleness of Christ; I who in your presence am lowly in you all, but continuously being absent am being bold (PI) into you all.

10:2 But, I am begging (PI) that I may not, continuously being present, to show courage to the confidence to which I am intending (PI) to be bold on any, continuously considering us as continuously walking according to the flesh.

10:3 For continuously walking in the flesh, we are not waging war (PI) according to the flesh;

10:4 for the weapons of our warfare are not of the flesh, but mighty to God toward the throwing down of strongholds,

10:5 continuously throwing down imaginations and every height continuously being exalted against the knowledge of God, and continuously leading into captivity every thought into the obedience of Christ;

10:6 and continuously having in readiness to defend the cause against all active disobedience, when your obedience may be made full (passive).

10:7 You all are looking (PI) according to appearance. If anyone trusts to himself to continuously be Christ's, let him continuously consider this again from himself, that, even as he (is) Christ's, so also we are Christ's.

10:8 For though I also may boast somewhat abundantly concerning our authority, (which the Lord gave into edification, and not into casting you all down) I will not be put to shame (passive),

10:9 that I may not seem as ever to continuously terrify you all through the letters.

10:10 That indeed the letters he is affirming (PI) (are) weighty and strong, but his bodily presence (is) weak, and his speech having been despised (passive).

10:11 Let him continuously consider this, that what we are now (PI) to word through letters continuously being absent, such (are we) also to deed continuously being present.

10:12 For we are not being bold (PI) to judge by or to compare ourselves to some of those continuously commending themselves. But they in themselves, continuously measuring themselves, and continuously comparing themselves to themselves, are being without understanding (PI).

10:13 But we will not boast into the immeasurable, but according to the measure of the allotment distributed to us, to reach even as far as you all.

10:14 For we are not as continuously reaching into you all. We are over-stretching (PI) ourselves. For as far as even to you all, we outstrip others in the Good News of Christ,

10:15 not continuously boasting into the immeasurable in other men's labors, but continuously having hope of a continuously growing up of your faith, to be magnified (passive) in you all according to the measurement of us into superabundance.

10:16 to preach the Good News into the parts beyond you all, not to boast in what is ready in another's allotment.

10:17 But "The one continuously boasting, let him continuously boast in the Lord."

10:18 For not the one continuously commending himself is the one approved, but whom the Lord is commending (PI).

11:1 I wish that you would bear with me to the little foolishness, but, and indeed, you all are bearing (PI) with me.

11:2 For I am being jealous (PI) over you all to jealousy of God. For I married you all to one husband, to present you a pure virgin to Christ.

11:3 But I am fearing (PI) lest somehow, as the serpent deceived Eve in his craftiness, thus your minds might be being corrupted (passive) from the faithful benevolence into Christ.

11:4 For if indeed the one continuously coming is preaching (PI) another Jesus, whom we did not preach, or if you all are receiving (PI) a different spirit, which you did not receive, or a different "good news", which you did not accept, you put up with that well.

11:5 For I am reckoning (PI) that I am not to be behind of the "super" apostles.

11:6 But even if (I am) unskilled to speech, but not to the knowledge, but in everything being revealed (passive) into you all in all (things).

11:7 Or did I commit a sin in continuously humbling myself that you all may be exalted (passive), that I preached to you all the Good News of God free of charge?

11:8 I robbed other assemblies, getting recompense toward service of you all.

11:9 And continuously being present unto you all and being in want (passive), I wasn't a burden to anyone, for the brothers coming from Macedonia, supplied the measure of my wants. In everything I kept myself not burdensome to you all, and I will keep (doing so).

11:10 The truth of Christ is being (PI) in me, that this boasting will not be blocked (passive) toward me in the regions of Achaia.

11:11 Why? Because I am not loving (PI) you all? God knows.

11:12 But what I am doing, and I will do, that I may cut off occasion of the ones that desire an occasion, that in which they are boasting, they may be found (passive) even as we.

11:13 For such false apostles, deceitful workers, are continuously changing their outward appearance into Christ's apostles.

11:14 And no wonder, for Satan is changing his outward appearance (PI) into an angel of light.

11:15 It is no great thing therefore if his servants also are being made in outward appearance (PI) (passive) as servants of righteousness, whose end will be according to their works.

11:16 I am saying (PI) again, no one may think me to continuously be foolish. But if not, yet receive me as foolish, that I also may boast a little.

11:17 Which I am speaking (PI), I am not speaking (PI) according to the Lord, but as in foolishness, in this the confidence of boasting.

11:18 Since many are boasting (PI) after the flesh, I will also boast.

11:19 For with relish you all are bearing with (PI) the foolish gladly, continuously being wise.

11:20 For you all are bearing (PI), if a man is enslaving (PI) you all, if anyone is devouring (PI) you all, if anyone is taking (PI) you all captive, if anyone is exalting (PI) himself, if anyone is striking (PI) you all into the face.

11:21 I am speaking (PI) according to disparagement, as that we were weak. But in which ever anyone may continuously be bold (in foolishness I am speaking (PI)), I am being bold (PI) also.

11:22 Hebrews they are being (PI). So am I. Israelites they are being (PI). So am I. Seed of Abraham they are being (PI). So am I.

11:23 Servants of Christ they are being (PI). (I am speaking (PI) as one continuously being beside himself) I am above them; in labors more abundantly, in beatings above measure, in prisons more abundantly, in deaths often.

11:24 Five times by the Jews I received forty (stripes) minus one.

11:25 Three times I was beaten (passive) with rods. Once I was stoned (passive). Three times I suffered shipwreck. I have been a night and a day in the bottom of the sea.

11:26 (I have been) to travels often, to perils of rivers, to perils of robbers, to perils of my countrymen, to perils out of the Gentiles, to perils in the city, to perils in the wilderness, to perils in the sea, to perils in false brothers;

11:27 in labor and travail, in watchings often, in hunger and thirst, in fastings often, in cold and nakedness.

11:28 Apart from those things that are outside, the opposition of me daily, anxiety of all the assemblies.

11:29 Who is being weak (PI), and I am not being weak (PI)? Who is being caused to stumble (PI) (passive), and I am not being incensed (PI) (passive)?

11:30 If I am to be continuously boasting, it is being necessary (PI) l boast of my weakness.

11:31 The God and Father of the Lord Jesus Christ, the One continuously being blessed forevermore, knows that I am not lying (PI).

11:32 In Damascus the governor of King Aretas guarded the city of the Damascenes continuously desiring to arrest me.

11:33 Through a window I was let down (passive) in a basket through the wall, and escaped his hands.

12:1 It is doubtless being not profitable (PI) to me to continuously boast. For I will come into visions and revelations of the Lord.

12:2 I know a man in Christ, fourteen years ago (whether in the body, I don't know, or whether out of the body, I don't know; God knows), such a one being caught up (passive) unto the third heaven.

12:3 I knew such a man (whether in the body, or outside of the body, I don't know; God knew),

12:4 that he was caught up (passive) into Paradise, and heard unspeakable words, which continuously not being lawful to a man to utter.

12:5 On behalf of such a one I will boast, but on my own behalf I will not boast, except in my weaknesses.

12:6 For if I may desire to boast, I will not be foolish; for I will speak the truth. But I am refraining (PI), so that no one may think more of me which he is seeing (PI) in me, or is hearing (PI) out of me.

12:7 Also to the exceeding greatness of the revelations, that I may not continuously be exalted excessively (passive), there was given (passive) to me a thorn in the flesh, a messenger of Satan, that he may continuously torment me, that I may not continuously be exalted excessively (passive).

12:8 Concerning this, I begged the Lord three times that it may depart from me.

12:9 He has said to me, "My grace is being sufficient (PI) to you, for my power is being made perfect (PI) (passive) in weakness." Most gladly then I will rather glory in my weaknesses, that the power of Christ may rest on me.

12:10 Therefore I am taking pleasure (PI) in weaknesses, in injuries, in necessities, in persecutions, in distresses, for Christ's sake. For when I may continuously be weak, then I am being (PI) strong.

12:11 I have become foolish in continuously boasting. You all compelled me, for I ought to have continuously been commended (passive) by you all, for in nothing was I inferior of the "super" apostles, even if I am being (PI) nothing.

12:12 Truly the signs of an apostle were worked (passive) in you all in all patience, in signs and wonders and mighty works.

12:13 For is there being (PI) anything in which you all were made inferior (passive) above the rest of the assemblies, if not that I myself was not a burden to you all? Forgive me this injustice.

12:14 Lo and behold, this is the third time I am being (PI) ready to come unto you all, and I will not be a burden of you all; for I am not seeking (PI) of you all, but you all. For the children not being obligated (PI) to continuously save up to the parents, but the parents to the children.

12:15 But I will most gladly spend and be spent (passive) for the sake of your souls. Even if I am continuously loving you all more abundantly, the less I am being loved (PI) (passive)?

12:16 But let it continuously be so, I did not burden you all. But, continuously being crafty, I caught you all to deception.

12:17 Did I defraud you all of anyone whom I have sent unto you all?

12:18 I exhorted Titus, and I sent the brother together with him. Did Titus defraud you all? Didn't we walk to the same spirit? Didn't we walk to the same steps?

12:19 Again, are you thinking (PI) that we are excusing ourselves (PI) to you all? In the sight of God we are speaking (PI) in Christ. But all, beloved, for your edifying.

12:20 For I am fearing (PI) lest somehow on coming, I may, find you all not the way I am wanting

(PI) to, and that I may be found (passive) to you all such as you are not desiring; lest somehow (there would be) strife, jealousy, outbursts of anger, factions, slander, whisperings, proud thoughts, riots;

12:21 not coming again, my God may humble me toward you all, and I will mourn for many of the ones having sinned already, and not repenting on the uncleanness and sexual immorality and lustfulness which they committed.

13:1 This is the third time I am coming (PI) unto you all. "On the mouth of two or three witnesses shall every word be established (passive)."

13:2 I have said beforehand, and I am predicting (PI), as when continuously being present the second time, and now, continuously being absent, I am writing (PI) to the ones having sinned before, and to all the rest, that, if I may come again, I will not spare;

13:3 Since you all are seeking (PI) a proof of Christ continuously speaking in me; Who into you all is not being weak (PI), but is being powerful (PI) in you all.

13:4 For even if He was crucified (passive) out of weakness, yet He is living (PI) out of the power of God. For we also are being weak (PI) in Him, but we will live with Him out of the power of God into you all.

13:5 Continuously test your own selves, if you all are being (PI) in the faith. Continuously test your own selves. Or are you all not knowing (PI) as to your own selves, that Jesus Christ is being (PI) in you all?—if any are not (PI) disqualified.

13:6 But I am hoping (PI) that you will know that we are not (PI) disqualified.

13:7 But now I am praying (PI) unto God that you all to do no evil; not that we may appear (passive) approved, but that you all may continuously do that which is honorable, but we may continuously be disqualified.

13:8 For we are not being able (PI) to do anything against the truth, but for the sake of the truth.

13:9 For we are rejoicing (PI) when we may continuously be weak, but you all may continuously be strong. But this we also are praying (PI) for, the perfecting of you all.

13:10 Through this cause I am writing (PI) these things continuously being absent, that continuously being present I may not deal sharply, according to the authority which the Lord gave me into building up, and not into tearing down.

13:11 Finally, brothers, continuously rejoice. You all be continuously being perfected (passive), you all be continuously being exhorted (passive), you all continuously have the same opinion, you all continuously live in peace, and the God of love and peace will be with you all.

13:12 Greet one another in a holy kiss.

13:13 All the saints are greeting (PI) you all.

13:14 The grace of the Lord Jesus Christ, the love of God, and the fellowship of the Holy Spirit with you all. Amen.

The second written (passive) unto Corinthians from Philippi of Macadonia through Titus and Lucas.

Introduction to Galatians

There is little dispute that the Apostle Paul wrote this epistle. It was probably his first letter. There is some doubt about when and from where it was written: either 48 AD from Galatia (which is a region and not a single city), or 55 AD from the city of Ephesus. It is quite short, but has an importance out of all proportion to its size.

You will note that the Epistles are not presented in the Bible in the same time order as they were written. For example, Romans was written in about 57 AD. Galatians was written first, but appears in most Bibles later than Romans. The sequence of the books is not important, and does not represent a development of the theology over time. Paul's theology was delivered to him directly and fully by revelation from Jesus Christ Himself at the beginning of his ministry (Galatians 1:12).

In this letter to the Galatians, Paul's major theme is that the law (trying hard to be good with your will power) is directly opposite to the Gospel (transformation into the image of Jesus). He is very clear that the Galatians cannot have both transformation and legalism (the law, Verse 2:21). He was very disturbed that it seemed that the Galatians were deserting the Gospel he had taught them for legalism (Verses 1:4-7; 3:1-5). He had personally been with them on his first missionary journey, and it is clear that he had taught them how to be transformed into the image of Jesus by forgiving and thus being forgiven by God; or he would not have been upset that they were abandoning what he had taught them, and were adopting legalism instead.

Without an awareness of the miraculous provision of the process of transformation into the image of Jesus (also referred to as "sanctification"), legalism is the only other option available for producing good behavior. That is why a lack of awareness of sanctification is such a slippery slope to legalism in our Western culture, where the will and the intellect are considered to be the only tools we need to live life.

Apparently it was also a slippery slope for the Galatians! That is why this Epistle is so important for us Western Christians: it is a warning that we need to understand and apply the Good News of sanctification to our lives. Otherwise the blood of Jesus will be of no benefit to us in this life. There were apparently Jews who were telling the Galatians that they needed physical circumcision. Physical circumcision is a symbol of making a commitment to the Law of Moses. Paul told the Galatians:

> *5:2 Behold, I, Paul, tell you that if you receive circumcision, Christ will profit you nothing.*
> *5:3 Yes, I testify again to every man who receives circumcision, that he is a debtor to do the whole law.*
> *5:4 You are alienated from Christ, you who desire to be justified by the law. You have fallen away from grace* (World English Bible).

Because you were probably raised in the Western World, and attended a Western church, you should pay especial attention to Paul's warning in this Epistle.

1:1 Paul, an apostle (not from men, neither through man, but through Jesus Christ, and God the Father, the One raising Him from the dead),

1:2 and all the brothers who are with me, to the assemblies of Galatia:

1:3 Grace to you all and peace from God the Father, and our Lord Jesus Christ,

1:4 the One giving Himself over our sins, that He Himself might rescue us out of this present evil age, according to the will of our God and Father—

1:5 to Whom (be) the glory into the ages of the ages. Amen.

1:6 I am marveling (PI) that you all are now so quickly turning away (PI) from the One calling you in the grace of Christ into a different "good news";

1:7 which is not being (PI) another. Only there are being (PI) ones continuously troubling you all, and continuously wanting to pervert the Good News of Christ.

1:8 But also if ever we, or an angel from heaven, may continuously preach to you all any "good news" other than that which we preached to you all, let him be continuously cursed.

1:9 As we have said before and I am saying (PI) again: if any man is bringing (PI) a "good news" other than that which you received, let him be continuously cursed.

1:10 For am I now persuading (PI) men, or God? Or am I striving (PI) to continuously please men? For if I still pleased men, I wouldn't ever be a servant of Christ.

1:11 But I am making (PI) known to you all, brothers, concerning the Good News being preached (passive) by me, that it is being (PI) not according to man.

1:12 For neither did I receive it to myself from man, nor was I taught it (passive), but through revelation of Jesus Christ.

1:13 For you all have heard of my way of living in time past in the Jews' religion, how that beyond measure I persecuted the assembly of God, and ravaged her.

1:14 And I advanced in the Jews' religion beyond many of my own age among my posterity, being continuously more exceedingly zealous of the traditions of my fathers.

1:15 But when it pleased God, the One separating me from my mother's womb, and calling me through His grace,

1:16 to reveal His Son in me, that I might continuously preach Him in the Gentiles, I didn't immediately confer with flesh and blood,

1:17 nor did I go up into Jerusalem to the ones (who were) apostles before me, but I went away into Arabia, and again I returned into Damascus.

1:18 Then after three years I went up into Jerusalem to visit Peter, and stayed with him fifteen days.

1:19 But of the other apostles I saw no one, except James, the Lord's brother.

1:20 But about the things which I am writing (PI) to you all, behold, before God, I'm not lying (PI).

1:21 Thereupon I came to the regions of Syria and Cilicia.

1:22 But I was continuously being unknown (passive) by face to the assemblies in Christ of Judea,

1:23 but they were only continuously hearing that "the one continuously persecuting us now is preaching (PI) the faith that he once ravaged."

1:24 And they glorified God in me.

2:1 Then after a period of fourteen years I went up again into Jerusalem with Barnabas, taking Titus also with me.

2:2 But I went up according to revelation, and I laid before them the Good News which I am preaching (PI) in the Gentiles, but privately before the ones continuously being respected, for fear that I might be continuously running, or had run, in vain.

2:3 Yet not even Titus, who was with me, continuously being a Greek, was compelled (passive) to be circumcised.

2:4 This was because of the false brothers secretly brought in, who stole in to spy out our liberty which we are having (PI) in Christ Jesus, that they might bring us into bondage;

2:5 to whom we gave no place in the way of subjection, not for an hour, that the truth of the Good News might continue unto you all.

2:6 But from the ones continuously seeming to continuously be someone (of what sort they at some time were it is making (PI) no difference to me; God is not taking account (PI) the outward appearance of a man) —for to me the ones continuously seeming to be of repute imparted nothing,

2:7 but to the contrary, perceiving that I had been entrusted (passive) (with) the Good News of the uncircumcision, even as Peter (with the Good News) of the circumcision

2:8 (for the One acting to Peter into the apostleship of the circumcision also acted to me into the Gentiles);

2:9 and them knowing the grace being given (passive) to me, James and Cephas and John, the ones continuously seeming to be pillars, gave to me and Barnabas the right hand of fellowship, that we (should go) into the Gentiles, but they into the circumcision.

2:10 only that we may continuously remember the poor--which also I was eager to do this same thing.

2:11 But when Peter came into Antioch, I resisted him to his face, because he was worthy of having been blamed (passive).
2:12 For before some people came from James, he ate together with the Gentiles. But when they came, he drew back and separated himself, continuously fearing the ones out of the circumcision.
2:13 And the rest of the Jews also played the hypocrite together with him (passive); so that even Barnabas was carried away (passive) with their hypocrisy.
2:14 But when I saw that they are not walking uprightly (PI) according to the truth of the Good News, I said to Peter before them all, "If you, continuously being a Jew, are living (PI) as the Gentiles (do), and not as the Jews do, why are you compelling (PI) the Gentiles to continuously live as the Jews do?
2:15 We, being Jews to nature, and not sinners out of the Gentiles,
2:16 knowing that a man is not being justified (PI) (passive) out of the works of the (OT) law but through faith of Jesus Christ, and we believed into Christ Jesus, that we might be justified (passive) out of faith of Christ, and not out of the works of the (OT) law, because every flesh will not be justified (passive) out of the works of the (OT) law.

2:17 But if we were continuously seeking to be justified (passive) in Christ, we ourselves also were found (passive) sinners, is Christ a minister of sin? Certainly not!
2:18 For if I am building up (PI) again those things which I demolished, I am showing (PI) myself a transgressor of the (OT) law.
2:19 For I, through the (NT) law, died to the (OT) law, that I might live to God.
2:20 I have been crucified (passive) to Christ, but I am no longer living (PI), but Christ is living (PI) in me. But that which I am now living (PI) in the flesh, in faith I am living (PI) to the Son of God, the One loving me and giving up Himself in behalf of me.
2:21 I am not making void (PI) the grace of God. For if righteousness (is) through the (OT) law, then Christ died for nothing!"
3:1 Foolish Galatians, who has bewitched you all not to continuously be persuaded (passive) to obey the truth, according to whose eyes Jesus Christ was openly set forth (passive) in you all having been crucified (passive)?
3:2 Only this I am wanting (PI) to learn from you all. Did you all receive the Spirit out of the works of the (OT) law, or out of hearing of faith?
3:3 Thus are you being (PI) so foolish? Having begun to Spirit,

are you all now being completed (PI) to flesh?

3:4 Did you suffer so many things in vain, if it is indeed also in vain?

3:5 Therefore the One continuously supplying the Spirit to you all, and continuously working power in you all, (does He do it) out of the works of the (OT) law, or out of hearing of faith?

3:6 Even as Abraham "believed God, and it was counted (passive) to him into righteousness."

3:7 Be knowing (PI) therefore that those out of faith, these are being (PI) children of Abraham.

3:8 But the Scripture, foreseeing that God is justifying (PI) the Gentiles out of faith, preached the Good News beforehand to Abraham, that "In you all the nations will be blessed (passive)."

3:9 So that the ones out of faith are being blessed (PI) (passive) together with faithful Abraham.

3:10 For as many as are being (PI) out of the works of the (OT) law are being (PI) under a curse. For it has been written (passive), "Cursed is everyone who is not persevering in all things having been written (passive) in the book of the (OT) law, to do them."

3:11 But that no man is being justified (PI) (passive) in the (OT) law with God is evident,

that, "The righteous will live out of faith."

3:12 But the (OT) law is not being (PI) out of faith, but, "The man doing them will live in them."

3:13 Christ redeemed us out of the curse of the (OT) law, becoming a curse on behalf of us. For it has been written (passive), "Cursed is everyone continuously hanging on a tree,"

3:14 that the blessing of Abraham might come into the Gentiles in Christ Jesus; that we might receive the promise of the Spirit through faith.

3:15 Brothers, I am speaking (PI) according to human terms, yet even a man's covenant, when it has been confirmed, no one is making it void (PI), or is adding to it (PI).

3:16 But the promises were spoken (passive) to Abraham and to his seed. He is not saying (PI), "And to seeds," as on many, but as on one, "And to your seed," which is being (PI) Christ.

3:17 But I am saying (PI) this. A covenant having been confirmed (passive) beforehand by God into Christ, the (OT) law, having come into existence four hundred thirty years after, is not annulling (PI), into to do away with the promise.

3:18 For if the inheritance is out of the (OT) law, it is no longer out of promise; but to Abraham, God has granted it through promise.

3:19 What then (is) the (OT) law? It was added (passive) because of transgressions, until the seed may come to Whom the promise has been made, having been ordained (passive) through angels in the hand of a mediator.

3:20 But a mediator is not being (PI) between one, but God is being (PI) one.

3:21 Is the (OT) law then against the promises of God? Certainly not! For if there had been given (passive) a (OT) law continuously being able to make alive, most certainly righteousness would have been out of the (OT) law.

3:22 But the Scriptures imprisoned together all things under sin, that the promise out of faith of Jesus Christ might be given (passive) to the ones continuously believing.

3:23 But before of the faith to come, we were kept imprisoned (passive) under the (OT) law, having been confined (passive) into the faith continuously being about to be revealed (passive).

3:24 So that the (OT) law has become our tutor into Christ, that we might be justified (passive) out of faith.

3:25 But (after) the coming of faith, we are no longer being (PI) under a tutor.

3:26 For you are all now being (PI) children of God, through faith in Christ Jesus.

3:27 For as many of you all as were baptized (passive) into Christ have put on Christ.

3:28 There is being (PI) neither Jew nor Greek, there is being (PI) neither slave nor free man, there is being (PI) neither male nor female; for you all are being (PI) one in Christ Jesus.

3:29 But if you all are of Christ, then you all are being (PI) Abraham's seed and heirs according to promise.

4:1 But I am saying (PI) that so long as the heir is being (PI) a child, he is being no different from (PI) a bondservant, though he continuously is being lord of all;

4:2 but is being (PI) under guardians and stewards until the day appointed by the father.

4:3 So we also, when we were children, we were having been enslaved (passive) under the elemental principles of the world.

4:4 But when the fullness of the time came, God sent out His Son, becoming out of a woman, becoming under the (OT) law,

4:5 that He might redeem the ones under the (OT) law, that we might receive the adoption of children.

4:6 But because you all are being (PI) children, God sent out the Spirit of His Son into the hearts of you all, continuously crying, "Abba, Father!"

4:7 So that you are no longer being (PI) a bondservant, but a son; but if a son, then an heir of God through Christ.

4:8 But then indeed, not having known God, you all were slaves to the ones not in nature continuously being gods.

4:9 But now that you all are knowing God, or rather being known by God, how are you all turning back (PI) again upon the weak and destitute elements, to which you all are again willing (PI) to again continuously be in bondage now?

4:10 You all are observing (PI) months, seasons, and years.

4:11 I am being afraid (PI) for you all, lest somehow I have toiled in vain into you all.

4:12 You all continuously be becoming as I, that I also (become) as you all, brothers. I am beseeching (PI) of you all. In nothing you all injured me,

4:13 but you all know that because of weakness of the flesh I preached the Good News to you all the first time.

4:14 And the trial of me in my flesh, you all didn't despise nor reject; but you all received me as an angel of God, as Christ Jesus.

4:15 The blessing then was what? For I am testifying (PI) to you all that, if possible, you all plucking out your eyes, and perhaps gave them to me.

4:16 So then, have I become your enemy by continuously being true to you all?

4:17 They are being zealous (PI) over you all in no good way, but they are desiring (PI) to alienate you all, that you all may continuously be zealous (over) them.

4:18 But (it is) always good to continuously be zealous in good, and not only when I am to continuously be present unto you all.

4:19 My little children, with whom I am again travailing in birth (PI) until, of Him, Christ may be formed (passive) in you all—

4:20 but I could wish to continuously be present unto you all now, and to change my tone, because I am being perplexed (PI) in you all.

4:21 Continuously be telling me, the ones continually desiring to continuously be under the (OT) law, you all are not hearing (PI) the (OT) law.

4:22 For it has been written (passive) that Abraham had two sons, one out of the handmaid, and one out of the free woman.

4:23 But the one indeed out of the handmaid was born (passive) according to the flesh, but the one out of the free woman (was born) through promise.

4:24 Which is being (PI) continuously allegorized (passive), for these are being (PI) two covenants. One indeed proceeding from Mount Sinai, continuously generating into bondage, which is being (PI) Hagar.

4:25 For this Hagar is being (PI) Mount Sinai in Arabia, but is corresponding to (PI) to the Jerusalem that exists now, yet she is being in bondage (PI) with her children.

4:26 But the Jerusalem that is above is being (PI) free, who is being (PI) the mother of us all.

4:27 For it has been written (passive), "Be rejoiced (passive), the one barren not the one continuously bringing forth. Break forth into rejoicing and cry aloud, not the one continuously travailing in birth, that many (are) the children of the desolate rather than of the woman continuously having the husband."

4:28 But we, brothers, as Isaac was, are being (PI) children of promise.

4:29 But even as then, the one being born according to the flesh persecuted the one (who was born) according to the Spirit, so also (it is) now.

4:30 But what is the Scripture saying (PI)? "Throw out the handmaid and her son, for the son of the handmaid emphatically will not inherit with the son of the free woman."

4:31 So then, brothers, we are not being (PI) children of a handmaid, but of the free (woman).

5:1 You all continuously stand firm therefore in the liberty (by which) Christ freed us, and you all don't be continuously entangled (passive) again to a yoke of slavery.

5:2 Behold, I, Paul, am telling (PI) you all that if you all may continuously receive circumcision (passive), Christ will profit you nothing.

5:3 Yet again I am testifying (PI) to every man who is continuously being circumcised (passive), that he is being (PI) a debtor to do the whole (OT) law.

5:4 You all were alienated (passive) from Christ, you all who are being justified (PI) (passive) in (OT) law. You all fell of grace.

5:5 For we, to the Spirit, out of faith are patiently awaiting (PI) the hope of righteousness.

5:6 For in Christ Jesus neither circumcision is having any force (PI), nor uncircumcision, but faith continuously working through love.

5:7 You all were racing well! Who interfered with you all not to be continuously persuaded (passive) to the truth?

5:8 The persuasion (is) not out of the One continuously calling you all.

5:9 A little leaven is leavening (PI) the whole lump.

5:10 I have confidence into you all in the Lord that you all will be of no other opinion. But the one continuously troubling you all will bear the judgment, whoever he may continuously be.

5:11 But I, brothers, if I am still preaching (PI) circumcision, why am I still being persecuted (PI) (passive)? Then the stumbling block of the cross has been removed (passive).

5:12 And I wish that those continuously disturbing you all would cut themselves off.

5:13 For you all brothers, were called (passive) unto freedom. Only don't (use) the freedom into an occasion to the flesh, but through love continuously be servants to one another.

5:14 For the whole (NT) law is being fulfilled (PI) (passive) in one word, in this: "You will love your neighbor as yourself."

5:15 But if you all are biting (PI) and are devouring (PI) one another, continuously be careful that you all aren't consumed (passive) by one another.

5:16 But I am saying (PI), you all continuously live your life in the Spirit, and you all won't fulfill the strong desire of the flesh.

5:17 For the flesh is lusting (PI) against the Spirit, but the Spirit against the flesh; yet these are being contrary (PI) to one another, that which ever (bad) you all may continuously will not to do, these you all may continuously do.

5:18 But if you all are being brought along (PI) (passive) in the Spirit, you all are not being (PI) under the (OT) law.

5:19 But the works of the flesh is being (PI) obvious, which is being (PI) adultery, sexual immorality, uncleanness, lustfulness,

5:20 idolatry, sorcery, hatred, strife, jealousies, outbursts of anger, rivalries, divisions, heresies,

5:21 envyings, murders, drunkenness, orgies, and things like these; to which I am forewarning (PI) you all, even as I also told before, that the ones continuously practicing such things will not inherit the Kingdom of God.

5:22 But the fruit of the Spirit is being (PI) love, joy, peace, patience, kindness, goodness, faith,

5:23 gentleness, and strength inside. The (NT) law is not being (PI) against such things.

5:24 But those of Christ crucified the flesh together with the passions and strong desires.

5:25 If we are living (PI) in the Spirit, in the Spirit we may continuously walk in orderly fashion.

5:26 We may not continuously beginning to become conceited, continuously provoking one another, continuously envying one another.

6:1 And brothers, if ever also a man may be overtaken (passive) in some error, you all the spiritual ones, must continuously restore such a one in a spirit of gentleness; continuously looking to yourself so that you also may not be tempted (passive).

6:2 Continuously bear one another's consequences of sin, and thus fulfill the (NT) law of Christ.

6:3 For if any man is imagining (PI) himself to continuously be something, continuously being nothing, he is deceiving (PI) himself.

6:4 But let each man continuously test his own work, and then he will boast into himself and not into another.

6:5 For each man will bear his own burden of responsibilities and failures.

6:6 But continuously let him who is continuously being taught (passive) the word share in all good things to the one continuously instructing.

6:7 Don't continuously be deceived (passive). God is not being mocked (PI) (passive), for whatever a man may be continuously sowing, this he will also reap.

6:8 That the one continuously sowing into his own flesh out of the flesh shall reap corruption. But the one continuously (sowing) into the Spirit, out of the Spirit will reap eternal life.

6:9 But (us) continuously doing the good, may not continuously lose courage, for to our own season we will reap (if) we are not continuously being made weary (passive).

6:10 So then, as we are having (PI) opportunity, we may continuously do good unto all, but especially unto those of the household of the faith.

6:11 See with what large letters I write to you all with my own hand.

6:12 As many as are desiring (PI) to look good in the flesh, these are compelling (PI) you all to continuously be circumcised (passive); only that they may not continuously be persecuted (passive) to the cross of Christ.

6:13 For not even the ones continuously being circumcised (passive) are keeping (PI) the (OT) law themselves, but they are desiring (PI) to continuously have you all circumcised (passive), that they may boast in your flesh.

6:14 But not to me to wish to continuously boast, if not in the cross of our Lord Jesus Christ, through whom the world has been crucified (passive) to me, and I to the world.

6:15 For in Christ Jesus neither circumcision is availing (PI) anything, nor uncircumcision, but a new creation.

6:16 And as many as live their lives to this rule, peace on them and mercy, and on the Israel of God.

6:17 Of the rest, let no one continuously be the source of grief to me, for I am bearing (PI) the marks of the Lord Jesus in my body.

6:18 The grace of our Lord Jesus Christ (be) with your spirit, brothers. Amen.

Was written (passive) from Rome to the Galatians.

(The last sentence in this verse is not in the WEB, because it is not in the Greek text the WEB used).

Introduction To Ephesians

This epistle was probably written in about 62 AD while Paul was in prison in Rome. He had personally spent about 3 years with the Ephesians about 10 years earlier, so he was very familiar with them and what they knew about the foundations of the faith.

He apparently felt that they needed to be reminded of some of the things he had taught them. It was not that Paul had learned more in those 10 years and was giving them some new information which he had discovered. He did not gain his knowledge of Christ by careful study over years. Rather, the living Christ personally imparted this knowledge to him by revelation:

> *For I neither received it from man, nor was I taught it, but it came through the revelation of Jesus Christ* (Galatians 1:12).

We do not have a record of what he taught them during the three years he was with them, but we can certainly assume that a major theme he would have emphasized is how they can have Jesus take away their sins. After all, that is why Jesus came to earth, suffered, died, rose again, and sent His Spirit: to provide a cure for sin. Without a doubt he would have also actively mentored them in this process.

From the contents of this letter, it would appear that the Ephesians needed to be reminded about some fundamentals of the faith. In Verses 1:4 through 1:9 he specifically talks about the fundamental importance of forgiveness of their sins. Interestingly, in this letter he does not specifically teach them HOW to do this – to forgive so they will be forgiven.

Why did he not teach them this in this letter? The answer is pretty simple: He had spent three years teaching them HOW to do this. He apparently did not feel that he needed to again teach them what he had already taught them. Rather, he needed to remind them of their need to do this, because it appears that they were drifting away from it. It was easy for them to become lax in this, because there were spiritual forces of darkness trying to lead them astray. Verses 6:10 through

6:18 are a strong reminder to them that they are indeed in a spiritual battle. They need to "accept the helmet of salvation" (not "take" – see my note at Verse 6:17) which Jesus has offered to them. Since they were already Christians, this can only be referring to the ongoing process of salvation, namely sanctification through forgiving and thus being forgiven of their sins. If they do not "accept" it, it will not occur; and they will be stuck in their sins and thus vulnerable to the influence of the Devil.

Of all the Epistles, this one has the greatest concentrated emphasis on sanctification.

1:1 Paul, an apostle of Christ Jesus through the will of God, to the saints continuously being in Ephesus, and to faithful in Christ Jesus:

1:2 Grace to you all and peace from God our Father and the Lord Jesus Christ.

1:3 The blessed God and Father of our Lord Jesus Christ, the One blessing us in every spiritual blessing in the heavenly places in Christ;

1:4 even as He chose us in Him before the foundation of the world, us to continuously be holy and without blemish in the very presence of Him in love;

1:5 having predestined us into adoption as children through Jesus Christ into Himself, according to the good pleasure of His desire,

1:6 into the praise of the glory of His grace, in which He greatly favored us in the One having been beloved (passive),

1:7 in whom we are having (PI) the redemption through His blood, the forgiveness of our sins, according to the abundance of His grace,

1:8 which He made to abound into us in all wisdom and prudence,

1:9 making known to us the mystery of His will, according to His good pleasure which He designed beforehand in Him

1:10 into the management of the full end of the times, to bring all things into one in Christ, both the things in the heavens, and the things on the earth, in Him;

1:11 in Him in Whom the lot has fallen upon us (passive) also having been foreordained (passive) according to the purpose of the One Who is continuously working all things according to the counsel of His will;

1:12 into us to continuously be into the praise of His glory, the ones having hoped in advance in Christ:

1:13 in Whom you all (Gentiles) also, hearing the word of the truth, the Good News of your salvation--in Whom, also believing, you were sealed (passive) to the Holy Spirit of promise,

1:14 Who is being (PI) a pledge into our inheritance, into the redemption of the purchased possession, into the praise of His glory.

1:15 Through this I also, hearing of the faith of you all in the Lord Jesus, and the love into all the saints,

1:16 I am not ceasing (PI) continuously giving thanks over you all, continuously making mention of you all upon my prayers,

1:17 that the God of our Lord Jesus Christ, the Father of glory, may give to you all a spirit of wisdom and revelation in the knowledge of Him;

1:18 the eyes of your understanding having been

enlightened (passive) with ongoing results into you all to perceive what is being the hope of His calling, and what (are) (PI) the riches of the glory of the inheritance of Him in the saints,
1:19 and what continuously is the exceeding greatness of His power into us, the ones continuously believing, according to that working of the strength of His might
1:20 which He worked in Christ, rousing Him out of the dead, and made Him to sit in His right hand in the heavenly places,
1:21 far above all rule, and authority, and power, and dominion, and every name continuously being named (passive), not only in this age, but also in that which is continuously coming.
1:22 And He put all under subjection under His feet, and gave Him head over all things to the assembly,
1:23 which is being (PI) His body, the fulfilling of the all, in all continuously making perfect.
2:1 And you all continuously being dead to the transgressions and the sins,
2:2 in which you all once walked according to the age of the world, according to the prince of the power of the air, of the spirit now continuously working in the children of disobedience;
2:3 in whom we also all once lived in the lust of our flesh, continuously doing the desires of the flesh and of the modes of thinking, and were children to nature of wrath, even as the rest.
2:4 But God, continuously being rich in mercy, through His great love with which He loved us,
2:5 and us continuously being dead to the trespasses, He made us alive together to the Christ. To grace you all are being (PI) having been saved (passive),
2:6 and He raised together, and seated together in the heavenly places in Christ Jesus,
2:7 that in the ages continuously coming He might show the continuously exceeding riches of His grace in kindness upon us in Christ Jesus;
2:8 for to the grace you all are ones being (PI) having been saved (passive) (4982) through the faith, and this not out of you all, (it is) the gift of God,
2:9 not out of works, so that not anyone may boast.
2:10 For, of Him, we are being (PI) His workmanship, being created (passive) in Christ Jesus toward good works, which God prepared before that in them we may be able to walk.
2:11 Therefore continuously remember that once you all, the Gentiles in the flesh, the ones continuously being called (passive) "uncircumcision" by the ones continuously being called (passive) "circumcision," in the flesh, made by hands;
2:12 that you all were in that time separate from (being) of

Christ, having been alienated (passive) of the commonwealth of Israel, and strangers of the covenants of the promise, continuously having no hope and without God in the world.

2:13 But now in Christ Jesus you all who once continuously being far off began to become near in the blood of Christ.

2:14 For He is being (PI) our peace, the One making both one, and breaking down the middle wall of partition,

2:15 nullifying in His flesh the hostility, the (OT) law of precepts in ordinances, that He might create in Himself toward one new man of the two, continuously making peace;

2:16 and might reconcile the both in one body to God through the cross, killing the hostility in it.

2:17 And coming, He announced peace to you all, the ones far and the ones near.

2:18 That through Him we are having (PI) our access, both in one Spirit unto the Father.

2:19 So then you all are being (PI) no longer strangers and foreigners, but fellow citizens of the saints, and members of the household of God,

2:20 being built (passive) on the foundation of the apostles and prophets, Christ Jesus Himself continuously being the chief cornerstone;

2:21 in Whom the whole building, continuously being fitted together (passive), growing (PI) into a holy temple in the Lord;

2:22 in Whom you all also are being built (PI) (passive) into a habitation of God in the Spirit.

3:1 Of this grace I, Paul, the prisoner of Christ Jesus on behalf of you all of the Gentile nations,

3:2 if it is so that you all have heard of the administration of the grace of God having been given (passive) to me into you all;

3:3 that according to revelation He made known to me the mystery, as I wrote before in few words,

3:4 unto which the ones continuously reading will be being able (PI) to perceive my understanding in the mystery of Christ;

3:5 which in other generations was not made known (passive) to the children of men, as it now has been revealed (passive) to His holy apostles and prophets in the Spirit;

3:6 the Gentiles to continuously be fellow heirs, and fellow members of the body, and fellow partakers of His promise in Christ Jesus through the Good News,

3:7 of which I began to be a minister, according to the gift of the grace of God being granted (passive) to me according to the working of His power.

3:8 To me, the very least of all saints, was this grace given (passive), to preach in the

Gentiles the unsearchable riches of Christ,

3:9 and to make all men see what is the fellowship of the mystery having been concealed (passive) from of the ages in God, the One creating all through Jesus Christ;

3:10 that it might be made known (passive) now to the principalities and the powers in the heavenly places through the assembly the manifold wisdom of God,

3:11 according to the purpose of the ages which He brought about in Christ Jesus our Lord;

3:12 in Whom we are having (PI) boldness and access in confidence through the faith of Him.

3:13 Therefore I am asking (PI) you all to not continuously lose heart in my troubles over you all, which is being (PI) your glory.

3:14 For this cause, I am bowing (PI) my knees unto the Father of our Lord Jesus Christ,

3:15 out of Whom every family in heaven and on earth is being named (PI) (passive),

3:16 that He may grant to you all, according to the riches of His glory to power, to be made strong (passive) through His Spirit into the inward man;

3:17 the Christ to dwell in your hearts through faith; having been rooted (perfect passive) and having been grounded (perfect passive) in love,

3:18 that you all may be strong to grasp together with all the saints what is the breadth and length and height and depth,

3:19 and to know the love of Christ, continuously surpassing of (intellectual) knowledge, that you all may be filled (passive) with all the fullness of God.

3:20 Now to the One continuously being able to do exceedingly above all which we are asking (PI) or are thinking (PI), according to the power continuously working in us,

3:21 the glory to Him in the assembly in Christ Jesus into all generations forever and ever. Amen.

4:1 I therefore, the prisoner in the Lord, am begging (PI) you all to live your lives suitably of the calling with which you all were called (passive),

4:2 with all modesty and humility, with patience, continuously bearing with one another in love;

4:3 continuously being eager to continuously keep the unity of the Spirit in the bond of peace,

4:4 one body, and one Spirit, even as you all also were called in one hope of your calling;

4:5 one Lord, one faith, one baptism,

4:6 one God and Father of all, the One over all, and through all, and in you all.

4:7 But to each one of us the grace was given (passive) according to the measure of the gift of Christ.

4:8 Therefore He is saying, (PI) "Ascending into heaven, He led captivity captive, and gave gifts to men."

4:9 But this, "He ascended," what is it being (PI) if not that also He descended first into the lower parts of the earth?

4:10 The One descending is also being (PI) the One ascending far above all the heavens, that He might fill all.

4:11 And He Himself gave indeed the apostles; also the prophets; also the evangelists; also the shepherds and teachers;

4:12 for the purpose of the completion of the perfecting of the saints, into the work of ministration in the Christian community, into the building up of the body of Christ;

4:13 until we all may attain into the unity of the faith, and of the knowledge of the Son of God, into a morally mature man, into the measure of the stature of the fullness of Christ;

4:14 that we may continuously no longer be children, being continuously tossed back and forth and being continuously carried about (passive) to every wind of teaching, in the trickery of men, in craftiness, for the purpose of the organized method of seduction of deception;

4:15 but continuously professing true doctrine in love, we may grow into Him the all, Who is being (PI) the Christ the head;

4:16 out of Whom all the body, is continuously being fitted (passive) and continuously being knit together (passive) through every adjoining joint of the supply, according to the active power in measure of one of each part, is making (PI) the growth of the body into a building of itself in love.

4:17 Then this I am saying (PI) and am testifying (PI) in the Lord, you all no longer to continuously live your lives according as also the rest of the Gentiles are walking (PI), in the futility of their natural faculty of conscious thought,

4:18 Having been darkened (passive) to the understanding, continuously being alienated (passive) of the life of God, because of the ignorance continuously being in them, because of the hardness of their hearts;

4:19 who being past feelings gave themselves up to an insatiable desire for pleasure, into work of all uncleanness in greed.

4:20 But you all did not thus know Christ;

4:21 if indeed you all heard Him, and were taught (passive) in Him, even as truth is being (PI) in Jesus:

4:22 you all to put away, as concerning your former way of life, the old man, the one continuously being corrupted (passive) according to the desires of deceit;

4:23 but to continuously be being renewed (passive) to the spirit of your moral consciousness,

4:24 and to put on the new man, being created (passive) according to God in righteousness and holiness of truth.

4:25 Therefore, putting away falsehood, continuously speak truth each one with his neighbor, because we are being (PI) members of one another.

4:26 "You all continuously be made angry (passive), and don't continuously sin." Don't continuously let the sun go down on your wrath,

4:27 neither continuously give place to the devil.

4:28 The one continuously stealing, continuously steal no more; but rather continuously labor, continuously the good to the hands, that he may continuously have to continuously give to the one continuously having need.

4:29 Every corrupt word continuously let not go out of your mouth, but if any good (word) toward edification of the personal need that it may give grace to the one continuously hearing.

4:30 And don't continuously grieve the Holy Spirit of God, in which you were sealed (passive) into the day of redemption.

4:31 Every bitterness and wrath and anger and outcry and slander, let be taken up and carried away (passive) from you all, together with all malice.

4:32 But continuously be kind into one another, tenderhearted, you all continuously forgiving to one another, even as God also in Christ forgave you all.

5:1 Therefore continuously begin to be imitators of God, as beloved children.

5:2 And you all continuously live your lives in love, even as Christ also loved us, and gave Himself up for us, an offering and a sacrifice to God into a sweet-smelling fragrance.

5:3 But sexual immorality, and all uncleanness, or covetousness, let it not continuously be mentioned (passive) in you all, as being proper (PI) to saints;

5:4 and filthiness, and foolish talking, and coarse wittiness, continuously not being appropriate; but rather thanksgiving.

5:5 For this you all are being (PI) continuously knowing, that every sexually immoral person, or unclean person, or covetous person, who is being (PI) an idolater, is having (PI) no inheritance in the Kingdom of Christ and of God.

5:6 Let no one continuously deceive you to empty words. For because of these things, the wrath of God is coming (PI) on the children of disobedience.

5:7 Therefore don't continuously be partakers together with them.

5:8 For you all were once darkness, but now light in the Lord. You all continuously live your lives as children of light, 5:9 for the fruit of the Spirit in all goodness and righteousness and truth, 5:10 continuously proving what is being (PI) well pleasing to the Lord. 5:11 And continuously have no fellowship to the unfruitful works of darkness, but rather even continuously show them to be wrong. 5:12 For the hidden things continuously coming to be of them, it is being (PI) vile even to continuously speak. 5:13 But all things, continuously being shown to be wrong (passive) under the light is being made manifest (PI) (passive), for every light is (PI) continuously being made manifest (passive). 5:14 Therefore He is saying (PI), "Awake, the one continuously sleeping, and arise out of the dead, and Christ will give light to you." 5:15 Therefore you all continuously watch carefully how you all are living your lives (PI), not as unwise, but as wise; 5:16 continuously redeeming the opportunity, because the days of your life are being (PI) evil. 5:17 Through this not continuously becoming foolish, but continuously understanding what the will of the Lord (is).

5:18 And you all to not continuously be made drunk (passive) to wine, in which is being (PI) dissipation, but you all continuously be being filled (passive) in the Spirit, 5:19 continuously speaking to one another to psalms, to hymns, and to spiritual songs; continuously singing, and continuously making melody in the heart of you all, to the Lord; 5:20 you all continuously giving thanks always concerning all, in the name of our Lord Jesus Christ, to the God and Father; 5:21 continuously being subject (passive) to one another in reverence to God. 5:22 Wives, continuously be subject to your own husbands, as to the Lord. 5:23 for this reason, the husband is being (PI) the head of the wife, as even Christ the head of the assembly, and He is being (PI) savior of the body. 5:24 But even as the assembly is being subject ((PI) (passive) to Christ, so also let the wives be to their own husbands in everything. 5:25 Husbands, continuously love your wives, even as Christ also loved the assembly, and gave Himself up for her; 5:26 that He might sanctify her, cleansing to the bath of water in word. 5:27 that He might present her to Himself glorious, not continuously having spot or

wrinkle or any such thing; but that she may continuously be holy and without blemish.
5:28 Even so husbands are owing (PI) to continuously love their own wives as their own bodies. The one continuously loving his own wife is loving (PI) himself.
5:29 For no man ever hated his own flesh; but is nourishing (PI) and is cherishing (PI) her, even as the Lord also the assembly;
5:30 because we are being members of His body, out of His flesh and out of His bones.
5:31 "Equally, of this a man will leave his father and mother, and will be joined (passive) toward his wife and the two will be into one flesh."
5:32 This mystery is being (PI) great, but I am speaking (PI) into Christ and into the assembly.
5:33 However, also even each one must thus continuously love his own wife as himself; but that the wife may continuously honor and respect her husband.
6:1 Children, continuously obey your parents in the Lord, for this is being (PI) right.
6:2 "Continuously honor your father and mother," which is being the first commandment in promise:
6:3 "that it may begin to be well to you, and you will be long-lived on the earth."
6:4 And the fathers, don't continuously provoke your children to wrath, but continuously nurture them in the

discipline and instruction of the Lord.
6:5 Servants, continuously obey to your masters according to the flesh, with fear and trembling, in singleness of your heart, as to Christ;
6:6 not in the way of service only when eyes are on you, as men pleasers; but as servants of Christ, continuously doing the will of God out of the soul;
6:7 with good will continuously doing service, as to the Lord, and not to men;
6:8 knowing that if ever each one might do any good, the same he will bring to himself from of the Lord, whether he is bound or free.
6:9 And the masters, continuously do the same things toward them, continuously giving up threatening, knowing that the Master of you all, as well as of them, is being (PI) in heaven, and there is being (PI) no partiality to Him in His sight.
6:10 Finally, my brothers, continuously be being made strong (passive) in the Lord, and in the power of His inherent strength.
6:11 Put on the whole armor of God, unto you all to continuously be enabled to stand unto the wiles of the devil.
6:12 For our combat is not being (PI) unto flesh and blood, but unto the principalities, unto the powers, unto the world's rulers of the darkness of this age, unto the

spiritual forces of the wickedness in the heavenly places.

6:13 Through this, you all take up the whole armor of God, that you all may be able to withstand in the evil day, and, having done all, to stand.

6:14 You all stand therefore, being girded about your loin in truth, and having put on the breastplate of righteousness,

6:15 and having fitted the feet in readiness of the Good News of peace;

6:16 Upon all, taking up the shield of faith, in which you all will be able to quench all the arrows having been made fiery (passive) of the evil one.

6:17 And you all accept the salvation helmet, and the sword of the Spirit, which spoken word is being (PI) of God;

6:18 through every prayer and petition, continuously praying in every occasion in the Spirit, into this same, continuously being watchful in all perseverance and requests concerning all the saints:

6:19 and over me, that to me utterance may be given (passive) in opening my mouth, in boldness to make known the mystery of the Good News,

6:20 for the sake of which I am being an ambassador (PI) in chains; that in it I may be bold as is being necessary (PI) (for) me to speak.

6:21 But that you all also may know my affairs, Tychicus, the beloved brother and faithful servant in the Lord, will make known to you all what all things I am doing (PI);

6:22 whom I have sent unto you all into this very purpose, that you may know about us, and that he may comfort your hearts.

6:23 Peace to the brothers, and love with faith, from God the Father and the Lord Jesus Christ.

6:24 The grace with all of the ones continuously loving our Lord Jesus Christ in incorruption.

Was written (passive) towards Ephesians from Rome through Tychicus.

Introduction to Philippians

There is little doubt that this letter was written by the Apostle Paul. He was in prison when he wrote it.

The very core of this letter is sanctification, transformation into the image of Jesus, which is more important than anything else to him. See Verses 3:8-21. In this there is great encouragement for us. It can be easy for us to feel like failures because we have not yet fully become like Jesus; but even Paul had not yet been fully perfected (Verse 3:12), but he pressed on.

It is also encouraging to know that it is God at work:

> 2:13 *For it **continuously** is God **continuously acting** in you **all** both to **continuously** will and to continuously work, for **the sake of** his good pleasure* (my translation).

He encouraged them to imitate him in this journey of sanctification (Verses 3:15-3:17). It is very important to understand that Paul is NOT telling them to imitate him by trying hard to act perfectly (Verse 3:12). He is coaching them to continue to have Jesus forgive their sins so that He can perfect them.

My introduction to this epistle is pretty brief, because there is little that is confusing in it that needs further explanation. Let it speak for itself.

1:1 Paul and Timothy, servants of Jesus Chris,; to all the saints in Christ Jesus to the ones continuously being in Philippi, with the overseers and servants:
1:2 Grace to you, and peace from God, our Father, and the Lord Jesus Christ.
1:3 I am thanking (PI) my God upon every remembrance of you all,
1:4 always in every request of mine for you all continuously making my requests with joy,
1:5 on your fellowship into the Good News from the first day until now;
1:6 being confident of this same thing, that the One beginning a good work in you all will complete it until the day of Jesus Christ.
1:7 even as it is being (PI) right to me to continuously have this opinion on account of all of you, because of you all to continuously have me in your heart, both in my bonds and the defense and confirmation of the Good News, you all continuously are being joint partakers of me of grace.
1:8 For God is being (PI) my witness, how I am longing (PI) for all of you in the tender mercies of Christ Jesus.
1:9 And this I am praying (PI), that your love may continuously abound still more and more in knowledge and all perception;
1:10 even to you all continuously approve the things continuously differing; that you may continuously be sincere and without stumbling into the day of Christ;
1:11 having been filled (passive) of the fruits of righteousness, which are through Jesus Christ, to the glory and praise of God.
1:12 But I am desiring (PI) you all to continuously know, brothers, that the things of me have turned out rather toward the progress of the Good News;
1:13 so that my bonds in Christ to become apparent in the whole palace guard, and to the rest;
1:14 and that most of the brothers in the Lord, being confident to my bonds, are more abundantly to continuously be bold to continuously speak the word without fear.
1:15 Some indeed are preaching (PI) Christ even out of envy and strife, but some also out of good will.
1:16 Indeed the ones preaching (PI) Christ out of contention not sincerely, continuously thinking to be continuously bringing affliction to my imprisonment;
1:17 but the ones out of love, knowing that I am being appointed (PI) into the defense of the Good News.
1:18 For what? Moreover, to every manner, whether to pretense or to truth, Christ is being proclaimed (PI) (passive). And I am rejoicing (PI) in this (being proclaimed), yes. Nevertheless, I will rejoice.

1:19 For I know that this will turn out to my salvation, through the supplication of you all and the supply of the Spirit of Jesus Christ,

1:20 according to my expectation and hope, that I will in no way be put to shame (passive), but in all boldness, as always, now also Christ will be magnified (passive) in my body, whether through life, or through death.

1:21 For the Christ to me (is) to continuously live, and gain to die.

1:22 But to continuously live in the flesh, to me this (is) fruit of work; and I am not knowing (PI) (1107) what I will choose.

1:23 For I am being perplexed (PI) (passive) out of the two, continuously having the desire to depart and to continuously be together with Christ, which is far better.

1:24 Yet, to continuously remain in the flesh is more needful because of you all.

1:25 And having this confidence, I know that I will remain, and will remain with you all, into your progress and joy of the faith,

1:26 that your rejoicing may continuously abound in Christ Jesus in me through my presence unto you all again.

1:27 Only worthily of the Good News of Christ, continuously conduct yourselves that, whether I come and see you or am continuously being absent, I may hear of your state, that you are standing firm (PI) in one spirit, with one soul continuously laboring for the faith of the Good News;

1:28 and in nothing continuously being frightened (passive) by the ones continuously opposing, which is being (PI) to them proof of destruction, but to you all of salvation, and this from God.

1:29 that it has been graced to you all because of Christ, not only to continuously believe into Him, but also to continuously suffer because of Him,

1:30 continuously having the same conflict which you all saw in me, and now are hearing (PI) in me.

2:1 If then any encouragement in Christ, if any comfort of love, if any fellowship of the Spirit, if any tender affections and compassions,

2:2 make my joy full, that you all may continuously be like-minded, continuously having the same love, continuously being of one accord, of one opinion;

2:3 nothing according to rivalry or through conceit, but to the humility, continuously deeming one another continuously being superior in rank of yourselves;

2:4 each of you not continuously looking to his own things, but each of you also (the things) of others.

2:5 For this, continuously be being thus minded (passive) in you all, which was also in Christ Jesus,

2:6 who, continuously existing in the form of God, didn't deem it robbery to continuously be equal to God,

2:7 but emptied Himself, taking the form of a servant, becoming in the likeness of men. And being found (passive) to appear as a man,

2:8 He humbled Himself, becoming obedient unto death, even the death of the cross.

2:9 For which God also highly exalted Him, and graced to Him the name which is above every name;

2:10 that in the name of Jesus every knee may bow, of those in heaven, those on earth, and those under the earth,

2:11 and every tongue may confess that Jesus Christ (is) Lord, to the glory of God the Father.

2:12 So that, my beloved, even as you all have always hearkened, not only as in my presence, but now much more in my absence, continuously work out your own salvation with fear and profound reverence.

2:13 For it is being (PI) God continuously acting in you all both to continuously will and to continuously work, for the sake of His good pleasure.

2:14 Continuously do all things without murmurings and disputes,

2:15 that you all may be beginning to be blameless and harmless, children of God without blemish in the midst of a crooked and having been perverted (passive) generation, in whom you are being seen (PI) (passive) as lights in the world,

2:16 continuously holding up the word of life; into a ground of glorying to me into the day of Christ, that I didn't run in vain nor labor in vain.

2:17 But, and if, I am being poured out (PI) (passive) on the sacrifice and service of your faith, I am rejoicing (PI), and am rejoicing together (PI) with you all.

2:18 But in the same way, you all also continuously rejoice, and continuously rejoice with me.

2:19 But I am hoping in the Lord Jesus to quickly send Timothy to you all, that I also may continuously be cheered up, knowing the concerns of you all.

2:20 For I am having (PI) no one else like-minded, who will genuinely care about you.

2:21 For they all are seeking (PI) of themselves, not of Jesus Christ.

2:22 But you are knowing (PI) the proof of him (Timothy), that, as a child to a father, he served together with me into the Good News.

2:23 Indeed I am hoping (PI) to send him at once, as soon as I may presently see the things concerning me.

2:24 But I trust in the Lord that I myself also will come shortly.

2:25 But I counted it necessary to send to you all Epaphroditus, my brother, fellow worker, fellow soldier, but your apostle and servant of my need;

2:26 since he was continuously longing for you all, and continuously being depressed, because you had heard that he was sick.

2:27 For also he was sick, nearly to death, but God had mercy to him; but not to him only, but to me also, that I might not have sorrow on sorrow.

2:28 Then I have sent him the more diligently, that, seeing him again, you all may rejoice, and I may continuously be the less sorrowful.

2:29 Then continuously receive him in the Lord with all joy, and continuously hold such in honor,

2:30 that through the work of Christ he came near unto death, not regarding his soul that he might supply to perfection the want of you all of the public office with respect to me.

3:1 Finally, my brothers, continuously rejoice in the Lord. To continuously write the same things to you all, to me indeed is not tiresome, but to you all safe.

3:2 Continuously beware of the dogs, continuously beware the evil workers, continuously beware the carnal circumcision.

3:3 For we are being (PI) the circumcision, the ones continuously worshipping to God to the Spirit, and continuously rejoicing in Christ Jesus, and not having confidence in the flesh;

3:4 and even I continuously having confidence also in the flesh. If any other man is thinking (PI) to have confidence in the flesh, I yet more:

3:5 circumcised the eighth day, out of the race of Israel, of the tribe of Benjamin, a Hebrew out of Hebrews; concerning the (OT) law, a Pharisee;

3:6 concerning zeal, continuously persecuting the assembly; concerning the righteousness in the (OT) law, becoming blameless.

3:7 But, what things were gain to me, these have I counted loss for Christ.

3:8 But most certainly, and I am counting (PI) all to be loss through the continuously being excellent knowledge of Christ Jesus, my Lord, through Whom I have suffered the loss (passive) of all, and am counting (PI) them to continuously be refuse, that I may gain Christ

3:9 and may be found (passive) in Him, not continuously having my righteousness out of the (OT) law, but through the faith of Christ, the out of God righteousness upon faith;

3:10 to know of Him, and the power of His resurrection, and the fellowship of His sufferings, continuously being conformed to His death;

3:11 if somehow I may attain into the rising up of the dead ones.

3:12 Not that I have already obtained, or have already been made perfect (passive) but I am pursuing (PI), if also I may take hold on that which also I was assuredly taken hold of (passive) by Christ Jesus.

3:13 Brothers, I am not regarding (PI) myself to have attained, but one thing. Indeed continuously caring nothing about the things behind, but continuously reaching forward to the things before,

3:14 I am pressing (PI) on toward the goal on the prize of the high calling of God in Christ Jesus.

3:15 Then as many as are perfect may continuously be of this opinion. And if in anything you all are thinking (PI) otherwise, God will also reveal that to you all.

3:16 Much more into which we have already attained, to continuously walk to the same principle, to continuously be to the same (principle).

3:17 Brothers, continuously be becoming imitators together of me, and continuously note the ones continuously living their lives in this way, even as you all are having (PI) us for an example.

3:18 For many are living their lives (PI), of whom I told you all often, but now also I am telling (PI) you all even continuously weeping, the ones enemies of the cross of Christ.

3:19 of whom the end is destruction, of whom the god is the belly, and the glory in their shame, the ones continuously devoted to earthly things.

3:20 For our citizenship is existing (PI) in heaven, out of which we also are eagerly waiting for (PI) a Savior, the Lord Jesus Christ;

3:21 Who will change the body of our humiliation into to be becoming conformed to the body of His glory, according to the operation of continuous power to continuously enable Him and to subject all to Himself.

4:1 So that, my brothers, beloved and longed for, my joy and crown, thus continuously stand firm in the Lord, my beloved.

4:2 I am exhorting (PI) Euodia, and I am exhorting (PI) Syntyche, to continuously be of the same opinion in the Lord.

4:3 And, I am begging (PI) you also, true yokefellow, continuously help these women, who labored together to me in the Good News, with Clement also, and the rest of my fellow workers, of whom the names are in the book of life.

4:4 Continuously rejoice in the Lord always! Again I will say, continuously rejoice!

4:5 Your gentleness let be known (passive) to all men, the near Lord.

4:6 In nothing be continuously anxious, but in everything, to prayer and petition with thanksgiving, continuously, let your requests be made known (passive) unto God.

4:7 And the peace of God, continuously surpassing all understanding, will guard your hearts and your thoughts in Christ Jesus.

4:8 Finally, brothers, whatever is being (PI) true, whatever honorable, whatever just, whatever pure, whatever lovely, whatever well-spoken of; if any virtue, and if any praise, continuously occupy yourselves about these.

4:9 which you all also learned, and received, and heard, and saw in me: be practicing (PI) these things, and the God of peace will be with you.

4:10 But I rejoiced in the Lord greatly, that now at length you all have caused your care over me to flourish again; to also continuously be disposed in behalf of me, but you all lacked opportunity.

4:11 Not that I am speaking (PI) in respect to lack, for I have learned in whatever (state) I am existing (PI) in, to continuously be content.

4:12 And I know to continuously be humbled (passive), and I know also to continuously superabound. In everything and in all I have been introduced to (passive) the secret both to be continuously filled (passive) and to continuously be hungry, and to continuously abound and to continuously be made wanting (passive).

4:13 I am being strong (PI) in Christ, the One continuously strengthening me.

4:14 Much more, you all did well sharing together my affliction.

4:15 But you yourselves also know, you Philippians, that in the beginning of the Good News, when I departed from Macedonia, no assembly shared to me into the matter of giving and of receiving but you all only.

4:16 That also in Thessalonica you sent once and twice to my need.

4:17 Not that I am seeking (PI) the gift, but I am seeking (PI) the fruit continuously increasing into your account.

4:18 But I am having received (PI) all things, and am superabounding (PI). I am filled (passive), receiving from Epaphroditus the things that came from you all, a sweet-smelling fragrance, an acceptable and well-pleasing sacrifice to God.

4:19 But my God will supply every need of yours according to His riches in glory in Christ Jesus.

4:20 But to our God and Father the glory into forever and ever! Amen.

4:21 Greet every saint in Christ
Jesus. The brothers who are with
me are greeting (PI) you all.
4:22 All the saints are greeting
(PI) you all, but especially those
out of Caesar's household.

4:23 The grace of the Lord of us,
Jesus Christ, (be) with all of you.
Amen.

Was written (passive) towards
the Philippians from Rome
through Epaphroditus.

Introduction To Colossians

THIS IS A VERY POWERFUL, BRIEF AND FOCUSED LETTER REGARDING TRANSFORMATION INTO THE IMAGE OF JESUS!

Our salvation has two parts.
- First, there is the one-time event when we made Jesus our Lord and received His Spirit. Then we can know that we will go to heaven when we die.
- Then second, there is the ongoing process of forgiving and thus being forgiven of our sins, which continues for the rest of our lives. In this process we are transformed into the image of Jesus.

In this epistle Paul has the ongoing process as a major focus. Since the Epistles are "situational" letters (they addressed specific situations going on in the various churches), it is apparent that he felt that the Colossians needed to be encouraged to keep focused on this miraculous provision that Jesus provides for them. Paul apparently was concerned that outside influences were attempting to get the Colossians to fall back into legalism instead of being transformed into the image of Jesus. His emphasis on this transformation will be evident to you as you read this translation.

Paul's emphasis on transformation into the image of Jesus and its results is contrasted with keeping the Law of Moses as a way to produce good behavior. You may be surprised at how prominent is this message here.

In America we are perhaps even MORE vulnerable to this temptation to try to keep the law in our own strength. We are surrounded by the Western Mindset which says that we are in control of our own lives, and that our intellect and will power are all that we need to live life. It is very hard to not be influenced by this view of life. It is very possible that your church has been influenced by it.

1:1 Paul, an apostle of Christ Jesus through the will of God, and Timothy our brother,

1:2 to the saints and faithful brothers in Christ at Colossae: Grace to you and peace from God our Father, and the Lord Jesus Christ.

1:3 We are thanking (PI) to God the Father of our Lord Jesus Christ, continuously praying about you all,

1:4 hearing of the faith of you all in Christ Jesus, and of the love towards all the saints,

1:5 because of the hope which is continuously being reserved for you all in the heavenly realms, of which you heard before in the word of the truth of the Good News,

1:6 of the One continuously coming into you all, and even also in all the world, and is now (PI) continuously bringing forth fruit and even also in you all, from which day you all heard and you all knew the grace of God in truth;

1:7 and even as you all learned from Epaphras our beloved fellow servant, who is being (PI) a faithful servant of Christ over you all,

1:8 the one also declaring to us the love of you all in the Spirit.

1:9 Through this, we also, since the day we heard, are not ceasing (PI) continuously praying over you all, and continuously requesting that you all may be filled (passive) with the knowledge of His will in all spiritual wisdom and understanding,

1:10 to live your life worthily of the Lord into all pleasing in every act, you all continuously bearing good fruit and continuously being grown (passive) into the knowledge of God;

1:11 Continuously being strengthened (passive) in all power, according to the might of the glory of Him, into all endurance and forbearance with joy;

1:12 continuously giving thanks to the Father, the One making us competent into the inheritance of the saints in light;

1:13 Who did deliver us out of the power of darkness, and did translate (us) into the Kingdom of the Son of His love;

1:14 in Whom we are having (PI) our redemption, through His blood, the forgiveness of our sins;

1:15 Who is being (PI) the image of the invisible God, the firstborn of all creation.

1:16 That in Him all was created (passive), all in the heavens and on the earth, the visible and the invisible, whether thrones or dominions or principalities or powers; all through Him and into Him has been created (passive).

1:17 And He is being (PI) before all, and all in Him is held together.

1:18 He is being (PI) the head of the body, the assembly, Who is being (PI) the beginning, the firstborn out of the dead; that He may be beginning to become continuously being first in all.

1:19 That all the fullness was pleased to dwell in Him;

1:20 and through Him to reconcile all into Himself, whether things on the earth, or things in the heavens, having made peace through the blood of His cross.

1:21 And you all in past times continuously having been alienated (passive) and enemies to your mind in your evil works, but now He reconciled

1:22 in the body of His flesh through death, to present you all holy and without blemish and blameless in His sight,

1:23 if indeed you all are remaining (PI) to the faith, having been grounded

(passive) and settled, and not being continuously moved away (passive) from the hope of the Good News of which you all heard, the One being proclaimed in all creation under heaven; of which I, Paul, came to be a minister.

1:24 Now I am rejoicing (PI) in my sufferings for the sake of you all, and I am filling up (PI) on my part that which is lacking of the afflictions of Christ in my flesh over His body, which is being (PI) the church;

1:25 of which I came to be a minister, according to the stewardship of God, the one being given to me into you all, to fulfill the decree of God,

1:26 the mystery having been hidden (passive) from the ages and from the generations. But now was made manifest (passive) to His saints,

1:27 to whom God desired to make known what are the riches of the glory of this mystery in the Gentiles, which is being (PI) Christ in you all, the hope of glory;

1:28 whom we are proclaiming (PI), continuously exhorting every man and continuously teaching every man in all wisdom, that we may present every man perfect in Christ Jesus;

1:29 into which I also am laboring (PI), continuously striving according to His working, continuously working in me mightily.

2:1 For I am desiring (PI) to have you all know I am having (PI) great struggle concerning you all, and the ones in Laodicea, and for as many as have not seen my face in the flesh;

2:2 that their hearts may be comforted (passive), being knit together (passive) in love, and into all riches of the full assurance of understanding, into the knowledge of the mystery of God, both of the Father and of Christ,

2:3 in Whom are being (PI) all the treasures of the wisdom and of the hidden knowledge.

2:4 But this I am saying (PI) that no one may continuously delude you all in persuasiveness of words.

2:5 For if I am being absent (PI) to the flesh, yet I continuously am together with you all to the spirit, I am (PI) rejoicing and continuously seeing your order, and the steadfastness of the faith of you all into Christ.

2:6 Then as you all received Christ Jesus, the Lord, be living your lives (PI) in Him,

2:7 having been rooted (passive) and continuously being built up (passive) in Him, and continuously being preserved (passive) in faith, even as you all were taught, continuously abounding in her in thanksgiving.

2:8 Be being careful (PI) that you all don't let anyone be continuously robbing you all through the philosophy and vain deceit, according to the tradition of men, according to the elements of the world, and not according to Christ.

2:9 That in Him all the fullness of the Godhead is dwelling (PI) bodily,

2:10 and you all are being (PI) made full (passive) in Him, Who is being (PI) the head of all principality and power.

2:11 In Whom you all were also circumcised (passive) with a circumcision not made with hands, in the putting off of the body of the sins of the flesh, in the circumcision of Christ;

2:12 you all being buried (passive) to Him in baptism, in which you all also were raised together with Him (passive) through faith of the

working of God, the One raising Him from the dead.
2:13 And you all continuously being dead in your trespasses and to the uncircumcision of your flesh. He made you all alive together with Him, Him forgiving to you all the trespasses,
2:14 wiping out the handwriting in ordinances which was against us; and He has taken (perfect tense) it out of the way, nailing it to the cross;
2:15 divesting of power and authority the principalities and the powers, He made a show of them in boldness, triumphing over them in it.
2:16 Let no one therefore be judging (PI) you all in food, or in drink, or in particulars of a feast day or a new moon or a Sabbath day,
2:17 which is being (PI) a shadow of the things continuously being about to come; but conversely the body is the possession of Christ.
2:18 Let no one be robbing (PI) you all of your prize in continuously willing seeing yourself as small and worshipping of the angels, continuously dwelling in the things which he has not seen, being continuously vainly puffed up (passive) under his fleshly mind,
2:19 and not continuously holding firmly to the Head, from whom all the body, being continuously supplied (passive) and being continuously knit together (passive) through the joints and ligaments, is growing (PI) with God's growth.
2:20 If you all die with Christ from the elements of the world, why, as though continuously living in the world, are you all being subject (PI) (passive) to ordinances?
2:21 "Don't handle, nor taste, nor touch"
2:22 (all of which is perishing (PI) from use), according to the precepts and doctrines of men?
2:23 Which things indeed are appearing (PI) like continuously having wisdom in self-imposed worship, and humility, and severity to the body; but aren't in any value toward the satisfying of the flesh.
3:1 If then you all were raised (passive) together with Christ, be seeking (PI) the things above, where Christ is being (PI), continuously sitting in the right hand of God.

3:2 You all be being disposed (PI) to the things that are above, not to the things that are on the earth.

3:3 For you all died, and your life has been and is hidden (perfect passive) with Christ in God.

3:4 When Christ, our life, may be made visible (passive), then you all will also be made visible (passive) with Him in glory.

3:5 Then put to death your members on the earth: sexual immorality, uncleanness, depraved passion, evil desire, and covetousness, which is being (PI) idolatry;

3:6 through which things' sake the wrath of God is coming (PI) on the children of disobedience.

3:7 You all also once lived your lives in those, when you all lived in them;

3:8 but now you all also put them all away: anger, wrath, malice, slander, and shameful speaking out of your mouth.

3:9 Don't be lying (PI) to one another, stripping off (aorist participle) the old man with his deeds,

3:10 and putting on (aorist participle) the new man, the one continuously being renewed (passive participle) into a knowledge according to the image of the One creating him,

3:11 where there is being (PI) not Greek and Jew, circumcision and uncircumcision, barbarian, Scythian, bondservant, freeman; but Christ the all, and in all.

3:12 Put on then, as God's chosen ones, holy and having been loved (passive), compassions of pity, kindness, lowliness, humility, and patience;

3:13 you all continuously bearing with one another, and you all continuously forgiving each other, if any man may continuously have a complaint against any; even as Christ also forgave you all, so you all also (do).

3:14 Yet over all to these, love, which is being (PI) the bond of the perfection.

3:15 And the peace of God be ruling (PI) in your hearts, into which also you all were called (passive) in one body; and thankful ones be becoming (PI).

3:16 The word of Christ be dwelling (PI) in you all richly; in all wisdom continuously teaching and continuously admonishing one another to psalms, hymns, and spiritual songs, continuously singing in grace in the hearts of you all to the Lord.

3:17 And whatever you all may continuously do, in word or in deed, (do) all in the name of the Lord Jesus, continuously giving thanks to God the Father, through Him.

3:18 Wives, be submitting (PI) to your husbands, as is fitting in the Lord.

3:19 Husbands, be loving (PI) your wives, and don't be being made bitter (PI) (passive) towards them.

3:20 Children, be obeying (PI) your parents in all things, for this is being (PI) well pleasing to the Lord.

3:21 Fathers, don't be provoking your children, so that they may not continuously be discouraged.

3:22 Servants, be obeying (PI) in all things those who are your masters according to the flesh, not in appearance, as men pleasers, but in singleness of heart, continuously fearing God.

3:23 And whatever you all may continuously do, be working (PI) out of your soul as to the Lord, and not to men,

3:24 you all having perceived from the Lord you all will receive the reward of the inheritance; for you all are

being slaves (PI) to the Lord Christ.

3:25 But the one continuously doing wrong will receive harm, and there is being (PI) no partiality.

4:1 Masters, be giving (PI) to your servants the just and equal, knowing that you all also are having (PI) a Master in heaven.

4:2 You all be persevering (PI) to prayer, continuously watching in the same in thanksgiving;

4:3 You all continuously praying together for us also, that God may open to us a door of the word, to speak the mystery of Christ, because of which I am also in bonds (passive);

4:4 that I may reveal it as it is being necessary (PI) for me to speak.

4:5 You all be living your lives (PI) in wisdom toward those who are outside, continuously redeeming the time.

4:6 Your speech always be in grace, having been seasoned (passive) to salt, you all to know how it is being necessary (PI) for you all to continuously answer to each one.

4:7 All my affairs will be made known to you all by

Tychicus, the beloved brother, and faithful servant, and fellow bondservant in the Lord.
4:8 Whom I sent to you all into this very purpose, that he may know your circumstances and he may comfort your hearts,
4:9 together with Onesimus, the faithful and beloved brother, who is being (PI) out of you all. They will make known to you all everything that is going on here.
4:10 Aristarchus, my fellow prisoner, is greeting (PI) you all, and Mark, the cousin of Barnabas (concerning whom you received directions, "if he comes to you all, receive him"),
4:11 and Jesus, the one continuously being called (passive) Justus. These continuously are my only fellow workers into the Kingdom of God who are of the circumcision, men who have been a comfort to me.
4:12 Epaphras, the one out of you all, a servant of Christ, is greeting (PI) you all, always continuously striving over you all in his prayers, that you all may stand perfect and having been filled (passive) in all the will of God.

4:13 For I am testifying (PI) to him, that he is having (PI) great zeal over you all, and for the ones in Laodicea, and the ones in Hierapolis.
4:14 Luke, the beloved physician, and Demas is greeting (PI) you all.
4:15 You all greet the brothers in Laodicea, and Nymphas, and the assembly that is in his house.
4:16 And when this letter may be read (passive) among you all, you all cause it to be read (passive) also in the assembly of the Laodiceans; and that you all also read the letter out of Laodicea.
4:17 And you all tell Archippus, "Be heeding (PI) the ministry which you have received in the Lord, that you may continuously fulfill it."
4:18 The salutation of me, Paul, to my own hand: be remembering (PI) my bonds. Grace be with you all. Amen.

Written (passive) from Rome through Tychicus and Onesimus.

Introduction To 1 Thessalonians

There is often some speculation about when a letter was written, but it appears that this letter was written around 50 AD. This makes it among the earliest letters of Paul that we have. As you read his Epistles, you will recognize that Paul's theology was always the same after his encounter with Jesus on the road to Damascus (Acts 9:3-6). It did not develop and mature over time. This is because he received his knowledge of the Good News directly from Jesus. See Galatians 1:12.

It is clear that Paul had previously spent time with the Thessalonians, and had taught them (Verses 4:1-4:3). Since it is clear that for Christians, the very center of the Good News (the word of God) is the provision for the ongoing forgiveness of their sins resulting in their sanctification, there can be no doubt that when Paul wrote this letter, the Thessalonians already knew HOW that is accomplished. Thus in this letter, Paul would NOT have needed to give them detailed instructions as to HOW sanctification is accomplished. But he did feel the need to encourage them to work out their sanctification, and to help them to realize that they need to support each other in this journey. There were persons trying to get them to abandon it.

A significant issue addressed in this letter relates to the coming of the Lord Jesus (the *parousia*). There are two aspects to this.
- First, He has already come and is here now. He sent His Holy Spirit into men, on the day of Pentecost (Acts 2:1-4), but also continues to be present and fills us more and more as we are sanctified (1 Thessalonians 2:19, 4:3, and 5:8-5:9). It seems clear that this is one aspect of His coming:

  > "Hence, for John Easter, Pentecost, and the parousia are not three separate events, but one and the same." (Bultmann, Theology of the New Testament, Part II, page 57).

- Then there is His Second Coming in the future, and the raising of the saved dead (Verses 4:14-17). This event is separate from the first event, and seems to be clearly described in these verses.

This letter is probably the clearest teaching in the Epistles that both aspects of His coming are true. It is an error to understand that only the Second Coming will occur. This is unfortunate; because if we believe that, we can be robbed of an awareness of His living presence being available to us NOW. See Verse 5:23.

1:1 Paul, and Silvanus, and Timothy, to the assembly of the Thessalonians in God the Father and the Lord Jesus Christ: Grace to you all and peace from God our Father and the Lord Jesus Christ.

1:2 We are always giving (PI) thanks to God about all of you, continuously mentioning you all in our prayers,

1:3 Continuously remembering without ceasing your work of faith and labor of love and patience of hope in our Lord Jesus Christ, before our God and Father.

1:4 We are having perceived, brothers loved by God, that you all are chosen,

1:5 that our Good News came unto you all not in word only, but also in power, and in the Holy Spirit, and in much assurance. You all know what kind of men we were in the presence of you all for your sakes.

1:6 And you all became imitators of us, and of the Lord, having received the word in much affliction, with joy of the Holy Spirit,

1:7 so that you all became an example to all the ones continuously believing in Macedonia and in Achaia.

1:8 For from you all the word of the Lord has been declared, not only in Macedonia and Achaia, but also in every place your faith toward God has gone out; so that we need not to continuously say anything.

1:9 For they themselves are reporting (PI) concerning us what kind of a reception we had unto you all; and how you all turned unto God from idols, to continuously serve to the continuously living and true God,

1:10 and to continuously wait for His Son out of the heavens, whom He raised out of the dead--Jesus, the One continuously delivering us from the wrath continuously coming.

2:1 For you yourselves know, brothers, our visit unto you all has not been for naught,

2:2 but having suffered before and been shamefully treated, as you know, in Philippi, we grew bold in our God to tell you all the Good News of God, in much conflict.

2:3 For our exhortation (is) not out of error, nor out of uncleanness, nor in deception.

2:4 But even as we have been approved by God to be entrusted (passive) with the Good News, so we are speaking (PI); not as continuously pleasing men, but God, the One continuously approving our hearts.

2:5 For neither were we at any time found in (using) words of flattery, as you know, nor in pretense of covetousness. God (is) witness,

2:6 nor continuously seeking glory out of men (neither from

you all nor from others), nor continuously being able to continuously be burdensome as apostles of Christ.

2:7 But we were gentle with you all, as ever a nursing mother may continuously cherish her own children.

2:8 Thus, continuously being affectionately desirous of you all, we were well pleased to impart to you all, not the Good News of God only, but also our own souls, because you had become very dear to us.

2:9 For you all are remembering (PI), brothers, our labor and travail; for continuously working night and day, for the purpose to not be burdensome to any of you all, we preached unto you all the Good News of God.

2:10 You all are witnesses with God, how holy, righteously, and blamelessly we were beginning to become to you all, the ones continuously believing.

2:11 As you all were aware, how we were continuously consoling and continuously comforting each one of you all, as a father of his own children,

2:12 and continuously witnessing unto you all to live your lives worthily of God, the One continuously calling you all into His own Kingdom and glory.

2:13 Through this we also are thanking (PI) God without ceasing, that, receiving from us the word of the message of God, you accepted it not as the word of men, but, as it is being (PI) in truth, the word of God, which also is working (PI) in you all, the ones continuously believing.

2:14 For you all, brothers, became imitators of the assemblies of God, of the ones continuously being in Judea in Christ Jesus; that you all also suffered the same things even by your own countrymen, even as they also did by the Jews;

2:15 and the ones killing both the Lord Jesus and their own prophets, and banishing us out, and not continuously pleasing God, and are contrary to all men;

2:16 continuously forbidding us to speak to the Gentiles that they may be saved (passive); to fill up their sins always. But wrath came unexpectedly on them into the uttermost.

2:17 But we, brothers, being bereaved (passive) from you all for a short season, in presence, not to heart, we tried even harder to see your face in great desire,

2:18 because we wanted to come unto you all--indeed, I, Paul, and once and again--and Satan hindered us.

2:19 For who is our hope, or joy, or crown of rejoicing? Or isn't it even you all in front of our Lord Jesus in His presence?

2:20 For you all are being (PI) our glory and our joy.

3:1 Therefore, by no means any longer continuously enduring, we thought it good to be left behind in Athens alone,

3:2 and sent Timothy, our brother and God's servant and fellow-worker in the Good News of Christ, for the purpose to establish you all, and to comfort you all concerning your faith;

3:3 that no one to be moved (passive) in these afflictions. For you all know that we are now appointed (PI) into this.

3:4 For even when we were unto you all, we told you all beforehand that we are being about (PI) to continuously be afflicted (passive), even as it happened, and you all know.

3:5 Because of this, I also no longer refraining, I sent for the purpose to know your faith, lest somehow the one continuously testing continuously tested you all in the past, and the toil of us may be becoming for naught.

3:6 But when Timothy came just now unto us from you all, and bringing us glad news of your faith and love, and that you all are having (PI) good memories of us always, continuously longing to see us, even as we also (long) to see you all;

3:7 for this cause, brothers, we were comforted (passive) over you all on all our distress and affliction through your faith.

3:8 That now we are living (PI), if you all may continuously stand fast in the Lord.

3:9 For what thanksgiving are we being able (PI) to render again to God about you all upon all the joy with which we are rejoicing (PI) for your sakes before our God;

3:10 night and day continuously praying exceedingly for the purpose of to be seeing the face of you all, and to perfect that which is lacking in your faith?

3:11 But our God and Father, and our Lord Jesus Christ, may direct our way unto you all;

3:12 but the Lord may increase and may superabound to love into one another, and toward all, even as we also do toward you all,

3:13 toward the end to establish your hearts blameless in holiness in front of our God and Father, in the presence of our Lord Jesus with all His saints.

4:1 Finally then, brothers, we are begging (PI) and exhorting (PI) you all in the Lord Jesus, that as you received of us how it is being necessary (PI) (for) you all to be living your lives and to continuously please God, that you all may superabound more and more.

4:2 For you know what instructions we gave you through the Lord Jesus.

4:3 For this is being (PI) the will of God: your sanctification. To continuously abstain from sexual immorality,

4:4 that each one of you to know how to possess himself of his own vessel in sanctification and honor,

4:5 not in the passion of lust, even as the Gentiles not being acquainted with God;

4:6 that no one to continuously transgress and to continuously take advantage of a brother or sister in this matter; because the Lord (is) the avenger in all these things, as also we forewarned you all and testified.

4:7 For God called us not for uncleanness, but in sanctification.

4:8 Surely then the one continuously rejecting is not rejecting (PI) man, but God, (the One) also giving His Holy Spirit into us.

4:9 But concerning brotherly love, you all are having (PI) no need (for me) to be continuously writing to you all; for you yourselves are being (PI) divinely instructed into to be continuously loving one another,

4:10 for indeed you all are doing (PI) it unto all the brothers who are in all Macedonia. But we are exhorting (PI) you all, brothers, to continuously be superabounding more and more;

4:11 and to continuously be being ambitious to continuously be quiet, continuously be being engaged to continuously work to your own hands, even as we instructed you;

4:12 that you all may continuously live your lives properly toward those who are outside, and you all may continuously be having need of nothing.

4:13 But I am not desiring (PI) you all to be ignorant, brothers, concerning those having been put to sleep (passive) that you all may not be grieved (passive) like the rest, the ones continuously having no hope.

4:14 For if we are believing (PI) that Jesus died and rose again, even so God will bring with Him the ones having been put to sleep (passive) through Jesus.

4:15 For this we are telling (PI) you all in the word of the Lord, that we, the ones continuously living, the ones continuously surviving into the coming of the Lord, may not precede the ones having been put to sleep (passive).

4:16 That the Lord Himself will descend from heaven in a shout, in the voice of the archangel, and in God's trumpet. And the dead in Christ will rise first,

4:17 then we, the ones continuously living, the ones continuously surviving, will be caught up together with them in the clouds, toward meeting the Lord in the air. And thus we will be with the Lord forever.

4:18 Therefore continuously comfort one another in these words.

5:1 But concerning the times and the seasons, brothers, you are having (PI) no need anything to continuously be written (passive) to you all.

5:2 For you yourselves know well that the day of the Lord is coming (PI) like a thief in the night.

5:3 For when they may continuously say, "Peace and safety," then sudden destruction is coming (PI) to them, like continuously having pain of childbirth in the belly; and they may in no way be escaping.

5:4 But you all, brothers, are not being (PI) in darkness, that the day may overtake you all like a thief.

5:5 You all are being (PI) children of light, and children of the day. We are not being (PI) of the night, nor of darkness,

5:6 so then we may not be continuously sleeping, as even the rest, but may we be continuously watching and may we continuously be sober.

5:7 For the ones continuously sleeping are sleeping (PI) in the night, and the ones continuously being drunk are being drunk (PI) of night.

5:8 But we continuously being of (the) day may continuously be sober, putting on the breastplate of faith and of love, and, the head protecting hope of salvation.

5:9 That God didn't appoint us into wrath, but into the obtaining of salvation through our Lord Jesus Christ,

5:10 the One dying for us, that, whether we may be continuously awake or may be continuously sleeping, we may live together with Him.

5:11 Therefore continuously exhort one another, and continuously build each other up, even as you all also are doing (PI).

5:12 But we are begging (PI) you all, brothers, to know the ones continuously laboring among you all, and are continuously being caring of you all in the Lord, and continuously admonishing you all,

5:13 and to continuously respect them extravagantly in love because of their work's sake. Continuously be at peace among yourselves.

5:14 But we are exhorting (PI) you all, brothers, be continuously admonishing the disorderly, continuously encourage the fainthearted, continuously support the weak, continuously be patient toward all.

5:15 Continuously see that no one may return evil for evil to anyone, but always continuously pursue that which is good, unto one another, and unto all.

5:16 Continuously rejoice always.

5:17 Continuously pray without ceasing.

5:18 In everything continuously give thanks, for this is the will of God in Christ Jesus into you all.

5:19 Don't continuously quench the Spirit.

5:20 Don't continuously despise prophesies.

5:21 Continuously examine all things, and continuously hold firmly that which is good.

5:22 Continuously abstain from every appearance of evil.

5:23 But the God of peace Himself may sanctify you all completely. And your whole spirit, soul, and body may be preserved blameless in the presence of our Lord Jesus Christ.

5:24 Faithful (is) the One continuously calling you all, Who will also do it.

5:25 Brothers, continuously pray about us.

5:26 Greet all the brothers in a holy kiss.

5:27 I am adjuring (PI) you all by the Lord that this letter to be read (passive) to all the holy brothers.

5:28 The grace of our Lord Jesus Christ be with you all. Amen.

Introduction to 2 Thessalonians

Second Thessalonians was written shortly after 1 Thessalonians. We don't know exactly how soon after, but it was not long

There is some similarity with 1 Thessalonians, and you might want to review my Introduction to it before going on.

Why did Paul feel that he needed to write to them so quickly? The letter speaks for itself.

Apparently the Thessalonians were suffering some affliction, and needed to be encouraged.

Part of the encouragement was to keep on with the Good News, meaning to continue to do what Paul had taught them, and they had observed Paul doing - namely to continuously apply the blood of Jesus to their sins so they could continuously be transformed into His image (Verses 1:8, 2:15-2:17, and 3:4).

Part of the encouragement was that Jesus is present with them currently (Verse 2:2).

They also need to be watchful, because the "man of sin" is coming, and will deceive some (Verse 2:3-2:8). He wanted to clarify what was coming in that regard

.

1:1 Paul, Silvanus, and Timothy, to the assembly of the Thessalonians in God our Father, and the Lord Jesus Christ:
1:2 Grace to you all and peace from God our Father and the Lord Jesus Christ.
1:3 We are being obligated (PI) to continuously give thanks to God for you all, brothers, even as it is being appropriate (PI), seeing that your faith is flourishing exceedingly (PI), and the love of each and every one of you towards one another is increasing (PI);
1:4 so that we ourselves to continuously boast in you all in the assemblies of God for your patience and faith in all your persecutions and in the afflictions which you all are enduring (PI).
1:5 (This is an) obvious sign of the righteous judgment of God, into the end that you may be counted worthy (passive) of the Kingdom of God, for which you all also are suffering (PI).
1:6 If so be that it is a righteous thing with God to repay affliction to the ones continuously afflicting you all,
1:7 and to give relief to you all, the ones continuously being afflicted (passive), rest together with us in the unveiling of the Lord Jesus from heaven with His angels of power,
1:8 continuously giving vengeance in fire of flame to the ones not being acquainted with God, and to the ones not continuously obeying to the Good News of our Lord Jesus,
1:9 who will pay the penalty: eternal destruction from the face of the Lord and from the glory of His might,
1:10 when He may come to be glorified in His saints, and to be admired in all the ones continuously believing (because our testimony to you all was believed) in that day.
1:11 To this end we are praying (PI) always about you all always, that our God may consider you all suitable of your calling, and may fulfill every desire of goodness and work of faith, in power;
1:12 that the name of our Lord Jesus may be glorified in you all, and you all in Him, according to the grace of our God and the Lord Jesus Christ.
2:1 But we are asking (PI) you all, brothers, for the sake of the presence of our Lord Jesus Christ, and our gathering together toward Him,
2:2 in order to not to be quickly shaken (passive) in your mind, nor to be continuously troubled (passive), either through spirit, or through word, or through letters as through us, that the day of Christ has become present and is continuing to be present;
2:3 (so that) not any one may deceive you all in any way, that the falling away may not come first, and the man of sin may be

revealed (passive), the son of destruction,

2:4 the ones continuously opposing and continuously being lifted up (passive) over all that is continuously being called (passive) god or that is worshiped; so that to be seated as God into the temple of God, continuously showing himself that he is being (PI) God.

2:5 Are you all not remembering (PI) that, when I was still continuously being with you all, I told you all these things?

2:6 And now you know the continuously restraining into the end, that him to be revealed (passive) in his own season.

2:7 For the mystery of lawlessness already is working (PI). Only there is One continuously restraining at present, until He may become to be out of the way.

2:8 And then the lawless one will be revealed, whom the Lord will destroy to the spirit of His mouth, and will do away with, to the manifestation of His coming;

2:9 whose coming is being (PI) according to the working of Satan in all power and signs and lying miracles,

2:10 and in all deception of wickedness in the ones continuously perishing themselves, instead of which they did not receive the love of the truth into them to be saved.

2:11 And because of this, God will send them a working of error, into them to believe to the lie;

2:12 that they all may be judged (passive), all the ones not believing to the truth, but delighting in unrighteousness.

2:13 But we are being bound (PI) to continuously always give thanks to God for you all, brothers having been loved (passive) by the Lord, because God chose you all from the beginning unto salvation in sanctification of the Spirit and to faith of the truth;

2:14 into which He called you all through our Good News, into the obtaining of the glory of our Lord Jesus Christ.

2:15 So then, brothers, continuously stand firm, and continuously hold the substance of the teachings which you all were taught (passive) by us, whether through word, or through letter.

2:16 But our Lord Jesus Christ Himself, and God our Father, the One loving us and giving us eternal comfort and good hope in grace,

2:17 may comfort your hearts and may establish you in every good work and word.

3:1 Finally, brothers, continuously pray concerning us, that the word of the Lord may continuously spread rapidly and may continuously be glorified (passive), even as also unto you all;

3:2 and that we may be delivered (passive) from unreasonable and evil men; for faith is not of all (men).

3:3 But the Lord is being faithful (PI), Who will establish you all, and guard you all from of the evil one.

3:4 But we have confidence in the Lord on you all, that you all both are doing (PI) and will do that which we are declaring (PI).

3:5 But may the Lord direct your hearts into the love of God, and into the patience of Christ.

3:6 But we are declaring to you all, brothers, in the name of our Lord Jesus Christ, to continuously withdraw yourselves from every brother who is continuously living disorderly, and not after the substance of the teachings which they received from us.

3:7 For you know how it is being necessary (PI) to continuously follow us as an example, that we didn't behave ourselves rebelliously in you all.

3:8 Neither did we eat bread from anyone's hand without paying for it, but in labor and toil, continuously working night and day to not be burdensome to any of you all:

3:9 not that we are not having (PI) the right, but that we may be giving to you all an example into you all to continuously imitate us.

3:10 For even when we were with you all, we announced this to you all: "If anyone is not willing (PI) to continuously work, neither let him continuously eat."

3:11 For we are hearing (PI) of some who walk in you all in a disorderly manner, not continuously working at all, but are continuously being busybodies.

3:12 But to those who are that way, we are announcing (PI) and exhorting (PI) through the Lord Jesus Christ, that with quietness continuously working, they may continuously eat their own bread.

3:13 But you all, brothers, you all may not be weary in continuously doing well.

3:14 But if any man is not hearkening to (PI) our word through this letter, continuously let (it) be a sign to you all and continuously have no company to him, that he may be being ashamed (passive).

3:15 And don't continuously count him as an enemy, but continuously admonish him as a brother.

3:16 But the Lord of peace Himself may give to you all peace by means of every kind, in every way. The Lord be with you all.

3:17 The greeting of me, Paul, to my own hand, which is being (PI) the sign in every letter: this is how I am writing (PI).

3:18 The grace of our Lord Jesus Christ be with you all. Amen.

The second written (passive)
unto the Thessalonians from
Athens.

Introduction To 1 Timothy

In reading 1 Timothy, it is very important to keep the circumstances in mind. Otherwise, one might think that the Apostle Paul is an advocate of good behavior, rather than transformation into the image of Jesus – which is the Good News.

The reason that this letter could be misleading is that the majority of it is indeed advice Paul is giving to Timothy about how to steward a church.

If we had the privilege of spending a couple of years with Paul, we would thoroughly understand the central nature of forgiveness of our sins, the resulting transformation into the image of Jesus, and how that is accomplished. This is also referred to as sanctification, and is the ongoing aspect of salvation.

Being "saved" has two aspects.
1. The first aspect is the one-time event of when we made Jesus our Lord. As a result of this, we know we will go to heaven when we die.
2. The second aspect is then the ongoing provision for our sins to be forgiven as we continuously forgive. As a result of this process, we are progressively transformed into the image of Jesus.

Because Paul knows that sanctification is the very essence of Christianity, in his presence he would have emphasized it, taught it, mentored it, and modeled it. Since Timothy was like a son to Paul, we can be sure that they had spent a lot of time together, and that therefore Timothy was fully aware of how sanctification works, of its importance, and would be practicing it.

Since Timothy already was fully aware of the centrality of sanctification, and how to accomplish it before Paul wrote this letter, Paul would have no reason to repeat those lessons to Timothy here. Rather, in this epistle, other than in the first chapter, Paul is mentoring Timothy in how to be an elder in his local church.

Likewise, by emphasizing advice about what to do in this letter, Paul was NOT saying that keeping rules of conduct is a central part of Christianity. In reality, mature Christian conduct is the result of earnestly and continuously practicing the sanctification process. Both he and Timothy know full well that consistent good behavior is only possible as "good fruit" from the "good root" of Jesus in us.

Likewise for us, when we read this letter, we need to keep a proper perspective. Sanctification is the center and heart of the Good News, not behavior. The behaviors that Paul talks about to Timothy in most of this letter are only continuously possible as "good fruit" from "good roots." The "good roots" are created as we forgive and are forgiven by Jesus; and then He comes and inhabits those places in us.

This letter has some important things to say, but its primary purpose is NOT to reveal to us how the sanctification process occurs. On the other hand, many of Paul's other letters are indeed much more focused on how we can be sanctified, and especially of its paramount importance.

Please keep this perspective clearly in mind as you read this letter.

1:1 Paul, an apostle of Christ Jesus according to the authority of God our Savior, and Christ Jesus our hope;

1:2 to Timothy, my true child in faith: Grace, mercy, peace, from God our Father and Christ Jesus our Lord.

1:3 As I urged you to stay in Ephesus, when I was continuously going into Macedonia, that you might charge some not to continuously teach differently,

1:4 neither to continuously pay attention to myths and endless genealogies, which are causing (PI) disputes, rather than edifying of God in faith

1:5 but love is being (PI) the goal of this charge, out of a pure heart and a good conscience and sincere faith;

1:6 from which some, focusing on the wrong goal were turned aside (passive) into vain talking;

1:7 continuously desiring to continuously be teachers of (NT) law, though they are continuously not understanding either what they are saying (PI), nor about what they are strongly affirming (PI).

1:8 But we have known and continue to know that the (NT) law (is) good, if ever anyone may continuously use it lawfully,

1:9 knowing this, that (OT) law is not being laid down to the just, but to the lawless and insubordinate, the ungodly and sinners, the unholy and profane, murderers of fathers and murderers of mothers, manslayers,

1:10 (for) the sexually immoral, homosexuals, slave-traders, liars, perjurers, and for any other thing being contrary (PI) to teaching, being continuously sound;

1:11 according to the Good News of the glory of the blessed God, with which I was entrusted (passive).

1:12 And I am having gratitude (PI) to the One enabling me, Christ Jesus our Lord, because He counted me faithful, appointing me into service;

1:13 formerly continuously being a blasphemer, a persecutor, and insolent. But I was shown mercy (passive), because I did it ignorantly in unbelief.

1:14 But the grace of our Lord abounded exceedingly with faith and of love in Christ Jesus.

1:15 The faithful saying and worthy of all acceptance, that Christ Jesus came into the world to save sinners; of whom I am being (PI) chief.

1:16 But for this cause I was shown mercy (passive), that in me first, Jesus Christ may display all His patience, for a pattern of the ones continuously being about to continuously believe on Him into eternal life.

1:17 But to the King of the ages, immortal, invisible, to God Who alone is wise, honor and glory forever and ever. Amen.

1:18 This instruction I am committing (PI) to you, my child Timothy, according to the continuously preceding prophecies over you, that in them you may continuously wage the good warfare;

1:19 continuously having faith and a good conscience; which some having thrust away concerning the faith, have made shipwrecks;

1:20 of whom is being (PI) Hymenaeus and Alexander; whom I delivered to Satan, that they may be taught (passive) not to continuously blaspheme.

2:1 I am exhorting (PI) therefore, first of all, that petitions, prayers, intercessions, and giving of thanks, be made for all men:

2:2 over kings and all the ones continuously being in high places; that we may continuously lead a tranquil and quiet life in all holiness and reverence.

2:3 For this (is) good and acceptable in the sight of God our Savior;

2:4 Who is desiring (PI) all people to be saved (passive) and come to knowledge of the truth.

2:5 For (there is) one God, and one mediator of God and of men, the man Christ Jesus,

2:6 the One giving Himself as a ransom over all; the testimony to its own times;

2:7 into which I was appointed (passive) a preacher and an apostle (I am telling (PI) the truth in Christ, not lying (PI)), a teacher of the Gentiles in faith and truth.

2:8 I am desiring (PI) therefore the men to be continuously praying in every place, continuously lifting up holy hands without anger and doubting.

2:9 And also in the same way, the women to continuously adorn themselves in decent clothing, with modesty and propriety; not just in braided hair, or gold, or pearls, or expensive clothing;

2:10 but (which is becoming (PI) to women continuously professing godliness) through good works.

2:11 Let a woman continuously learn in quietness in all subjection.

2:12 But I am not permitting (PI) to a woman to continuously teach, nor to be continuously domineering of a man, but to continuously be in quietness.

2:13 For Adam was first formed (passive), then Eve.

2:14 And Adam wasn't deceived (passive), but the woman, being deceived (passive), was beginning to become in transgression;

2:15 but she will be saved through the childbearing, if they may continue in faith and love, and sanctification with sobriety.

3:1 The saying (is) fruitful: if a man is seeking (PI) of being an elder, he is desiring (PI) a good work.

3:2 The elder therefore to continuously be without reproach, the husband of one wife, temperate, sensible, modest, hospitable, good at teaching;

3:3 not a drinker, not violent, not greedy for money, but gentle, not quarrelsome, not covetous;

3:4 continuously presiding over his own house well, continuously having children in subjection with all reverence;

3:5 (but if a man has not known how to preside over his own house, how will he take care of the assembly of God?)

3:6 not a new convert, that being puffed up he may fall into the same condemnation of the devil.

3:7 But it is being necessary (PI) him also to continuously have a good testimony from those who are outside, that he may not fall into reproach and the snare of the devil.

3:8 Servants, in the same way, must be reverent, not double-tongued, not addicted to much wine, not greedy for money;

3:9 continuously holding the mystery of the faith in a pure conscience.

3:10 But let them also first continuously be tested (passive); then let them continuously serve, continuously being blameless.

3:11 Their wives in the same way must be reverent, not slanderers, temperate, faithful in all things.

3:12 Let servants continuously be husbands of one wife, continuously presiding well over their children and their own houses.

3:13 For the ones serving well are gaining (PI) to themselves a good standing, and great boldness in the faith in Christ Jesus.

3:14 These things I am writing (PI) to you, hoping to come unto you shortly;

3:15 but if I may be continuously being tardy, that you may know how it is being imperative (PI) to continuously behave themselves in the house of God, which is being (PI) the assembly of the continuously living God, the pillar and ground of the truth.

3:16 And without controversy, great is being (PI) the mystery of holiness: God was revealed (passive) in the flesh, justified in the spirit, was seen (passive) by angels, was preached (passive) in the nations, was believed (passive) in the world, and was received (passive) up in glory.

4:1 But the Spirit is saying (PI) expressly that in later times some will fall away of the faith, continuously paying attention to seducing spirits and doctrines of demons,

4:2 in hypocrisy of lying, having been branded (passive) in their own conscience as with a hot iron;

4:3 continuously forbidding to continuously marry and to

continuously abstain of foods which God created into partaking with thanksgiving to the ones believing and having known the truth.

4:4 Seeing that every creature of God (is) good, and nothing is to be rejected, continuously being taken with thanksgiving.

4:5 For it is being sanctified (PI) (passive) through the word of God and of prayer.

4:6 Continuously suggesting to the brothers of these things, you will be a good servant of Christ Jesus, continuously being trained to the words of the faith, and of the good teaching which you have followed and continue to follow.

4:7 But continuously refuse profane and old wives' fables, but continuously exercise yourself toward holiness.

4:8 For bodily exercise is being (PI) beneficial toward a few things, but holiness is being (PI) beneficial toward all (things), continuously having promise of the life now, and of that which is to come.

4:9 This saying (is) faithful and worthy of all acceptance.

4:10 For into this we both are laboring (PI) and being reproached (PI) (passive), because we trust on the continuously living God, Who is being (PI) Savior of all men, especially of those who believe.

4:11 Continuously declare and continuously teach these things.

4:12 Continuously let no man despise your youth; but continuously be an example of the ones believing, in word, in your way of life, in love, in spirit, in faith, and in purity.

4:13 Until I am coming (PI), continuously pay attention to reading, to exhortation, to teaching.

4:14 Don't be continuously neglecting of the gift in you, which was given to you through prophecy, with the laying on of the hands of the elders.

4:15 You continuously be continuously diligent in these things. Give yourself wholly to them, that your progress may continuously be revealed in all.

4:16 Continuously pay attention to yourself, and to your teaching. Continuously be persisting in these things, for in continuously doing this you will save both yourself and the ones continuously hearing of you.

5:1 You may not rebuke an older man, but continuously exhort him as a father; the younger men as brothers;

5:2 the elder women as mothers; the younger as sisters, in all purity.

5:3 Continuously honor widows, the ones really being widows.

5:4 But if any widow is having (PI) children or grandchildren, let them continuously learn first to continuously show piety (in) their own family, and to continuously repay to the

parents, for this is being (PI)
good and acceptable in the sight
of God.
5:5 But the one being a widow
indeed, and being left alone
(passive) relies on God, and is
remaining (PI) to petitions and to
prayers of night and of day.
5:6 But the one continuously
living in pleasure has died while
continuously living.
5:7 Also continuously declare
these things, that they may
continuously be without
reproach.
5:8 But if anyone is not
providing (PI) for his own, and
especially of the family
members, he has denied the faith,
and is being (PI) worse of an
unbeliever.
5:9 Let no one be continuously
being enrolled (passive) as a
widow under sixty years old,
having been the wife of one man,
5:10 continuously being
approved (passive) in good
works, if she has brought up
children, if she has been
hospitable to strangers, if she has
washed the saints' feet, if she has
relieved the ones continuously
being afflicted (passive), and if
she has diligently followed to
every good work.
5:11 But continuously refuse
younger widows, for when they
may have grown wanton to the
Christ, they are desiring (PI) to
marry;

5:12 continuously having
condemnation, seeing that they
have rejected their first faith.
5:13 But at the same time, idle
ones they are also learning to be
(PI), continuously going about
the homes, but not only idle, but
also gossips and busybodies,
continuously saying things not
continuously being proper.
5:14 I am desiring (PI) therefore
that the younger widows to
continuously marry, to
continuously bear children, to
continuously manage the
household, to continuously give
no opportunity of reviling to the
one continuously opposing
grace.
5:15 For already some have been
turned aside (passive) after
Satan.
5:16 If any man or woman who
believes is having (PI) widows,
let them continuously relieve
them, and don't continuously let
the assembly be burdened
(passive); that it might relieve
the ones who are widows indeed.
5:17 Let the elders, the ones
presiding well be counted worthy
of double honor, especially the
ones continuously laboring in the
word and teaching.
5:18 For the Scripture is saying
(PI), "You shall not muzzle the
ox continuously threshing the
grain." And, "The laborer (is)
worthy of his wages."
5:19 Don't continuously receive
an accusation against an elder, if

without (the word) of two or three witnesses.

5:20 The ones continuously sinning, continuously reprove in the sight of all, that the rest also may continuously have reverence.

5:21 I am bearing witness (PI) in the sight of God, and Christ Jesus, and of the chosen angels, that you may keep these things without prejudice, continuously doing nothing according to partiality.

5:22 Lay hands hastily to no one, neither continuously be a participant to other men's sins. Continuously keep yourself pure.

5:23 No longer continuously drink water only, but continuously use a little wine because of your stomach's sake and your frequent infirmities.

5:24 The sins of some men are being (PI) manifest before all, continuously preceding them into judgment, but some also are following their example (PI).

5:25 In the same way is being (PI) the evident good works, and those which are continuously being otherwise, is not being able (PI) to be hid.

6:1 Whoever are being (PI) bondservants under the yoke continuously count their own masters worthy of all honor, that the name of God and the teaching may not continuously be blasphemed (passive).

6:2 But the ones continuously having believing masters, let them continuously not despise, because they are being (PI) brothers, but rather let them continuously serve them, because they who receive the benefit of their service are being (PI) believing and beloved. Continuously teach and continuously exhort these things.

6:3 If anyone is teaching (PI) differently and is not coming (PI) to sound words, to the words of our Lord Jesus Christ, and to the teaching according to holiness,

6:4 he has been lifted up in pride (passive), continuously being versed in nothing, but continuously being obsessed about questionings and controversies, out of which is coming (PI) envy, strife, insulting, evil suspicions,

6:5 unprofitable disputes to be corrupted throughout (passive) of people of corrupt mind and being deprived (passive) of the truth, continuously supposing holiness to continuously be means of gain. Continuously withdraw yourself from such.

6:6 But holiness with contentment is being (PI) great gain.

6:7 For we brought nothing into the world, and (it is) evident we are not being able (PI) to carry anything out.

6:8 But continuously having food and clothing, we will be content to these.

6:9 But the ones continuously desiring to continuously be rich are falling (PI) into temptation and a snare and many foolish and harmful desires, which are drowning (PI) men in ruin and destruction.

6:10 For the love of money is being (PI) a root of all kinds of evil, of which some have been led astray (passive) from the faith, and have pierced themselves through to many sorrows.

6:11 But you, man of God, continuously flee these things, but continuously follow righteousness, holiness, faith, love, patience, and gentleness.

6:12 Continuously fight the good fight of faith. Lay hold of the eternal life to which you were called (passive), and you confessed the good confession in the sight of many witnesses.

6:13 I charge (PI) you in the sight of God, the One continuously giving life to all (things), and of Christ Jesus, the one testifying on Pontius Pilate the good confession,

6:14 that you keep the precept without spot, blameless, unto the appearing of our Lord Jesus Christ;

6:15 which to its own times He will show. The blessed and only Ruler, the King of the ones continuously being kings, and Lord of the ones continuously being lords;

6:16 the only One continuously having immortality, continuously dwelling in unapproachable light; Whom no man has seen, nor is able (PI) to see: to Whom honor and eternal power. Amen.

6:17 Continuously charge to the rich ones in this present age not to continuously be haughty, nor to rely in the uncertainty of riches, but in the continuously living God, the One continuously providing to us richly everything to enjoy;

6:18 to continuously be doing good acts, to continuously be rich in good works, ready to distribute, willing to continuously be liberal contributors;

6:19 continuously laying up to themselves a good foundation into the time which is continuously impending, that they may lay hold of eternal life.

6:20 Oh Timothy, guard that which is committed to you, continuously turning away from the profane chatter and oppositions of the knowledge which is falsely so called;

6:21 which some continuously professing about the faith have erred concerning the faith. Grace be with you. Amen.

The first unto Timothy. Was written from Laodicea which is being (PI) the mother city of Phrygia of Pacatiana.

Introduction To 2 Timothy

It is clear that this letter was written to Timothy by the Apostle Paul some time after he wrote 1 Timothy. It is not clear how much later it was written, but it was probably written within a year or two.

As with 1 Timothy, in this letter Paul would not have needed to teach Timothy in detail HOW to be sanctified, as he would undoubtedly have taught him this in detail when they were together. The purpose of this letter is primarily to explain in more detail how to lead a Christian church. Paul is NOT advocating to either Timothy or us that keeping a list of rules is being central to the Good News.

See the Introduction to 1 Timothy for more details.

Again, it is important to keep in mind Paul's purpose in writing this letter. It is therefore important to NOT conclude that because he does not here emphasize the details of how we are to be transformed into the image of Jesus, that this process is not central to the Good News.

1:1 Paul, an apostle of Jesus Christ through the will of God, according to the promise of the life which is in Christ Jesus,

1:2 to Timothy, my beloved child: Grace, mercy, and peace, from God the Father and Christ Jesus our Lord.

1:3 I am thanking (PI) to God, to whom I am serving (PI) from my forefathers, in a pure conscience. As unceasing I am having (PI) the remembrance about you in my petitions, night and day

1:4 continuously longing to see you, having been reminded (passive) of your tears, that I may be filled (passive) with joy;

1:5 continuously getting reminder of the sincere faith that is in you; which lived first in your grandmother Lois, and your mother Eunice, and, I have been persuaded (passive), that in you also.

1:6 Because of which cause, I am reminding (PI) you to continuously stir up the gift of God which is being (PI) in you through the laying on of my hands.

1:7 For God didn't give to us a spirit of fear, but of power, and of love, and of sound judgment.

1:8 Then you may not be being made ashamed (passive) of the testimony of our Lord, nor of me His prisoner; but endure hardship to the Good News in accord with the power of God,

1:9 the One saving us and calling us to a holy calling, not according to our works, but according to His own purpose and grace, being given (passive) to us in Christ Jesus before time was,

1:10 but being manifest (passive) now through the appearing of our Savior, Christ Jesus, the One indeed abolishing death, but illuminating life and immortality through the Good News.

1:11 Into which I was appointed (passive) a preacher, and an apostle, and a teacher of the Gentiles.

1:12 Through that reason I also am suffering (PI) these things. Yet I am not being ashamed (PI), for I have known and continue to know Him to Whom I have believed and continue to believe, and I have been persuaded (passive) that He is being able (PI) to guard that which I have committed unto that day.

1:13 Continuously be having a pattern of words of which you have heard beside me, in faith and love in Christ Jesus.

1:14 That good thing which was committed to you, guard through the Holy Spirit, the One continuously dwelling in us.

1:15 This you have known and continue to know, that all who are in Asia were turned away (passive) from me; of whom is being (PI) Phygelus and Hermogenes.

1:16 May the Lord grant mercy to the house of Onesiphorus, that he often refreshed me, and was not made ashamed (passive) of my chain,

1:17 but coming to be in Rome, he sought me diligently, and found me

1:18 (the Lord grant to him to find the Lord's mercy in that day); and in how many things he served in Ephesus, you are knowing (PI) very well.

2:1 You therefore, my child, be continuously strengthened (passive) in the grace in Christ Jesus.

2:2 And the things which you have heard from me among many witnesses, these commit to faithful men, who will be able to teach others also.

2:3 You therefore must endure hardship, as a good soldier of Christ Jesus.

2:4 No one continuously being a soldier on duty is being entangled (passive) to the manner of life practices, that he may please the one enlisting.

2:5 Also, if anyone may continuously compete in athletics, he is not being crowned (passive) unless he may compete by the rules.

2:6 The continuously toiling farmers must be (PI) the first to continuously partake of the crops.

2:7 Continuously consider what I am saying (PI), for may the Lord give you understanding in all.

2:8 Continuously remember Jesus Christ, the One having been roused out of the dead, out of the seed of David, according to my Good News,

2:9 in which I am suffering (PI) hardship unto chains as a criminal. But God's word isn't chained.

2:10 Because of this I am enduring (PI) all things because of the chosen ones, that they also may obtain the salvation which is in Christ Jesus with eternal glory.

2:11 This saying (is) faithful: "For if we died with Him, we will also live together with Him.

2:12 If we are enduring (PI), we will also reign with Him. If we are denying (PI) Him, that One also will deny us.

2:13 If we are being faithless (PI), that One is remaining (PI) faithful. To disown Himself, He is not being able (PI)."

2:14 Continuously remind them of these things, continuously charging them in the sight of the Lord, to not continuously argue about words, into nothing profitable, on to destruction of the ones continuously hearing.

2:15 Make every effort to do your best to present yourself approved to God, a workman unashamed, continuously properly handling the Word of Truth.

2:16 But continuously shun profane chatter, for they will increase further of ungodliness,

2:17 and their word will consume like gangrene, of whom

is being (PI) Hymenaeus and Philetus;

2:18 who have deviated concerning the truth, continuously saying that the resurrection is already past, and are overthrowing (PI) the faith of some.

2:19 However, God's firm foundation stands, continuously having this seal, "The Lord knew the ones continuously being of Him," and, "Let every one continuously naming the name of the Lord depart from unrighteousness."

2:20 But in a large house there is being (PI) not only golden vessel and silver, but also wooden and earthenware, and which indeed into honor, but some into dishonor.

2:21 If anyone therefore may purge himself from these, he will be a vessel into honor, having been sanctified (passive), and suitable to the master's use, having been prepared (passive) for every good work.

2:22 But continuously flee from youthful desires; but continuously pursue righteousness, faith, love, peace with the ones continuously calling on the Lord out of a pure heart.

2:23 But continuously refuse foolish and ignorant questionings, knowing that they are generating (PI) strife.

2:24 But it is being necessary (PI) the Lord's servant not to continuously quarrel, but to be gentle towards all, able to teach, patient,

2:25 in gentleness continuously correcting the ones continuously opposing him: lest at any time God may give to them repentance into a full knowledge of the truth,

2:26 and they may recover themselves out of the devil's snare, having been taken captive (passive) by him to his will.

3:1 But continuously know this, that in the last days, grievous times will come.

3:2 For men will be selfish, lovers of money, boastful, arrogant, blasphemers, disobedient to parents, unthankful, unholy,

3:3 without natural affection, unforgiving, adversaries, without uncontrollable, fierce, no lovers of good,

3:4 traitors, headstrong, conceited, lovers of pleasure rather than lovers of God;

3:5 continuously holding the external appearance of holiness but denying the power of it. Continuously turn away from these, also.

3:6 For out of these are being (PI) the ones continuously creeping into houses, and continuously capturing foolish women having been loaded (passive) down to sins, continuously being led away to various lusts,

3:7 always continuously learning, and never continuously being able to come into the knowledge of the truth.

3:8 But by which method Jannes and Jambres opposed Moses, thus these also are opposing (PI) the truth; men being corrupted (passive) in mind, rejected as to the faith, are rejected.

3:9 But they will proceed no further. For their folly will be evident to all men, as theirs also came to be.

3:10 But you did follow to my teaching, to the conduct, to the purpose, to the faith, to the patience, to the love, to the steadfastness,

3:11 to the persecutions, to the sufferings: such things that happened to me in Antioch, in Iconium, in Lystra. I endured those persecutions. And out of them all the Lord delivered me.

3:12 But, and all the ones continuously willing to continuously live godly in Christ Jesus will suffer being persecuted (passive).

3:13 But evil men and impostors will grow on the worse, continuously deceiving and continuously being deceived.

3:14 But you continuously remain in (the things) which you have learned and have been assured of (passive), knowing of Whom you have learned.

3:15 And from infancy, you have known and continue to know the holy Scriptures continuously being able to make you wise into salvation through faith in Christ Jesus.

3:16 Every writing, God-inspired and useful, toward teaching, toward reproof, toward correction, and toward instruction in righteousness,

3:17 that the man of God may continuously be perfect, having been thoroughly equipped (passive) toward every good work.

4:1 I earnestly exhort you therefore in the sight of God and the Lord Jesus Christ, the One continuously being about to continuously judge the ones continuously living and the dead in accordance with His appearing and His Kingdom:

4:2 preach the word; be urgent opportunely and inappropriately; reprove, rebuke, exhort, in all patience and teaching.

4:3 For the time will come when they will not receive the continuously being sound teaching, but, having ears itching to be told something pleasing (passive), will heap up to themselves teachers after their own desires;

4:4 and indeed will turn away their hearing of the truth, but shall be turned aside (passive) to fables.

4:5 But you continuously be sober in all things, suffer hardship, do the work of an evangelist, fulfill your ministry.

4:6 For I am already being offered (PI) (passive), and the time of my departure is imminent.

4:7 I have fought the good fight. I have finished the course. I have kept the faith.

4:8 From now on, there is being stored up (PI) to me the crown of righteousness, which the Lord, the righteous judge, will give to me in that day; but not to me only, but also to all the ones having loved (perfect participle) His appearing.

4:9 Be diligent to come unto me soon,

4:10 for Demas left me, loving this present world, and went into Thessalonica; Crescens into Galatia, Titus into Dalmatia.

4:11 Only Luke is being (PI) with me. Taking up Mark, continuously bring him with you, for he is being (PI) useful to me into service.

4:12 But I sent Tychicus into Ephesus.

4:13 Continuously bring the cloak which I left in Troas with Carpus when you are coming, and the books, especially the parchments.

4:14 Alexander, the coppersmith, did much evil to me. The Lord will repay to him according to his works,

4:15 of whom you also must continuously beware; for he greatly opposed our words.

4:16 In my first defense, no one came to help me, but all left me. May it not be reckoned to them.

4:17 But the Lord stood by me, and strengthened me, that through me the message might be fully proclaimed (passive), and that all the Gentiles might hear; and I was delivered (passive) out of the mouth of the lion.

4:18 And the Lord will deliver me from every evil work, and will save me into His heavenly Kingdom; to whom (be) the glory forever and ever. Amen.

4:19 Greet Prisca and Aquila, and the house of Onesiphorus.

4:20 Erastus remained in Corinth, but I left Trophimus in Miletus continuously being sick.

4:21 Be diligent to come before winter. Eubulus is greeting (PI) you, and Pudens, and Linus, and Claudia, and all the brothers.

4:22 The Lord Jesus Christ be with your spirit. The grace be with you all. Amen.

The second unto Timothy, being selected (passive) first elder of the church of the Ephesians, was written (passive) from Rome when Paul stood before Caesar Nero of a second time.

Introduction To Titus

This letter was written for a similar purpose as were 1 Timothy and 2 Timothy. Paul was a close friend of Titus, and had obviously spent a significant amount of time with him. While with him, Paul would have mentored him the in process of sanctification, as that is the very essence of the Good News and thus of a Christian life.

Because of this, as with 1 Timothy, Paul would not have had to teach Titus HOW to be sanctified in this letter. His purpose here was to teach Titus about how to lead a Christian church.

Titus was probably written between the time Paul wrote 1 Timothy and when he wrote 2 Timothy. When reading this letter it is very important to keep Paul's purpose in mind. Do not expect this to be detailed guide as to HOW to be transformed into the image of Jesus.

As in 1 Timothy and 2 Timothy, Paul does in fact here give Titus a list of things to do and to not do. But it is important to NOT then conclude that the essence of the Christian life is keeping a list of rules. Both Paul and Titus know full well that is not the case. Rather, his behavior as described here must be "good fruit" from a "good root." If these behaviors are not present, then Titus will need to look for the "bad root." Titus would know full well how to do this, because Paul was a close friend, and would have taught him HOW.

Please keep this in mind as you read this letter.

Also refer to the "Introduction To 1 Timothy" for more details. These two letters have very similar purposes.

1:1 Paul, a servant of God, namely an apostle of Jesus Christ, according to the faith of God's chosen ones, and the knowledge of the truth which is according to holiness,

1:2 upon hope of eternal life, which God, Who cannot lie, promised before time began;

1:3 but to His own time revealed His word in the message with which I was entrusted (passive) according to the commandment of God our Savior;

1:4 to Titus, my true child according to a common faith: Grace, mercy, peace from God the Father and the Lord Jesus Christ our Savior.

1:5 I left you in Crete for this reason, that you may set in order the things continuously lacking, and may appoint elders in every city, as I directed you;

1:6 if anyone is being blameless (PI), the husband of one wife, continuously having children who believe, not in accusation of loose or unruly behavior.

1:7 For it is being necessary (PI) the overseer to be blameless, as God's steward; not self-pleasing, not easily angered, not given to wine, not violent, not greedy for dishonest gain;

1:8 but hospitable, a lover of good, sober-minded, fair, holy, strong inside;

1:9 continuously upholding according to the teaching of the faithful word, that he may continuously be able to continuously exhort in the teaching continuously being sound, and to continuously convict the ones continuously contradicting.

1:10 For there are also being (PI) many unruly men, vain talkers and deceivers, especially the ones out of the circumcision,

1:11 whose mouths it is being imperative (PI) to continuously be stopping, who are subverting (PI) whole houses, continuously teaching things which it is being imperative (PI) they ought not, for dishonest gain's sake.

1:12 One of them, a prophet of their own, said, "Cretans are always liars, evil beasts, and idle gluttons."

1:13 This testimony is being (PI) true. For this cause, continuously reprove them sharply, that they may continuously be sound in the faith,

1:14 not continuously paying attention to Jewish fables and commandments of men, the ones continuously turning away from the truth.

1:15 To the pure ones, all (things) are indeed pure; but to the ones having been defiled (passive) and unbelieving, nothing is pure; but their mind and their conscience has been defiled (passive).

1:16 They continuously profess that they know God, but to their works they are denying (PI) (him), continuously being abominable, and disobedient, and unfit for any good work.

2:1 But you continuously say what is being proper (PI) to the teaching continuously being sound,

2:2 that older men to continuously be temperate, sensible, sober-minded, continuously sound to the faith, to love, to patience:

2:3 and that older women likewise in behavior as becomes the sacred, not slanderers nor enslaved to much wine, teachers of that which is good;

2:4 that they may continuously train the young women to continuously love their husbands, to love their children,

2:5 sober-minded, chaste, workers at home, kind, continuously being in subjection to their own husbands, that God's word may not continuously be blasphemed (passive).

2:6 Likewise, continuously exhort the younger men to continuously be sober-minded;

2:7 about all (things) showing yourself an example of good works; in your teaching with integrity, seriousness, incorruptibility,

2:8 sound speech that can't be condemned; that the one out of adversity may be being ashamed (passive), continuously having no evil thing to continuously say about you all.

2:9 Servants to continuously be in subjection to their own masters, to be well-pleasing in all things; not continuously contradicting;

2:10 not continuously stealing, but continuously showing all good fidelity; that they may continuously dignify the teaching of God, our Savior, in all things.

2:11 For the grace of God has appeared, bringing salvation to all men,

2:12 Continuously instructing us to the intent that, denying ungodliness and worldly desires, we may live soberly, righteously, and godly in this present time;

2:13 continuously looking for the blessed hope and appearing of the glory of our great God and Savior, Jesus Christ;

2:14 Who gave Himself for us, that He may redeem us from all iniquity, and may purify to Himself a people for His own possession, zealous of good works.

2:15 Continuously say these things and continuously exhort and continuously reprove with all authority. Continuously let no man despise you.

3:1 Continuously remind them to continuously be in subjection to authorities and to those with executive power, to continuously be obedient, to continuously be ready unto every good work,

3:2 to continuously speak evil of no one, not to continuously be contentious, to be gentle, showing all humility toward all men.

3:3 For we were also once foolish, disobedient, continuously being deceived (passive), continuously serving various desires and pleasures, in malice and envy, hateful, and continuously hating one another.

3:4 But when the kindness of God our Savior and His love toward mankind was made to appear (passive),

3:5 not out of works in righteousness, which we did ourselves, but according to His mercy, He saved us, through the washing of regeneration and renewing by the Holy Spirit,

3:6 whom He poured out on us richly, through Jesus Christ our Savior;

3:7 that, being justified (passive) to His grace, we may be made heirs according to the hope of eternal life.

3:8 This saying (is) faithful, and concerning these things I am desiring (PI) you to affirm confidently, so that the ones having believed God may continuously be careful to continuously be diligent to care of good works. These things are being good (PI) and profitable to men;

3:9 but continuously shun foolish questionings, and genealogies, and strifes, and disputes about the (OT) law; for they are being (PI) unprofitable and vain.

3:10 Continuously avoid a factious man after a first and second warning;

3:11 knowing that such a one has been perverted (passive), and is sinning (PI), continuously being self-condemned.

3:12 When I will send Artemas unto you, or Tychicus, be diligent to come unto me in Nicopolis, for I have determined to winter there.

3:13 Send forward Zenas, the lawyer, and Apollos speedily, that nothing may be continuously lacking to them.

3:14 But continuously let our people also learn to continuously be diligent to care of good works into necessary uses, that they may not continuously be unfruitful.

3:15 All who are with me are greeting (PI) you. Greet the ones continuously loving us in faith. Grace (be) with you all.
Amen.

Toward Titus of the Cretian church, having been selected (passive) foremost elder. Was written (passive) from Nicopolis of Macedonia.

Introduction To Philemon

The Epistle to Philemon is different than all the rest of the Apostle Paul's letters that we have in the New Testament.

It seems that Onesimus was a slave who had escaped from his master, Philemon, perhaps having robbed him in the process.

At some point, Onesimus had come into contact with Paul, and had become a Christian. From the letter, it is clear that Philemon was also a Christian, and had a prior relationship with Paul.

In this letter, Paul is sending Onesimus back to Philemon; and he wants Philemon to receive him back; still as a slave, but also as a Christian brother. Paul also twists Philemon's arm to convince him not to hold anything against Onesimus.

> "Did Philemon respond as Paul wished? We may safely assume that he did. Otherwise he would surely have suppressed the letter, and we would know nothing about it." (Carson, Moo, and Morris, pages 388-389).

Do not expect to find much in this letter which is instruction as to how to be sanctified, or relating to its importance. That was not Paul's purpose in this letter.

I have included it in this translation simply because it is a part of the New Testament Epistles.

1:1 Paul, a prisoner of Christ Jesus, and the brother Timothy, to Philemon, our beloved fellow worker,

1:2 and to the beloved and Apphia, to Archippus, our fellow soldier, and to the assembly in your house:

1:3 Grace to you and peace from God our Father and the Lord Jesus Christ.

1:4 I am thanking (PI) my God always, continuously making mention of you in my prayers,

1:5 hearing of your love, and the faith which you are having (PI) toward the Lord Jesus, and unto all the saints;

1:6 that the fellowship of your faith may become effective, in the knowledge of every good thing which is in you all into Christ Jesus.

1:7 For we are having (PI) much joy and comfort in your love, that the compassions of the saints have been refreshed (passive) through you, brother.

1:8 Therefore, I am continuously having much boldness in Christ to continuously enjoin you that which is appropriate,

1:9 for love's sake I rather am begging (PI), continuously being such a one as Paul, the aged, but now also a prisoner of Jesus Christ.

1:10 I am begging (PI) you about my child, whom I begot in my chains, Onesimus,

1:11 who once was useless to you, but now is useful to you and to me,

1:12 whom I sent back. But you receive him, that is being (PI) my own heart,

1:13 whom I desired to continuously keep unto me, that on your behalf may continuously serve me in my chains of the Good News.

1:14 But I was willing to do nothing without your consent, that your goodness would not be according to necessity, but according to free will.

1:15 For perhaps through this he was separated (passive) for a while, that you might have him forever,

1:16 no longer as a slave, but more than a slave, a beloved brother, especially to me, but how much rather to you, and in the flesh and in the Lord.

1:17 If then you are having (PI) me a partner, receive him as you would receive me.

1:18 But if he has wronged you in anything, or is owing (PI), continuously put that to my account.

1:19 I, Paul, wrote this to my own hand: I will repay it (that I may not continuously say to you that you are owing (PI) to me even your own self).

1:20 Yes, brother, I may obtain profit of you in the Lord. Refresh my compassion in the Lord.

1:21 Having confidence to your obedience to the truth, I

you will do even beyond what I am saying (PI).

1:22 But also, continuously prepare a guest room to me, for I am hoping (PI) that through your prayers I will be restored (passive) to you.

1:23 Epaphras, my fellow prisoner in Christ Jesus, is greeting (PI) you,

1:24 (as do) Mark, Aristarchus, Demas, and Luke, my fellow workers.

1:25 The grace of our Lord Jesus Christ (be) with your spirit. Amen.

Was written (passive) unto Philemon from Rome through Onesimus, a servant.

Introduction to Hebrews

This Epistle is the most thorough and definitive description of the fact that Jesus Christ provides the ONLY way for our sins to be forgiven.

Traditionally this letter was believed to have been written by the Apostle Paul. The message is definitely congruent with his other letters. Periodically there has been some questioning of this, because the Greek writing style is not his. One proposed explanation to this is that Paul wrote it in Hebrew, which would make sense because he wrote it to Hebrew Christians. Since the writing style is similar to that of Luke, it is postulated that Luke then translated it into Greek for the use of other churches. Regardless of who wrote it, it was very early accepted as being inspired by God and written by an Apostle.

I realize there are these questions of authorship, but I am going to go with the long tradition of the Apostle Paul being the author.

All the Epistles were written to address specific problems in churches. In this case, Paul is addressing the problem that Jewish Christians had of leaving behind the Old Testament ways and continuously applying the blood of Jesus to their sins. They seemed to have a tendency to drift back into the Old Testament beliefs with which they grew up. He wants them to then truly grasp how much more magnificent is their possession of forgiveness of sins through Jesus' sacrifice than the previous provision for holiness through the Old Testament sacrifices.

Jesus Christ did not just suddenly appear out of nowhere. This book shows that God had been miraculously preparing the way for Him for a very long time. There are accurate prophesies in the Old Testament of the coming Messiah. That is one of the powerful evidences of the truth of Christianity: it has a long history leading up to His appearance, and this long history has been validated over and over again by not only the Old Testament, but also archaeology and other ancient records.

The most important thing to keep in mind as you read the book to the Hebrews is that **it was written to Hebrew Christians.** Therefore the writer knew that the audience would be very familiar with Old Testament history, and the Law of Moses, and the temple sacrifices. He would not have written this way to gentiles, who would know nothing of that. He also knows that some of them would be reluctant to completely let go of their Old Testament ways in order to embrace Jesus Christ as the Messiah. He wants to convince them that Jesus' provision for taking away our sins REPLACES the Old Testament provision, and so they must abandon the laws of Moses.

It is clear from the detailed discussion in this letter of the Levitical priesthood and Old Testament provision for sin, that at the time this letter was written the temple sacrifices were still going on in Jerusalem. This would mean it was written before 70 AD when the Romans destroyed the temple and temple sacrifices ceased. Of course, the writer of this letter would have had no idea that what he was writing about Levitical priests and the temple sacrifices for sin would soon cease and never be resumed. This of course adds importance to the eternal priesthood of Jesus, which outlived the temple, and Who is still available to us almost 2,000 years later.

Paul wants to connect Jesus Christ with the Old Testament, so that these Hebrew readers will accept what He does for us in taking away our sins. Because of the intended audience, this connection is so important in this letter that he spends a bit over 9 chapters to convince them from their own scriptures. He explains how the blood of Jesus takes away our sins, whereas the blood of bulls and goats did not do that, and how supernatural is this new way. He also knows that they would be used to trying to keep the law with their will power, which is what Old Testament believers had to do.

Then starting in Chapter 10 Paul changes the emphasis, and speaks eloquently of the process of transformation into the image of Jesus.

He makes it very clear, in no uncertain terms, how important it is for them to appropriate the forgiveness of sins that Jesus Christ has miraculously provided.

In Verses 10:28-31 he warns against counting the blood of Jesus as ordinary, and the very serious consequences of not counting it as crucial. In Verses 12:1-15 he explains in a powerful way that they need to "run with endurance the race that is set before us." (Verse 12:1); and that if they persist, they will be "partakers of His holiness" (Verse 12:10).

In summary, the epistle to the Hebrews says three things:
1. **Sin is our fundamental problem, and Jesus came to provide the only way to take away our sins.**
2. **We then MUST act by first forgiving to have Him do it.**
3. **If we don't apply the blood of Jesus, we are trampling Him underfoot, and we will suffer.**

1:1 God, speaking to the fathers in the prophets in many parts and in many ways,

1:2 on the last of these days spoke to us in the Son, Whom He appointed heir of all, through whom also He made the ages.

1:3 Who continuously being the radiance of His glory, and the very image of His substance, and continuously upholding all to the word of His power, through Himself making purification of our sins, sat down at the right hand of the Majesty in high places;

1:4 becoming so much better of the angels, as much as He inherited a more excellent name than them.

1:5 For to which of the angels said He at any time, "You are being (PI) My Son. Today I have begotten you"? And again, "I will be to Him unto a Father, and He will be unto me a Son?"

1:6 But again, when He may bring in the firstborn into the world He is saying (PI), "Let all the angels of God worship Him."

1:7 And of the angels He is saying (PI), "The One continuously making His angels spirits, and His ministers a flame of fire."

1:8 But unto the Son, "Your throne, O God, into the age of the age. The scepter of uprightness (is) the scepter of Your Kingdom.

1:9 You (Jesus) loved righteousness, and hated iniquity; through this, God anointed You, Your God (anointed You) with the olive oil of joy near Your partners."

1:10 And, "You, Lord, according to the beginnings (plural) founded the earth. And the heavens are being (PI) the works of Your hands.

1:11 They will perish, but You are continuing (PI). And they all will be made old (passive) like a garment does.

1:12 And as a mantle, You will roll them up, and they will be changed (passive); but You are being (PI) the same. And Your years will not fail."

1:13 But which of the angels has He told at any time, "You may continuously sit out from (as a source) My right hands, until I may make Your enemies the footstool of Your feet?"

1:14 Are they not all being (PI) ministering spirits, continuously being sent out (passive) into the ones continuously being about to continuously enjoy salvation?

2:1 Because of this, it being exceedingly necessary (PI) to continuously heed to the things being heard (passive) lest we may drift away.

2:2 For if the word being spoken (passive) through angels became certain, and every transgression and disobedience received a just recompense;

2:3 how will we escape neglecting of so vast a salvation--which at the first to continuously having been spoken (passive) through the Lord, was confirmed (passive) into us by the ones hearing?

2:4 God also continuously testifying with them, both to signs and wonders, and to various powerful works, and of gifts of the Holy Spirit, according to His own will?

2:5 For He didn't subject to angels the world continuously being about to come, of which we are speaking (PI).

2:6 But one has somewhere testified, continuously saying, "What is man being(PI), that You are being mindful (PI) of him? Or the Son of Man, that You are caring for Him?

2:7 You made Him a little lower than the angels. To glory and honor You crowned Him and You placed on Him the works of Your hands.

2:8 You have put all things in subjection under His feet." For to subject to Him all, He left nothing that is not subject to Him. But now we are not seeing (PI) all having been subjected (passive) to Him,

2:9 But we are seeing (PI) the One having been made (passive) a little lower than the angels, Jesus, because of the suffering of death, having been crowned (passive) to glory and honor, that to the grace of God He might taste of death for everyone.

2:10 For it was conspicuous to Him, for Whom (are) all things, and by Whom (are) all things, leading into glory many children, to make perfect the Author of their salvation through sufferings.

2:11 For both the One continuously sanctifying and the ones continuously being sanctified (passive) are all out of One, through which cause He is not being ashamed (PI) to continuously call them brothers,

2:12 continuously saying, "I will declare Your name to My brothers. In the midst of the congregation I will sing (to) You."

2:13 And again, "I will be having confidence on Him." And again, "Behold, I and the children whom God has given Me."

2:14 Since then the children have shared of flesh and of blood, and He also Himself in the same way partook of the same, that through death He might bring to nothing the one continuously having the power of death, this is being(PI), the devil,

2:15 and might deliver these, whoever, to fear of death, through all their lifetime were held to be continuously living of a slavish spirit

2:16 For most certainly, He is not taking upon Himself (PI) angels, but is taking upon Himself (PI) the seed of Abraham.

2:17 Whence He was obligated according to all things to be made (passive) like His brothers, that He might become a merciful and faithful high priest towards God, into to continuously be the propitiate (passive) for the sins of the people.

2:18 For in that He Himself has suffered being tempted (passive), He is being able (PI) to help the ones continuously being tempted (passive).

3:1 Whence, holy brothers, partakers of a heavenly calling, consider the Apostle and High Priest of our confession, Jesus Christ;

3:2 continuously being faithful to the One appointing Him, as also was Moses in all his house.

3:3 For He has been counted worthy (passive) of more glory than Moses, inasmuch as the One building is having (PI) more honor than the house.

3:4 For every house is being built (PI) (passive) by someone; but the One constructing all (is) God.

3:5 And Moses indeed was faithful in all his house as a servant, unto a testimony of those things which were to be spoken (passive),

3:6 but Christ as a Son over His house; Whose house we are being, (PI) if we may hold fast confidence and the glorying of our hope firm unto the end.

3:7 Wherefore, even as the Holy Spirit is saying (PI), "Today if you may hear His voice,

3:8 You all may not continuously harden your hearts, as in the bitter provocation, like as in the day of the trial in the wilderness,

3:9 where your fathers tested Me, they proved Me, and saw My works for forty years.

3:10 Wherefore I was displeased to that generation, and I said, 'They are being strayed (PI) (passive) to their heart, but they didn't know My ways;'

3:11 as I swore in My passion, 'If they will enter into My rest.'"

3:12 Continuously beware, brothers, lest perhaps there be in any one of you all, in the evil heart of unbelief, to withdraw from the continuously living God;

3:13 but continuously exhort one another throughout each day, until which day is being called (PI) (passive) "today;" that not any out of you all may be hardened (passive) to the deceitfulness of sin.

3:14 For we have begun to be partakers of Christ, if we may hold fast the beginning of the confidence unto the end that does not fail:

3:15 in continuously being said (passive), "Today if you all may hear His voice, you all may not continuously harden your hearts, as in the bitter provocation."

3:16 For any hearing were bitter? But not all the ones coming out of Egypt through Moses?

3:17 But to whom was He displeased forty years? If not to the ones sinning, whose bodies fell in the wilderness?

3:18 But to whom did He swear to not enter into His rest, if not to the ones being disobedient?

3:19 And we are seeing (PI) that they were not able to enter in because of unbelief.

4:1 Then may we be afraid of continuously being left (passive) of a promise to enter into His rest, any out of you all may continuously seem to come short of it.

4:2 For also we are (PI) having been brought (passive) the well message, even as they also; but hearing the word of the tidings didn't profit them, not having been mixed (passive) to faith to the ones hearing.

4:3 For the ones believing are entering (PI) into that rest, even as He has said, "As I swore in My passion, if they will enter into My rest;" although the works were coming to be from the foundation of the world.

4:4 For He has said somewhere about the seventh day, "And God rested in the seventh day from all His works;"

4:5 and in this again, "If they will enter into My rest."

4:6 Since then it is being made to remain (PI) (passive) for some to enter into her, and the ones formerly being brought (passive) the good news failed to enter because of disobedience,

4:7 He again is defining (PI) a certain day, today, continuously saying in David after so long a time (just as has been said

(passive)), "Today if you all may hear His voice, you all may not continuously harden your hearts."

4:8 For if Joshua had given them rest, he would not even have spoken afterward of a day after these.

4:9 Therefore the Sabbath rest is being left (PI) (passive) to the people of God.

4:10 For the one entering into His rest also has himself rested from his own works, even as God from out of His own.

4:11 Then we may be diligent to enter into the rest, that anyone may not fall in the same example of disobedience.

4:12 For the word of God is continuously living, and active, and sharper superior than any two-edged sword, and continuously piercing until the dividing of both soul and spirit, of both joints and marrow, and is able to discern of thoughts and of intentions of the heart.

4:13 And there is being (PI) no creature that is hidden in His sight, but all (are) naked and having been laid open (passive) to His eyes, the word toward us.

4:14 Continuously having then a great high priest, the One having passed through the heavens, Jesus, the Son of God, we may continuously hold tightly of the confession.

4:15 For we are not having (PI) a high priest continuously not being able to sympathize to our infirmities, but having been tried (passive) like all (men) similar yet apart from sin.

4:16 Then we may continuously draw near with boldness to the throne of grace, that we may receive mercy, and may find grace into well-seasoned, timely help.

5:1 For every high priest, continuously taken (passive) out of men, is being appointed (PI) (passive) over men in (things) pertaining unto God, that he may continuously offer both gifts and sacrifices for sins.

5:2 Continuously being able to continuously be moderate to the ones continuously being ignorant, and continuously being strayed (passive), since he also is being surrounded (PI) with weakness.

5:3 And because of this, he is being obligated (PI), as concerning the people thus also about himself, to continuously offer sacrifices for sins.

5:4 And nobody is taking (PI) this honor to himself, but the one continuously being called (passive) by God, just like Aaron was.

5:5 So also Christ didn't glorify Himself to be made a high priest, but the One speaking unto Him, "You are being (PI) My Son. Today I have begotten You."

5:6 And as He is saying (PI) also in another place, "You (are a) priest into eternity according to the order of Melchizedek."

5:7 Who in the days of His flesh, offering both prayers and petitions with strong crying and tears unto the One continuously being able to continuously save Him out of death, and having been heard (passive) from His reverent submission,

5:8 though continuously being a Son, He learned obedience from what He suffered.

5:9 And having been made perfect, He became the source of eternal salvation to all the ones continuously obeying to Him,

5:10 being named (passive) by God a high priest after the order of Melchizedek.

5:11 About whom many words to us, and hard to continuously interpret, since you all have become dull to hearing.

5:12 For also because of the time, you all continuously being obligated to be teachers, you all again having (PI) need of someone to continuously teach you all. What (are) the rudiments of the beginning principles of the oracles of God? And you all have come to continuously having need of milk, and not of solid food.

5:13 For everyone continuously partaking of milk is inexperienced of the word of righteousness, for he is being (PI) a baby.

5:14 But solid food is being (PI) of the ones full grown by means of the practiced faculties having been exercised (passive) are continuously having discernment of both good and of bad.

6:1-2 Therefore you all abandoning the word of the beginning of the Christ, you all may continuously be brought (passive) toward perfection; you all not continuously throw away again a foundation of repentance away from dead works, and also (repentance away from) of belief upon God of the teaching of baptisms, of laying on of hands, of resurrection of the dead, and of eternal judgment.

6:3 And this will we do, if God may continuously permit.

6:4 For (it is) impossible, the ones once being enlightened (passive) and tasted of the heavenly free gift, and beginning to become partakers of the Holy Spirit,

6:5 and tasting the good word of God, and the powers of the age continuously being impending.

6:6 and falling away, again to continuously renew them into repentance; the ones continuously crucifying the Son of God to themselves, continuously putting Him to open shame.

6:7 For the land drinking the rain continuously coming often on it, and continuously bringing forth a crop suitable to those through whom it is also being tilled(PI), is receiving (PI) blessing from God;

6:8 but continuously bringing thorns and thistles, it is rejected and near of curse, of whom the end into be burned.

6:9 But, beloved, we have been persuaded (passive) concerning you all about the better things, and of you all continuously having salvation, if we are also speaking (PI) thus.

6:10 For God is not unrighteous, to forget your work and the labor of love which you all showed into His name, serving the saints, and continuously serving.

6:11 But we are desiring (PI) that each one of you all to continuously show the same diligence toward the full assurance of hope even until the end,

6:12 that you all may not be sluggish, but imitators of the ones who through faith and patience continuously inheriting the promises.

6:13 For God promising to Abraham, since He had no one of greater to swear, He swore by Himself,

6:14 continuously saying, "Surely continuously blessing I will bless you, and continuously multiplying I will multiply you."

6:15 And thus, being patient, he obtained the promise.

6:16 For men indeed are swearing (PI) by a greater, the oath into confirmation to end of every controversy.

6:17 In which God, far more is continuously intending to show to the heirs of the promise the immutability of His counsel, interposed to oath;

6:18 that through two immutable matters, in which it is impossible (for) God to lie, we may continuously have a strong encouragement, to ones fleeing for refuge to take hold of the hope continuously lying before (them).

6:19 Which (hope) we are having (PI) as an anchor of the soul, both sure and on which one can rely, and continuously entering into the interior of the veil;

6:20 where a forerunner Jesus entered for us, becoming a high priest into forever after the order of Melchizedek.

7:1 For this Melchizedek, king of Salem, priest of God Most High, who meeting together with Abraham continuously returning from the slaughter of the kings and blessing him,

7:2 to whom also Abraham divided a tenth part from all (first, indeed continuously being translated, king of righteousness, but then also king of Salem, which is being (PI) king of peace;

7:3 without father, without mother, without genealogy, continuously having neither beginning of days nor end of life, but made very much like the Son of God), is remaining (PI) a priest into continually.

7:4 But be considering (PI) how great this man was (Melchizedek), to whom also Abraham, the patriarch, gave a tenth out of the best spoils.

7:5 And the ones indeed out of the sons of Levi continuously obtaining the priest's office are having (PI) a commandment to continuously take tithes from the people according to the (OT) law, this is being (PI), their brothers, even the ones having come out of the body of Abraham,

7:6 but the one not continuously being reckoned by descent (passive) out of them, (Melchizedek) has received tithes from Abraham, and has blessed the one (Abraham) continuously having the promises.

7:7 But without any dispute the lesser is being blessed (PI) (passive) by the greater.

7:8 And here indeed people continuously dying are receiving (PI) tithes, but there one continuously being witnessed (passive) that he is living (PI).

7:9 And as to say, through Abraham also Levi, the one continuously receiving tithes, has paid tithes,

7:10 for he was still in the body of his father when Melchizedek met him.

7:11 If indeed then perfection was through the Levitical priesthood (for under it the people have received the (OT) law), what further need was there for another priest to continuously arise after the order of

Melchizedek, and not to continuously be called (passive) after the order of Aaron?

7:12 For the priesthood continuously being changed (passive), there is of necessity beginning to become (PI) a change made also of the (OT) law.

7:13 For on whom these things are being said (PI) (passive) belonged to another tribe, from which no one has attended to the altar.

7:14 For it is evident that our Lord has sprung out of Judah, into which tribe Moses spoke nothing concerning priesthood.

7:15 And this is being (PI) still more abundantly evident, if according to the likeness of Melchizedek another priest is arising (PI),

7:16 Who has begun to become, not according to the (OT) law of a fleshly commandment, but according to the power of an endless life:

7:17 for it is being testified (PI) that, "You (are) a priest forever, according to the order of Melchizedek."

7:18 For indeed there is beginning to be (PI) an annulling of a continuously preceding commandment because of its weakness and uselessness

7:19 (for the (OT) law made nothing perfect), but a bringing in of a better hope, through which we are drawing near (PI) to God.

7:20 And inasmuch as (it is) not apart from oath, (for those indeed are (PI) beginning to become priests apart from oath),

7:21 But through the One continuously saying an oath unto Him "The Lord swore and will not regret, 'You (are) a priest forever, according to the order of Melchizedek.'"

7:22 By so much, Jesus has become the surety of a better covenant.

7:23 And many, indeed, are (PI) having become priests, because they are to continuously be hindered (passive) to continuously remain because of death.

7:24 But He, because He is to continuously live forever, is having (PI) His priesthood unchangeable.

7:25 Therefore He is also being able (PI) to continuously save into the uttermost the ones continuously coming to God through Him, seeing that He is always continuously living into continuously making intercession over them.

7:26 For such a high priest became conspicuous to us: holy, guiltless, undefiled, having been separated (passive) from sinners, and beginning to become higher of the heavens;

7:27 Who is not having (PI) necessity daily, like the high priests, previously to continuously offer up sacrifices, first for their own sins, and then (for) the sins of the people. For He did this once for all, offering up Himself.

7:28 For the (OT) law is appointing (PI) men high priests continuously having weakness, but the word of the oath after the (NT) law appoints the Son forever having been perfected (passive).

8:1 But on the main point continuously being said, we are having (PI) such a high priest, Who sat down in the right hand of the throne of the Majesty in the heavens,

8:2 a servant of the sanctuary, and of the true tabernacle, which the Lord made firm, not man.

8:3 For every high priest (is appointed) into to continuously offer both gifts and sacrifices being placed down (PI) (passive). Therefore it is necessary that this One also to continuously have something which He may offer.

8:4 For indeed if He were on earth, He would not ever be a priest at all, there continuously being of priests continuously offering the gifts according to the (OT) law;

8:5 who (the Levitical priests) are serving (PI) a copy and shadow of the heavenly things, even as Moses was warned (passive) by God when he was continuously being about to continuously make the tabernacle, for He is saying (PI), "Continuously see, you may make everything according to the pattern being shown (passive) to you in the mountain."

8:6 But now He has obtained of a more excellent ministry, by so much as He is being (PI) also the mediator of a better covenant, which on better promises has been established (passive).

8:7 For if that first one was faultless, then no place would have been demanded (passive) (2212) for a second.

8:8 For continuously finding fault to them, He is saying (PI), "Behold, the days are coming (PI)," is saying (PI) the Lord, "and I will make a new covenant on the house of Israel and on the house of Judah;

8:9 not according to the covenant which I made to their fathers, in the day of My taking hold of their hand to lead them out of the land of Egypt; that they didn't continue in My covenant, and I did not regard them," is saying (PI) the Lord.

8:10 "That this covenant that I will make (FI) to the house of Israel. After those days," is saying (PI) the Lord; "Continuously imparting My (NT) laws into their mind, I will also write (FI) them on their heart. And I will be (FI) to them into God, and they will be (FI) into to Me people.

8:11 They may not teach every man his fellow citizen, and every man his brother, continuously saying, 'Know the Lord,' that all

will know Me, from the least of them to the greatest of them.
8:12 That I will be merciful to their injustice and of their sins and of their lawlessness. I may be reminded (passive) of them no more."
8:13 In to continuously be saying, "A new (covenant)," He has made old the first. But the (one) continuously being made old (passive) continuously being aged, is near of vanishing away.
9:1 Then indeed also the first covenant had ordinances of divine service, and an earthly sanctuary.
9:2 For a tabernacle was prepared (passive). In the first part were the lampstand, the table, and the show bread; which is being called (PI) (passive) the Holy Place.
9:3 But after the second veil (was) the tabernacle, the one continuously being called (passive) the Holy of Holies,
9:4 continuously having a golden censer of incense, and the ark of the covenant having been overlaid (passive) on all sides to gold, in which was a golden pot continuously holding the manna, and Aaron's rod that budded, and the tablets of the covenant;
9:5 but above her cherubim of glory continuously overshadowing the mercy seat, of which it is not being (PI) now to continuously say in detail.
9:6 But of these things having been thus prepared (passive), the priests continually are passing (PI) into the first tabernacle, continuously accomplishing the divine services,
9:7 but into the second only the high priest, once of the year, not without blood, which he is offering (PI) for himself, and the sins of the people.
9:8 This continuously making evident of the Holy Spirit not as yet to having been manifest (passive) of the way of the holies of the first tabernacle continuously still having standing (in a person's life,.
9:9 which parable into the present age, according to which both gifts and sacrifices are being offered (PI) (passive) that are continuously not being able according to conscience, to make perfect the one continuously offering divine service;
9:10 only on foods and drinks and various washings and fleshly ordinances, continuously laying upon (them) unto the time of reformation.
9:11 But Christ coming as a high priest of the continuously coming good things, through the greater and more perfect tabernacle, not made of hands, this is not being (PI) of this creation,
9:12 nor yet through the blood of goats and calves, but through His own blood, He entered once for all into the Holy Place, finding eternal redemption.

9:13 For if the blood of goats and bulls, and the ashes of a heifer continuously sprinkling the ones having been defiled (passive), is sanctifying (PI) toward the cleanness of the flesh:

9:14 how much more the blood of Christ, Who through the eternal Spirit offered Himself without blemish to God, will definitely cleanse the conscience of you all from dead works into to continuously serve the continuously living God!

9:15 And because of this, He is being (PI) the mediator of a new covenant, so that of His death coming into existence, into redemption of the transgressions upon the first covenant, the ones having been called (passive) may receive the promise of the eternal inheritance.

9:16 For where a last will and testament (is), it is necessary to continuously be bringing in the death of him who made it.

9:17 For a will is in force on the dead ones since it is never being in force (PI) when the one making the covenant is living (PI).

9:18 Whereupon neither the first covenant has been dedicated (passive) without blood.

9:19 For every precept being spoken (passive) by Moses to all the people according to the (OT) law, taking the blood of the calves and the goats, with water and scarlet wool and hyssop, and sprinkled both the book itself and all the people,

9:20 continuously saying, "This (is) the blood of the covenant which God has commanded unto you all."

9:21 Also he sprinkled the tabernacle and all the vessels of the ministry in the same way to the blood.

9:22 And according to the (OT) law, nearly everything is being cleansed (PI) (passive) in blood, and apart from shedding of blood there is becoming (PI) no remission.

9:23 Then it was necessary indeed that the examples of the things in the heavens to continuously be cleansed (passive) themselves; but the heavenly things to better sacrifices than these.

9:24 For Christ hasn't entered into holy places made with hands, which are representations of the true, but into the heaven itself, now to appear to the presence of God for us;

9:25 nor yet that He may continuously offer Himself often, as the high priest is entering (PI) into the holy place every year in others' blood,

9:26 since He must to be suffering often from the laying down of the world. But now once on the end of the ages, He has been revealed (passive) into repudiation of sin through the sacrifice of Himself.

9:27 And inasmuch as it is being appointed (PI) to men to die once, but after this, judgment, 9:28 thus the Christ, having been offered (passive) once in order to bear the sins of many, out of a second time, will be seen (passive) apart from sin, to those who are continuously expectantly waiting for Him unto salvation.

10:1 For the (OT) law, continuously having a shadow of the continuously impending good things (not the very image of the (good) things to be done), according to the same sacrifices which they are offering (PI) every year, is never being able (PI) to make perfect those continuously drawing near.

10:2 Else wouldn't they ever cease continuously being offered (passive), because the ones continuously worshipping, having been once cleansed (passive), would not to continuously have had consciousness of sins?

10:3 But in them (those sacrifices there is) a yearly remembrance of sins.

10:4 For it is impossible for the blood of bulls and goats to continuously take away sins.

10:5 Therefore continuously coming into the world, He is saying (PI), "Sacrifice and offering you did not will, but you prepared a body to Me;

10:6 About whole burnt offerings and sacrifices concerning sin You had no pleasure.

10:7 Then I said, 'Behold, I am arriving (PI) (in the volume of the book it has been written (passive) concerning me) to do Your will, O God.'"

10:8 Previously continuously saying, "Sacrifices and offerings and whole burnt offerings and about sin You didn't desire, neither had pleasure which according to the (OT) law are being offered (PI) (passive),

10:9 then He has said, "Behold, I am arriving (PI) to do Your will, God." He is taking away (PI) the first, that He may establish the second,

10:10 In which will we are being (PI) "having been set apart (perfect passive)" through the offering of the body of Jesus Christ once for all.

10:11 And indeed every priest stood daily continuously serving and often continuously offering the same sacrifices, which are never being able (PI) to take away sins,

10:12 but He, offering one sacrifice for sins forever, sat down in the right hand of God;

10:13 henceforth continuously waiting (expectantly) until His enemies may be made (passive) the footstool of His feet.

10:14 For to one offering He has perfected into the end the ones continuously being sanctified (passive).

10:15 But the Holy Spirit also is testifying (PI) to us, for after to have declared,

10:16 "This is the covenant that I will make unto them: 'After those days,' the Lord is saying (PI), 'continuously imparting My (NT) laws on their hearts, and on their minds I will write them."

10:17 "And I may not be reminded (passive) still of their sins and of their lawlessness."

10:18 But where remission of these, (there is) no longer offering for sin.

10:19 Continuously having therefore, brothers, boldness into the entrance in of the holies in the blood of Jesus,

10:20 which He dedicated for us, through a recently slain and continuously living way, through the veil, this is being (PI) His flesh;

10:21 and a great priest over the house of God,

10:22 we may continuously draw near with a true heart in assurance of faith, our hearts having been sprinkled (passive) from an evil conscience, and the body having been washed (passive) with pure water,

10:23 we may continuously hold fast the confession of our hope without wavering; for faithful (is) the One promising.

10:24 And we may continuously consider one another for the purpose to stir up one another of love and of good works,

10:25 not continuously forsaking the assembling of ourselves, according as the custom (is) to some, but continuously exhorting; and so much more, in as much as you all are seeing (PI) the Day continuously approaching.

10:26 For of our continuously sinning voluntarily, deliberately after to actively take the knowledge of the truth, sacrifice no longer is being left (PI) (passive) concerning sins,

10:27 but a certain fearful expectation of judgment, and a fierceness of fire continuously being about to continuously devour the adversaries.

10:29 To how much of worse punishment, are you all thinking (PI), will be counted worthy (passive) the one trampling on the Son of God, and counting the blood of the covenant in which He was sanctified (passive) a common thing, and treading with reproach the Spirit of grace?

10:30 For we know the One saying (PI), "Vengeance belongs to Me, I will repay." The Lord is saying. And again, "The Lord will judge His people."

10:31 Fearful to be falling into the hands of the continuously living God.

10:32 But continuously remember the former days, in which, being enlightened (passive), you all endured a fight of afflictions;

10:33 as to this, indeed you all continuously being made a public spectacle (passive) to both reproaches and oppressions; but as to this, becoming partakers of the ones continuously being so used.

10:34 For you all also had compassion to my chains, and with joy you all accepted the plundering of the things you were continuously possessing, continuously knowing to continuously have in yourselves a better possession and a continuously enduring one in the heavens.

10:35 Therefore not to throw away your boldness, which is having (PI) a great reward.

10:36 For you all are having (PI) need of endurance so that, doing the will of God, you all may receive the promise.

10:37 "For yet a little while, the One continuously coming will come, and will not wait.

10:38 But the righteous will live out of faith, and if he may shrink back, My soul is having no pleasure (PI) in him."

10:39 But we are not being (PI) of shrinking back into destruction, but of faith into the procuring by Jesus of the soul.

11:1 But faith is being (PI) assurance of things continuously hoped for (passive), certain persuasion of things continuously not seen (passive).

11:2 For in this, the elders were testified to (passive).

11:3 To faith, we are understanding (PI) the ages to have been framed (passive) to the word of God, into the (things) continuously being seen (passive), (these things) not to have begun to become out of things continuously being visible.

11:4 To faith, Abel offered to God a more excellent sacrifice than Cain, through which he was testified (passive) to continuously be righteous, God continuously testifying on his gifts; and through it he, being dead, still is speaking (PI).

11:5 To faith, Enoch was taken away (passive), not to experience death, and he was not found (passive), because God translated him. For he had been witnessed (passive) before his translation to have been well pleasing to God.

11:6 But without faith it is impossible to please well. For the one continuously coming to God, it is being necessary (PI) to believe that He is existing, and that He is beginning to be (PI) a rewarder to the ones continuously seeking Him.

11:7 To faith, Noah, being warned (passive) about things not yet continuously being seen (passive), moved with reverence and awe, prepared an ark into the saving of his house, through which He condemned the world, and became heir of the righteousness according to faith.

11:8 To faith, Abraham, continuously being called (passive), obeyed to go out into the place which he was to continuously receive into an inheritance. And he went out, not continuously knowing where he was going (PI).

11:9 To faith, he lived as an alien into the land of promise, as in a land not his own, dwelling in tents, with Isaac and Jacob, the heirs with him of the same promise.

11:10 For he looked to the city continuously having the foundations, of which the builder and maker is God.

11:11 To faith also Sarah received strength for the casting or implanting of seed, and she brought forth a child when she was past age, since she counted the One promising faithful.

11:12 Therefore also from one were begotten these, and of one having been deadened (passive), as many as the stars of the sky to multitude, and as innumerable as the sand which is by the sea shore.

11:13 These all died in faith, not obtaining the promises, but having seen them and embraced them from afar, and having confessed that they were being (PI) strangers and pilgrims on the earth.

11:14 For the ones continuously saying such things are making apparent (PI) that they are seeking (PI) a country of their own.

11:15 And if indeed they had been thinking of that country from which they went out, they would have had an opportunity to return.

11:16 But now they are desiring (PI) a better country, that is being (PI), a heavenly one. Therefore God is not being ashamed (PI) of them, to be continuously called (passive) their God, for He prepared a city for them.

11:17 To faith, Abraham, continuously being tested, offered up Isaac. And the one receiving promises offered up the only begotten son;

11:18 of whom it was said (passive), "In Isaac will your seed be called (passive);"

11:19 concluding that the able God is also able to be continuously rousing out of the dead, from whence also he received him in parable.

11:20 To faith, Isaac blessed Jacob and Esau, even concerning things continuously being impending.

11:21 To faith, Jacob, continuously dying, blessed each of the sons of Joseph, and worshiped, (leaning) on the top of his staff.

11:22 To faith, Joseph, continuously nearing the end of his life, remembered the departure of the children of

Israel, and gave instructions concerning his bones.

11:23 To faith, Moses, being born (passive), was hidden for three months by his parents, because they saw that he was a beautiful child, and they were not afraid of the king's commandment.

11:24 To faith, Moses, becoming great, refused to be continuously called (passive) the son of Pharaoh's daughter,

11:25 choosing rather to continuously share ill treatment to God's people, than to continuously enjoy the pleasures of sin for a time;

11:26 accounting the reproach of Christ greater riches than the treasures in Egypt; for he looked into the reward.

11:27 To faith, he left Egypt, not fearing the wrath of the king; for he endured, as continuously seeing Him Who is invisible.

11:28 To faith, he kept the Passover, and the sprinkling of the blood, that the One continuously destroying the firstborn may not touch them.

11:29 To faith, they passed through the Red Sea as through dry (land), of which (land) the Egyptians tried getting were swallowed up (passive).

11:30 To faith, the walls of Jericho fell down, being surrounded (passive) on seven days.

11:31 To faith, Rahab the prostitute, didn't perish to the ones being disobedient, receiving the spies with peace.

11:32 And what still may I continuously say? For the time will be lacking for me continuously relating about Gideon, Barak, besides also Samson, and Jephthah, David, besides also Samuel, and of the prophets;

11:33 who, through faith subdued kingdoms, worked righteousness, obtained promises, stopped the mouths of lions,

11:34 quenched the power of fire, escaped the edge of the sword, from weakness were made strong (passive), grew mighty in battle, routed camps of aliens.

11:35 Women received their dead out of resurrection. But others were tortured (passive), not accepting the deliverance, that of a better resurrection they may gain.

11:36 But others were tried of mocking and scourging, but moreover of bonds and of imprisonment.

11:37 They were stoned (passive). They were sawn apart (passive). They were tempted (passive). They died in murder of the sword. They went around in sheep skins, in goat skins; being continuously destitute (passive), being continuously afflicted (passive), being continuously ill-treated (passive),

11:38 of whom the world was not worthy, continuously being caused to wander (passive) in deserts, and to mountains, and to caves, and to the holes of the earth.

11:39 And these all, being testified (passive) through of the faith, didn't receive the promise

11:40 of God providing some better thing on account of us, that they may not be made perfect (passive) apart from us.

12:1 Therefore we also, continuously having so vast a cloud of witnesses continuously surrounding to us, putting off every weight and the easily besetting sin, may we continuously race through patience the race continuously lying before us,

12:2 Continuously looking into Jesus, the author and perfecter of the faith, Who for the joy continuously lying before Him endured the cross, despising the shame, and is seated in the right hand of the throne of God.

12:3 For you all consider the One having endured such reproach of sinners into Himself, that you all may not be weary continuously being exhausted (passive) to your souls.

12:4 You all have not yet resisted unto blood, continuously striving against the sin;

12:5 and you all have been made oblivious (passive) of the exhortation which is reasoning (PI) to you all as to children,

"My son, don't continuously take lightly the chastening of the Lord, nor continuously be made faint (passive) when you are continuously being reproved (passive) by Him;

12:6 For whom the Lord is loving (PI), He is chastening (PI), but He is scourging (PI) every son whom He is receiving (PI)."

12:7 If you all are enduring (PI) discipline, God is bringing it (PI) to you all as to sons, for what son is there being (PI) whom his father is not disciplining (PI)?

12:8 But if you all are being (PI) without discipline, of which all have become partakers, then you all are being (PI) illegitimate, and not sons.

12:9 Furthermore, we indeed had the fathers of our flesh as discipliners, and we respected them. Shall we not much rather be in subjection to the Father of spirits, and live?

12:10 For they indeed, for a few days, disciplined us as continuously seeming good to them; but the One (God) (disciplines us) toward continuously being profitable, for the purpose (of us) to partake of His holiness.

12:11 But all discipline indeed unto the present is not seeming (PI) to continuously be joyous but grievous; yet afterward it is yielding (PI) the peaceful fruit of righteousness to those having been exercised (passive) of her.

12:12 Therefore, you all lift up the enfeebled (passive) hands and the having been paralyzed (passive) knees,

12:13 and you all make straight paths to your feet, that the lame one (foot) may not be turned aside (passive), but rather may be healed (passive).

12:14 Continuously eagerly pursue (1377) peace in the midst of all, and indeed the sanctification apart from which no man will see the Lord,

12:15 continuously looking carefully not anyone continuously falling short from the grace of God; not any root of bitterness continuously springing up may continuously trouble you, and through this many may be defiled (passive);

12:16 Not any sexually immoral person, or profane person, like Esau, who sold his birthright for one meal.

12:17 For you all know that also, afterwards continuously willing to inherit the blessing, he was rejected (passive), for he found no place of repentance, and even seeking it diligently with tears.

12:18 For you all have not come to a mountain continuously being touched (passive), and to have been burned (passive) to fire, and to blackness, and to darkness, and to storm,

12:19 and the sound of a trumpet, and the voice of words; which the ones hearing begged that no word to be added (passive),

12:20 for they could not bear the thing continuously being commanded (passive), "If even an animal may come in contact of the mountain, it shall be stoned (passive), or be shot down (passive) to a dart;"

12:21 and so fearful was the appearance, that Moses said, "I continuously am terrified (passive) and trembling."

12:22 But you all have come to Mount Zion, and to the city of the continuously living God, to heavenly Jerusalem, and to innumerable multitudes of angels,

12:23 to the general assembly and to the assembly of the firstborn having been written in heavens (plural), to God the Judge of all, to the spirits of just men having been made perfect (passive),

12:24 and to Jesus, the mediator of a new covenant, and to the blood of sprinkling continuously speaking better than that of Abel.

12:25 Continuously see that you all may not refuse the One continuously speaking. For if they didn't escape, refusing the one continuously warning on the Earth, how much more the ones continuously turning from the One of the heavens,

12:26 Whose voice shook the earth then, but now He has promised, continuously saying, "Yet once more I am shaking

(PI) not only the earth, but also the heaven (singular)."

12:27 But the "Yet once more," is signifying (PI) the removal from one place to another of those things continuously being shaken (passive) as of things that have been made (passive), that those things which are not continuously being shaken (passive) may remain.

12:28 Therefore, continuously be taking into one's possession a kingdom unshakable. May we continuously have grace, through which we may continuously serve to God acceptably, with fellowship of reverence and of piety,

12:29 for also our God (is) a continuously consuming fire.

13:1 Continuously have brotherly love remain.

13:2 Don't continuously forget of hospitality to strangers, for through this, some were oblivious when lodging angels.

13:3 Continuously be mindful of those in bonds as having been bound with them; of the ones continuously being ill-treated (passive), as you all are also continuously being in the body.

13:4 The honorable marriage in all, and the bed undefiled: but God will judge the sexually immoral and adulterers.

13:5 The mode of thinking, not fond of money, continuously being content (passive) to the things continuously present, for He has said, "No, in no way may I be lax regarding you, neither in no way may I forsake you."

13:6 So that continuously having good courage to continuously say, "The Lord (is) helper to me and I will not fear. What can man do to me?"

13:7 Continuously remember the ones continuously leading of you all, who spoke to you all the word of God, of whom continuously considering the outcome of their turning about, continuously imitate their faith.

13:8 Jesus (is) Christ, yesterday and today, and (is) Himself into forever.

13:9 You all don't continuously be carried about to various and strange teachings, for (it is) good the heart to be continuously established (passive) to grace, not to food, in which the ones so living their lives were not benefited.

13:10 We are having (PI) an altar out of which the ones continuously offering divine service to the holy tabernacle are having (PI) no right to eat.

13:11 For of these the blood of animals is being carried (PI) (passive) into the holy place through the high priest concerning sin, the bodies of these are being burned (PI) (passive) outside of the camp.

13:12 Therefore Jesus also, that He might sanctify the people through His own blood, suffered outside of the gate.

13:13 Now then we may continuously go out unto Him outside of the camp, continuously bearing His reproach.

13:14 For we are not having (PI) here a continuously enduring city, but we are seeking the one continuously being about to come.

13:15 Through Him, then, we may continuously offer up a sacrifice of praise to God continually, this is being (PI), the fruit of lips, continuously openly proclaiming allegiance to His name.

13:16 But of doing good and sharing, you all don't continuously forget. For to such sacrifices God is being well pleased (PI) (passive).

13:17 You all continuously be persuaded to the ones continuously going before you all, and continuously defer to them, for they are watching (PI) on behalf of your souls, as those giving account, that they may continuously do this with joy, and not with continuous groaning, for that would be unprofitable for you all.

13:18 Continuously pray about us, for we are persuaded that we are having (PI) a good conscience, continuously desiring to continuously be turned around (passive) to live honorably in all things.

13:19 But I am urging (PI) strongly to do this, that I may be restored (passive) to you all sooner.

13:20 But the God of peace, the One leading up out of the dead, the great Shepherd of the sheep in the blood of an eternal covenant, our Lord Jesus,

13:21 make you perfect and complete in every good work to do His will, continuously working in you all the well pleasing in His sight, through Jesus Christ, to whom the glory into forever and ever. Amen.

13:22 But I am exhorting (PI) you all, brothers, continuously hold up the word of exhortation, for also I have written to you all in few words.

13:23 You all are knowing (PI) the brother Timothy having been freed (passive) with whom, if he may continuously come shortly, I will see you all.

13:24 Greet the ones continuously leading you all, and all the saints. The ones from Italy are greeting (PI) you all.

13:25 The Grace with you all. Amen.

Was written (passive) towards the Hebrews from Italy through Timothy.

(This last sentence is not in the Greek manuscript that the WEB used.)

Introduction To James

THIS IS AN IMPORTANT AND HIGHLY ANOINTED EPISTLE.

THE DANGER:
The danger in this epistle is that it might seem to be advocating good works as the goal. For instance:

> *Thus also faith by itself, if it does not have works, is dead. But someone will say, "You have faith, and I have works." Show me your faith without your works, and I will show you my faith by my works* (James 2:17-2:18).

However, James could not possibly be advocating that we prove that we have faith by our works. This is a God inspired letter, and that idea would contradict a huge message of the epistles.

THE ANSWER
Christian faith is belief that Jesus came to provide the only way to take away our sins. If we forgive others, He has the power to forgive us; and He will then <u>always</u> do so. When we are thus forgiven, our 'bad root" is removed, and the "good root" of Jesus will take its place. In that area we will have been transformed into the image of Jesus. Jesus in that place will <u>always</u> produce good works ("good fruit").

Therefore, our faith will <u>always</u> produce good works <u>if we will apply</u> our faith to our sins. If there are no good works, then the process of transformation into His image has not taken place.

You will see James speak of this process of sanctification throughout the letter.

In this letter there is a particular danger to understand James to be telling Christians to focus on producing good behavior. This is in error, and is of particular danger to Christians who live in the Western culture where it is believed that the intellect and will power are the tools to use to live life. James is speaking of continuously producing "good fruit" that can ONLY occur as a result of the "good root" of

Jesus being present in the Christian as a result of their transformation into the image of Jesus.:

James was an Apostle to the Jews, and so this letter was directed at Christians who had been Jews, located throughout the world. Since these Christians had been raised under the Old Testament Law of Moses, they would have a tendency to try to live their Christian lives in the same way as they had been doing as Jews, namely keeping the Law with their will power. In this epistle he then emphasized the difference between the OT law and the NT provision.

You may also note that the epistle of Hebrews was also directed at Hebrews, and that writer spent the first 10 chapters of that epistle explaining how different and more powerful is the NT provision than was the OT law. Both writers realized that the Jews had a lot of unlearning to do.

Without an understanding of the central importance of sanctification (the process of our transformation into the image of Jesus, also called the process of being saved), it is easy to conclude that James is promoting self-effort as a way to prove we have faith. Most English translations seem to have this self-effort as the message. Presumably the translators were influenced by the Western Mindset, which assumes that we do life through intellect and will power. With this Western Mindset influencing translations, no wonder Christians read it this way; and then, thinking that the Lord is telling them to produce good behavior, they try to be good with their will power – and of course fail over and over again (see Romans 7:15). It is tragic.

The Good News is that we can indeed be transformed into the image of Jesus, and then good behavior will spontaneously occur. Hopefully, my translation will help you to see this.

This epistle is generally accepted to have been written by James, the natural half-brother of Jesus. They had the same mother (Mary), but a different father. The father of Jesus was the Holy Spirit. The father of James was Joseph, Mary's husband.

1:1 James, a servant of God and of the Lord Jesus Christ, to the twelve tribes which are in the Dispersion: to continuously be rejoicing.

1:2 Count it all joy, my brothers, when you all might fall into various tests,

1:3 continuously knowing that the testing of the faith of you all is producing (PI) endurance.

1:4 But continuously let endurance have its perfect work, that you all continuously may be perfect and complete, in nothing continuously being made to lack (passive).

1:5 But if any of you all is being made to lack (PI) (passive) wisdom, let him continuously ask of God, continuously giving to all liberally and without continuously reproaching; and it will be given (passive) to him.

1:6 But let him continuously ask in faith, continuously without any doubting, for the one continuously doubting has been like a wave of the sea, continuously being driven (passive) by the wind and continuously being tossed (passive).

1:7 For continuously let that man not think that he will receive anything from the Lord.

1:8 A double-minded, doubting man (is) unstable in all his ways.

1:9 But let the low degree brother be continuously boasting in his high position;

1:10 But the rich man (is) in a humble state, because like the flower in the grass, he will pass away.

1:11 For the sun arises with the scorching heat, and did wither the grass, and the flower of it falls off, and the beauty of its appearance perished. So also the rich man shall be made to fade away (passive) in his pursuits.

1:12 Blessed is the man enduring (PI) trial, that when he is beginning to become tested, he will receive the crown of life, which the Lord promised to the ones continuously loving Him.

1:13 Let no man continuously say when he is continuously being tested (passive), "I am being tested (PI) (passive) from God," for God is being (PI) incapable of being tempted to do evil, but He is tempting (PI) no one.

1:14 But each one is being tested (PI) (passive) by his own strong desire, he is continuously being drawn away (passive) and continuously being enticed (passive).

1:15 Then the strong desire, seizing and holding (him) fast, is bringing forth (PI) sin; and the sin, having been (passive) full grown, is bringing forth (PI) death.

1:16 Don't continuously be deceived (passive), my beloved brothers.

1:17 Every good gift and every perfect gift is being (PI) from above, continuously coming down from the Father of lights, with whom there is being (PI) no variableness, nor turning shadow.

1:18 Being willing, He brought us forth by the word of truth into us, to continuously be a kind of first fruit of His creatures.

1:19 So, then, my beloved brothers, every man continuously be swift to hear, slow to speak, and slow to anger;

1:20 for the anger of man is not producing the righteousness of God.

1:21 Therefore, putting away all filthiness and overflowing of wickedness, in humility receive the implanted word, continuously being able to save your souls.

1:22 But continuously be doers of the word, and not only hearers, continuously deluding your own selves.

1:23 That if anyone is being (PI) a hearer of the word and not a doer, he is like a man continuously looking at his natural face in a mirror;

1:24 for he saw himself, and has gone away, and immediately forgot what kind of man he was.

1:25 But the one looking into the perfect (NT) law of freedom, and is remaining, not becoming a hearer who forgets, but a doer of the work, this man will be blessed in what he does.

1:26 If anyone in you all is thinking (PI) himself to continuously be religious while not continuously bridling his tongue, but is continuously deceiving his heart, the religion of this one (is) useless.

1:27 Pure religion and undefiled before our God and Father is being (PI) this: to continuously visit the fatherless and widows in their affliction, (and) to continuously keep himself unstained from the world.

2:1 My brothers, don't continuously be holding the

faith of our Lord Jesus Christ of glory in favoritism.

2:2 For if a man with a gold ring, in fine clothing, may enter your synagogue, a poor man in filthy clothing also may enter;

2:3 and you all may pay special attention to the one continuously wearing fine clothing, and you all may say, "You continuously sit here in a good place;" and you all may tell the poor man, "Stand there," or "Continuously sit under my footstool;"

2:4 haven't you all made a distinction in yourselves, and you all became judges, of evil thoughts?

2:5 Listen, my beloved brothers. Didn't God choose the poor ones of this world rich in faith, and heirs of the Kingdom which He promised to the ones continuously loving Him?

2:6 But you all have dishonored the poor man, not the rich who are oppressing (PI) you all, and they are dragging (PI) you all into the courts.

2:7 Are they not blaspheming (PI) the honorable name, the One being called upon (passive) over you all?

2:8 However, if you all are accomplishing to perfection (PI) the (NT) royal law, according to the Scripture, "You will love your neighbor as yourself," you all are doing (PI) well.

2:9 But if you all are showing partiality (PI), you all are committing (PI) sin, being continuously convicted (passive) by the (OT) law as transgressors.

2:10 For whoever will keep the whole (OT) law, but will fall into sin in one (point), he has become guilty of all.

2:11 For the One saying, "You might not commit adultery," also said, "You might not commit murder." But if you will not commit adultery, but you will murder, you have become a transgressor of the (OT) law.

2:12 So you all continuously speak, and thus continuously do, as ones continuously being about to continuously be judged (passive) through the (NT) law of freedom.

2:13 For uncompassionate judgment to the one not doing mercy, and mercy is triumphing (PI) over judgment.

2:14 What advantage (is it), my brothers, if ever a man continuously claims to continuously have faith, but may continuously not to continuously have works? The faith is not being able (PI) to save him.

2:15 Yet if ever a brother or sister may continuously be naked and may continuously be continuously made lacking (passive) of the nourishment of the day,

2:16 but someone out of you all may say to them, "You all continuously go away in peace, you all continuously be warmed (passive), and you all continuously be satisfied (passive);" yet you all not give to them the necessities of the body, what advantage (is it)?

2:17 Thus also faith, if it may continuously not have works, it is being (PI) dead according to itself.

2:18 But someone will say, "You are having (PI) faith, and I am having (PI) works." Show to me your faith without works, and I out of my works will show to you my faith.

2:19 You are believing (PI) that God is being (PI) one. You are doing (PI) well. The demons also are believing (PI), and are shuddering (PI) in fear.

2:20 But are you being willing (PI) to know, o vain man, that faith apart from works is being (PI) dead?

2:21 Wasn't Abraham our father justified (passive) out of works, offering up Isaac his son on the altar?

2:22 That you are seeing (PI) that faith worked together with his works, and out of the works faith was made complete (passive);

2:23 and the Scripture was fulfilled (passive), the one continuously saying, "Yet Abraham believed God, and it was accounted (passive) to him into righteousness;" and he was called (passive) friend of God.

2:24 Indeed now you all are seeing (PI) then that out of works, a man is being justified (PI) (passive), and not only out of faith.

2:25 But also in the same way, wasn't Rahab the prostitute also justified (passive) out of works, receiving the messengers, and sending them out to a different way?

2:26 For just as the body apart from the spirit is being (PI) dead, thus also faith apart from works is being (PI) dead.

3:1 Not many of you all continuously begin to be teachers, my brothers, knowing that we will receive heavier judgment.

3:2 For in many things we all are stumbling (PI). If anyone is not stumbling (PI) in word, this one (is) a perfect man, able to bridle the whole body also.

3:3 Behold, we are putting (PI) bits into the mouths of the horses unto them to be continuously yielded (passive) to us, and we are guiding (PI) their whole body.

3:4 Behold, the ships also, continuously being so big and continuously being driven by fierce winds, are being guided (PI) (passive) by a very small rudder, wherever the impulse of the one continuously steering may continuously wish.

3:5 So the tongue is being (PI) also a little member, and is boasting greatly (PI). See a small fire is lighting (PI) how great a forest.

3:6 And the tongue (is) a fire, the world of iniquity in our members. In this way the tongue is constituted (PI) (passive), continuously defiling the whole body, and continuously setting on fire the course of the species, and is continuously being set on fire (passive) from Gehenna.

3:7 For every nature of animal, birds, creeping things, and things in the sea, is being tamed (PI) (passive), and has been tamed (PI) (passive) to the human nature.

3:8 But nobody is being able (PI) to tame the tongue of humans. (It is) untamable evil, full of deadly poison.

3:9 In it we are blessing (PI) the God and Father, and in it we are cursing (PI) men, the ones having become according to the likeness of God.

3:10 Out of the same mouth is coming forth (PI) blessing and cursing. My brothers, these things are not needing (PI) to continuously begin to be.

3:11 Is any spring sending out from the same opening the fresh and the bitter?

3:12 A fig tree is not being able (PI), my brothers, to produce olives, or a grape vine figs. Thus no spring (is able) to yield both salt and fresh water.

3:13 Who (is) wise and understanding in you all? Let him show out of his good conduct his deeds in gentleness of wisdom.

3:14 But if you all are having (PI) bitter jealousy and only self interest in the heart of you all, don't continuously boast and don't continuously lie against the truth.

3:15 This wisdom is not being (PI) from above, but is continuously being down on earth, sensual, and demonic.
3:16 For where jealousy and rivalry (are), there is tumult and every evil deed.
3:17 But the wisdom from above is indeed being (PI) first pure, then peaceful, gentle, reasonable, full of mercy and good fruits, without partiality, and without hypocrisy.
3:18 But the fruit of righteousness is being sown (PI) (passive) in peace in the ones continuously making peace.
4:1 From what place do wars and fightings in you all (come from)? Don't they come from out of your pleasures of the continuous warring in your members?
4:2 You all are longing after (PI) and are not having (PI). You all are killing (PI) and are coveting, (PI) and are not being able (PI) to obtain. You all are fighting (PI) and making war (PI). You all are not having (PI), but because to continuously ask you all (do) not.
4:3 You all are asking (PI), and are not receiving (PI), because you all are asking (PI) evily, so that you may spend it in your pleasures.
4:4 You adulterers and adulteresses, don't you all know that fondness of the world is being (PI) enmity of God? Whoever then may want to continuously be a friend of the world is being made (passive) (PI) enemy of God.
4:5 Or are you all thinking (PI) that the Scripture is saying (PI) in vain, "The Spirit Who lives in us is yearning (PI) towards jealousy"?
4:6 But He is giving (PI) more grace. Therefore He is saying (PI), "God is resisting (PI) the proud ones, but is giving (PI) grace to the humble."
4:7 You all be being subject (passive) therefore to God. You all resist the devil, and he will definitely flee from you all.
4:8 You all draw near to God, and He will draw near to you all. Cleanse your hands, you sinners; and purify your hearts, you double-minded.
4:9 Lament and mourn, and weep. Let your laughter be being turned (passive) to mourning, and your joy to gloom.
4:10 You all be being humbled (passive) in the sight

of the Lord, and He will exalt you all.

4:11 You all don't be continuously speaking against one another, brothers. The one continuously speaking against a brother and continuously judging his brother, is speaking against (PI) the (NT) law and is judging (PI) the (NT) law. But if you are judging (PI) the (NT) law, you are not being (PI) a doer of the (NT) law, but a judge.

4:12 Only One is being (PI) the lawgiver, the One continuously being able to save and to destroy. Who are you being (PI) who is judging (PI) another?

4:13 Continuously come now, the one continuously saying, "Today or tomorrow we may go into this city, and we will spend a year there, we will trade, and we will make a profit."

4:14 You all who are not knowing (PI) of the tomorrow. For what (is) your life? For you all are being (PI) a vapor, continuously appearing for a little time, and then continuously being disappeared (passive).

4:15 Instead you all ought to continuously say, "If the Lord may will, and we will live, and we will do this or that."

4:16 But now you all are boasting (PI) in your ostentations. All such boasting is being (PI) evil.

4:17 To the one therefore knowing to continuously do good, and continuously not doing (it), to him it is being (PI) sin.

5:1 Now continuously bring the rich ones. You all weep, continuously howling on the misery continuously coming on you all.

5:2 Your wealth is rotted and your garments become moth-eaten.

5:3 Your gold and your silver have been corroded (passive), and their corrosion will be into a testimony to you all, and will eat your flesh like fire. You all have laid up your treasure in the last days.

5:4 Behold, the wages of the laborers, the ones mowing your fields, the ones having been defrauded of what belongs to him (passive) from you all, is crying out (PI), and the cries of the ones reaping have entered into the ears of the Lord of the angelic hosts.

5:5 You all live luxuriously on the earth, and you all live in pleasure. You all nourish your hearts as in a day of slaughter.

5:6 You all have condemned, you all have murdered the righteous one. He is not resisting (PI) to you all.

5:7 You all be patient therefore, brothers, until the presence of the Lord. Behold, the farmer is waiting for (PI) the precious fruit of the earth, continuously being patient upon Him, until he may receive the early and late rain.

5:8 You all also be patient. You all strengthen your hearts, because the presence of the Lord definitely has drawn near and remains near.

5:9 Don't continuously grumble, brothers, against one another, so that you may not be judged (passive). Behold, the judge stands before the door.

5:10 Take, brothers, for an example of suffering and of patience, the prophets who spoke in the name of the Lord.

5:11 Behold, we are calling (PI) them blessed the ones continuously enduring. You all have heard of the endurance of Job, and you all have perceived the Lord in the outcome, that the Lord is being (PI) full of compassion and mercy.

5:12 But above all things, my brothers, don't continuously swear, neither by heaven, nor by the earth, nor by any other oath; but continuously let your "yes" be "yes," and your "no," "no"; so that you all don't fall under judgment.

5:13 Is any in you all suffering afflictions (PI)? Let him continuously pray. Is any being cheerful (PI)? Let him continuously sing praises.

5:14 Is any in you all being weak (PI)? Let him call for the elders of the assembly, and let them pray over him, anointing him to oil in the name of the Lord,

5:15 and the prayer of faith will save the one continuously weary, and the Lord will raise him up. And if he may continuously be having done sins, he will be forgiven (passive).

5:16 Continuously confess your offenses to one another, and you all continuously pray over one another, that you all may be healed (passive). The petition of a just one continuously acting is being very strong (PI).

5:17 Elijah was a man with like feelings to us, and in prayer he prayed of no rain, and it didn't rain on the earth for three years and six months.

5:18 And he prayed again, and the sky gave rain, and the earth brought forth her fruit. 5:19 Brothers, if any in you all may wander from the truth, and someone might turn him back,

5:20 let him continuously know that the one turning back a sinner out of straying of his way will save a soul out of death, and will cover a multitude of sins.

Introduction To 1 Peter

It is generally accepted that this letter was written by the Apostle Peter, one of the original 12 Apostles. Therefore, the author personally knew Jesus Christ when He was in His ministry on earth.

Some theologians object to Peter being the author, because this theology is so much like that of the Apostle Paul. This is a pretty ridiculous argument. If both Paul and Peter were anointed by the Lord in writing their letters, one should expect their theology to be very similar. This objection probably actually affirms the accuracy of both writers.

You will see that Peter well understands our need of a savior Who can take away our sins. Then we will have the mind of Christ, and good behavior will result. Because of the Western Mindset of most English translators, it is very easy to think that Peter is focusing on good behavior which we bring about with our intellect and will power. See specifically Verses 2:21, 2:25, 4:17, and 5:6. But actually, Peter is focusing on our transformation into the image of Jesus. Then continuous good behavior is evidence of the transformation having taken place.

After all, Peter well understood the forgiveness of sins, and the power that results when we are filled with the Spirit. As the fear-filled man in Mark 14:71-72, he was forgiven by Jesus (implied in John 21:15-17), was then filled with His Spirit in Acts 2:4, and became a courageous defender of the faith in Acts 2:14-40. He would have known that a miracle occurred in himself. Why would he expect it to be any different for us? He would have known that we also need the miracle of the blood of Jesus to change us. His transformation was so amazing that he couldn't take credit for it. Therefore it is not possible that he would teach the church to produce good works in their own strength.

Hopefully, my translation and commentary will make this clear. Keep this in mind as you read it.

1:1 Peter, an apostle of Jesus Christ, to the chosen ones who are living as foreigners of the Dispersion of Pontus, Galatia, Cappadocia, Asia, and Bithynia,
1:2 according to the foreknowledge of God the Father, in sanctification of the Spirit, into obedience and sprinkling of the blood of Jesus Christ. Grace to you all and peace be multiplied (passive).
1:3 Blessed be the God and Father of our Lord Jesus Christ, the One according to His great mercy regenerating us into a continuously living hope through the resurrection of Jesus Christ out of the dead,
1:4 into an incorruptible and undefiled and unfading inheritance having been kept (passive) in Heavens (plural) into you all,
1:5 being continuously guarded (passive) in the power of God through faith into salvation ready to be revealed (passive) in the last time.
1:6 In which you all are continuously rejoicing briefly at present, if it is (PI) continuously needing to be, you have been being put to grief (passive) in various trials,
1:7 that the genuineness of the faith of you all, which is more precious than gold continuously being perished (passive) through fire, but continuously being tested (passive), may be found (passive) into praise and glory,
and honor in revelation of Jesus Christ—
1:8 Whom not seeing, you all be loving (PI); into Whom, though now you all aren't continuously seeing Him, yet continuously believing, you all are rejoicing (PI) greatly to joy unspeakable and being glorified (passive)--
1:9 continuously receiving the end goal, the faith of you all, the salvation of souls.
1:10 Concerning this salvation, the prophets sought and searched diligently, prophesying about the grace into you all,
1:11 continuously searching into who or what season the Spirit of Christ, which was in them, pointed out, continuously predicting the sufferings into Christ, and the glories after these.
1:12 To them it was revealed (passive), that not to themselves, but to us, they ministered them, which now was announced (passive) to you all through those preaching the Good News to you all, in the Holy Spirit being sent out (passive) from heaven; into which angels are desiring (PI) to look.
1:13 Therefore, girding up the loins of your minds, being continuously sober and unwavering, set your hope on the grace continuously being brought (passive) to you all in the revelation of Jesus Christ—
1:14 as children of obedience, not continuously conforming to

your former lusts in your ignorance,

1:15 but down from the One calling you all is holy, you yourselves also be beginning to be holy in all of your manner of life;

1:16 For this reason it has been written (passive), "Holy ones be beginning to be, because I am being (PI) holy."

1:17 And if you all are calling (PI) on Him as Father, the One continuously judging impartially on account of each man's work, in reverential fear of the duration of your human life, be turned back (passive):

1:18 knowing that you all were redeemed (passive), not with corruptible things, with silver or gold, out of the useless way of life handed down from your fathers,

1:19 but to the precious blood of Christ, as of a faultless and pure lamb;

1:20 the One having been foreknown (passive) indeed before the foundation of the world, but being revealed (passive) on the end of times because of you all,

1:21 the ones continuously believing through Him into God, the One rousing Him out of the dead, and giving Him glory; so that your faith and hope to continuously be into God.

1:22 Having purified your souls in your obedience of the truth through the Spirit into sincere brotherly affection, love one another from the heart earnestly, continually:

1:23 continuously having been born again (passive), not out of corruptible seed, but of incorruptible, through the continuously living word of God, and continuously remaining into forever.

1:24 For, "All flesh is like grass, and all of man's glory like the flower of the grass is withered (passive). The grass and its flower falls off;

1:25 but the Lord's word is enduring (PI) forever." But this is being (PI) the word, the Good News being preached (passive) into you all.

2:1 Putting away therefore all wickedness, all deceit, hypocrisies, and envies, and all evil speaking,

2:2 as newborn babies, long for the reasonable, without guile rudiment of Christianity, that in it you all may be being grown (passive).

2:3 if that the good Lord you have experienced:

2:4 the ones continuously moving near unto a continuously Living Stone, having been rejected (passive) indeed by men, but near to God, chosen, precious.

2:5 You all also, as continuously living stones, are being built up (PI) (passive) a spiritual house, a holy priesthood, to offer up spiritual sacrifices, acceptable to God through Jesus Christ.

2:6 Through which also it is being contained (PI) in Scripture, "Behold, I am laying (PI) in Zion a Chief Cornerstone, chosen, precious: and the one continuously believing on Him may not be disgraced (passive)."

2:7 Honor then to you all, to the ones continuously believing; but to the ones continuously disbelieving, "which stone the ones continuously building the house rejected became into the head of the corner,"

2:8 and, "a stone of stumbling, and a rock of offense." Who all are stumbling (PI) to the word, continuously being disbelieving, into which also they were appointed (passive).

2:9 But you all, a chosen race, a royal priesthood, a holy nation, into a people acquired, so that you all may proclaim the excellence of the One calling you all out of darkness into His marvelous light:

2:10 who in time past were no people, but now God's people, the ones not having been shown mercy (passive) but now being shown mercy (passive).

2:11 Beloved, I am begging (PI) you all as foreigners and pilgrims, to continuously abstain of fleshly lusts, which are warring (PI) against the soul;

2:12 you all continuously having good behavior in the nations, so in that in which they are speaking against (PI) you all as evildoers, they may out of your good works, being spectators, they may glorify God in the day of visitation.

2:13 Therefore you all be subject (passive) to every human creation because of the Lord: whether to the king, as continuously being superior;

2:14 or to governors, as continuously being sent (passive) through him into vengeance of evildoers but praise of doers of good.

2:15 That this is being (PI) the will of God, those continuously doing good to continuously put to silence the ignorance of foolish men:

2:16 as free, and not continuously having freedom as a cloak of wickedness, but as bondservants of God.

2:17 You all honor all. Continuously love the brotherhood. Continuously reverence God. Continuously honor the king.

2:18 Servants, be continuously being in subjection to your masters in all fear; not only to the good and gentle, but also to the wicked.

2:19 For grace this is commendable if someone is enduring (PI) pain, continuously suffering unjustly, because of conscience of God.

2:20 For what credit (is it) if, ones continuously sinning and continuously being buffeted (passive) patiently endure? But if the ones continuously doing good and continuously suffering patiently endure, this is grace with God.

2:21 For to this you all were called (passive), because Christ also suffered for us, continuously leaving to us an example, that you all may follow to His steps,

2:22 Who did not sin, "neither was deceit found (passive) in His mouth."

2:23 Who, continuously being reviled (passive), didn't revile back. Continuously suffering, didn't threaten, but committed Himself to the One continuously judging righteously;

2:24 Who carried up our sins in His body on the tree, that the ones dying to sins, might live to righteousness; of Whom to His stripes you all were healed (passive).

2:25 For you all were continuously being strayed (passive) like sheep; but now have been turned back (passive) on the Shepherd and Overseer of your souls.

3:1 In the same way, wives, continuously be being subject (passive) to your own husbands; and that, if any (husbands) are being disbelieving (PI) to the Word, they may be won (passive) through the behavior of their wives without a word;

3:2 seeing your pure behavior in respect.

3:3 Of who continuously let it be not just the outward adorning of braiding the hair, and of wearing jewels of gold, or of putting on fine clothing;

3:4 but in the hidden person of the heart, in the incorruptibility of a gentle and quiet spirit, which is being (PI) in the sight of God very precious.

3:5 For thus once also the holy women, the ones continuously hoping on God adorned themselves, continuously being subject (passive) to their own husbands:

3:6 as Sarah obeyed Abraham, continuously calling him master, of whom you all were made to become (passive) children, continuously doing good, and not continuously fearing in any terror.

3:7 You husbands, in the same way, continuously living with them according to knowledge, continuously giving honor to the woman, as to the weaker vessel, and as also joint heirs of the grace of life; into your prayers to continuously not be hindered (passive).

3:8 But finally, all be like-minded, compassionate, loving as brothers, tenderhearted, courteous,

3:9 not continuously rendering evil in place of evil, or insult in place of insult; but instead continuously blessing; knowing that into this were you called (passive), that you may inherit a blessing.

3:10 For, "The one continuously purposing to continuously love life, and see good days, let him keep his tongue from evil, and his lips to not speak guile.

3:11 Each one turn away from evil, and each one do good. Seek peace, and pursue her.

3:12 Because the eyes of the Lord (are) on the righteous, and His ears open into their prayer; but the face of the Lord (is) on the ones continuously doing evil."

3:13 And who is the one evil treating you all, if you all may become followers of the good?

3:14 But even if you all may be suffering (PI) for righteousness, you all are blessed. "But don't be afraid of them, neither may you all be troubled (passive)."

3:15 But you all sanctify the Lord God in your hearts; but always speak a defense to everyone continuously asking you all a word concerning the hope in you all, with humility and reverence:

3:16 continuously having a good conscience; that, in which they may continuously speak against you all as evildoers, they may be shamed (passive), the ones continuously insulting your good way of life in Christ.

3:17 For it is better, if the will of God is being willing (PI), the ones continuously doing good to continuously suffer than for continuously doing evil.

3:18 Seeing that Christ also suffered for sins once, the righteous One for the sake of unrighteous ones, that He might bring us to God; being put to death (passive) to the flesh, but being made alive (passive) to the spirit;

3:19 in which He also went and preached to the spirits in prison,

3:20 the ones being dis-believers, once the longsuffering of God waited in the days of Noah, the ark continuously being built (passive), few, that is being (PI), eight souls, were saved (passive) through water.

3:21 To which also baptism (is) a representation saving (PI) us -- not the putting away of the filth of the flesh, but the answer of a good conscience into God, through the resurrection of Jesus Christ,

3:22 Who is being (PI) in the right hand of God, going into heaven, angels and authorities and powers being made subject (passive) to Him.

4:1 Then the suffering of Christ for us to the flesh, you all also arm yourselves with the same mind; that the one suffering in the flesh has ceased of sin;

4:2 into no longer still to the desires of humans to pass the rest (of) time in the flesh, but to the will of God.

4:3 For we, suffice to us having passed the time of life having

carried out the desire of the
Gentiles, in lewdness, lusts,
drunken binges, orgies,
carousings, and abominable
idolatries.

4:4 In which they are being made
to think (PI) (passive) of you all
not continuously running with
them into the same excess of riot,
continuously blaspheming:

4:5 who will give account to the
One continuously having
readiness to judge the
continuously living and the dead.

4:6 For into this also is brought
the Good News even to the dead,
that they may be judged
(passive) indeed as men to the
flesh, but may continuously live
as to God to the spirit.

4:7 But the end of all things is
near. Therefore you all be of
sound mind, and sober into
prayer.

4:8 But above all, into
yourselves continuously having
earnest love that the love will
cover a multitude of sins.

4:9 You all be hospitable into
one another without grumbling.

4:10 As each has received a gift,
be continuously serving it into
one another, as good managers
of the diverse grace of God.

4:11 If anyone is speaking (PI),
as the very words of God. If
anyone is serving (PI), let it be
out of the strength which God is
supplying (PI), that in all, God
may be continuously glorified
(passive) through Jesus Christ, to
Whom is being (PI) the glory

and the dominion forever and
ever. Amen.

4:12 Beloved, don't continuously
be astonished (passive) to the
fiery trial continuously beginning
to come in you all, to test you all,
as though a strange thing is
continuously happening to you
all.

4:13 But because you all are
partaking (PI) to the sufferings of
Christ, continuously rejoice; that
in the revelation of His glory you
also may rejoice, continuously
exulting.

4:14 If you all are being insulted
(PI) (passive) in the name of
Christ, blessed are you all that
the Spirit of glory and of God is
resting (PI) on you all. On their
part He is being blasphemed (PI)
(passive), but on your part He is
being glorified (PI) (passive).

4:15 For let none of you
continuously suffer as a
murderer, or a thief, or an evil
doer, or a meddler in other men's
matters.

4:16 But (if one of you suffers)
as a Christian, let him
continuously not be ashamed;
but let him continuously glorify
God in this matter.

4:17 For this reason (it is) the
time to begin of the judgment to
separate out from the household
of God. But if first of all out
from us, what will be the end of
the ones continuously being
stubborn to the Good News of
God?

4:18 And if the righteous with difficulty is being saved (PI) (passive), where will the ungodly and sinner appear?

4:19 And so that the ones continuously suffering according to the will of God, as to a faithful Creator, continuously have their souls delivered (passive), in doing good.

5:1 I am exhorting (PI) the elders in you all, a fellow elder, and a witness of the sufferings of Christ, and participant of the glory continuously being about to continuously be revealed (passive).

5:2 Shepherd the flock of God which is in you all, continuously exercising the oversight, not of compulsion, but voluntarily, not for dishonest gain, but willingly;

5:3 neither as continuously being lords of the inheritance, but continuously becoming examples of the flock.

5:4 And being manifested (passive) of the Chief Shepherd, you all will receive the crown of glory that doesn't fade away.

5:5 Likewise, all you younger ones, be subject (passive) to the elder. But all of you continuously be being subject (passive) to one another, you all clothed of humility, that "God is resisting (PI) the proud, but is giving (PI) grace to the humble."

5:6 Be being humbled (passive) therefore under the mighty hand of God, that He may exalt you all in due time;

5:7 casting all your worries on Him, that He is caring (PI) about you all.

5:8 You all be sober and vigilant. Be watchful. Your adversary, the devil, is walking around (PI) as a continuously roaring lion, continuously seeking whom he may devour.

5:9 Whom resist steadfast to your faith, knowing that your brothers in the world to be continuously undergoing (passive) of the same sufferings.

5:10 But may the God of all grace, the One calling us into His eternal glory in Christ Jesus, the ones suffering briefly, He may perfect, establish, strengthen, and give you all a good foundation.

5:11 To Him the glory and the power forever and ever. Amen.

5:12 Through Silvanus, our faithful brother, as I am considering (PI) him, I have written to you briefly, continuously exhorting, and continuously testifying this to continuously be the true grace of God into which you all stand.

5:13 The (church) in Babylon, chosen together with you all, is greeting (PI) you all; and so does Mark, my son.

5:14 Greet one another in a kiss of love. Peace to you all, to the ones in Christ Jesus. Amen.

Introduction To 2 Peter

Again, keep in mind that the Apostle Peter well knew the power of the blood of Jesus to take away our sins and then fill us with the Holy Spirit. He was a spiritual weakling when Jesus was about to be crucified, and denied Him three times. But after the Holy Spirit was shed abroad as described in Acts 2:1 through 2:4, he became a fearless and powerful apostle.

Clearly, this letter was written after 1 Peter; but it has not been possible to determine when.

Verses 1:1 through 1:12 are a FANTASTIC EXPLANATION OF THE IMPORTANCE OF SANCTIFICATION, and what a wonderful gift it is to us!

These verses are the heart of this letter.

Later on he tells them to watch out for false prophets (Verse 2:1), and explains that it will not go well for those people.

Let Peter's words inspire you to diligently pursue your own sanctification!

1:1 Simon Peter, a servant and apostle of Jesus Christ, to those who having obtained through God's divine allotment an equally precious faith to us in the righteousness of our God and Savior, Jesus Christ:

1:2 Grace to you all and peace be multiplied (passive) in the knowledge of God and of Jesus our Lord,

1:3 so as all of His divine power toward life and holiness having been graciously given to us, through the knowledge of the One calling us (genitive case) by means of glory and of virtue;

1:4 Through which to us has been given (passive) the greatest and precious promises; that through these you all may be beginning to be participants of the divine nature, escaping of the corruption in the world in (its) strong desire of corruption.

1:5 And in the same manner also this, you all in addition bringing forth all diligence in your faith in virtue, also in the virtue, knowledge;

1:6 also in the knowledge, strength; also in the strength the endurance; also in the endurance Godliness;

1:7 also in holiness brotherly affection; also in brotherly affection, love.

1:8 For to these things you all continuously existing and increasing (PI), you all not continuously constituted idle nor unfruitful into the knowledge of our Lord Jesus Christ.

1:9 For to whom these things are not present (PI) is blind (PI), continuously closing his eyes, getting oblivious of the cleansing of his old sins.

1:10 Therefore rather, brothers, be diligent to continuously make your calling and election confirmed. For continuously doing these things, you all may never stumble.

1:11 For thus to you all will be richly supplied (passive) the entrance into the eternal Kingdom of our Lord and Savior, Jesus Christ.

1:12 Therefore I will not be negligent to continuously remind you all about these things, even though the ones being aware and continuing to be aware, and the ones having been established and continuing to be established (passive) in the truth continuously being present.

1:13 But I am thinking (PI) right, on as long as I am (PI) in this tent, to continuously stir you all in reminder;

1:14 knowing that near at hand is being (PI) the putting off of my tent, even as our Lord Jesus Christ made clear to me.

1:15 Yet, I will also make every effort to continuously have you all, always after my departure, to continuously make mention of these things.

1:16 For not following cunningly devised fables, we made known to you all the power and presence of our Lord Jesus Christ, but onlookers beginning to become of His majesty.

1:17 For receiving of God the Father as the source, honor and glory, of the voice being carried (passive) to Him by so great of Majestic Glory, "This is being (PI) My beloved Son, into Whom I have been well pleased."

1:18 And this voice we heard coming out of heaven, ones continuously being together with Him in the holy mountain.

1:19 And we are having (PI) the more sure word of prophecy; to which you all are doing (PI) well continuously heeding, as to a lamp continuously shining in a dark place, until of which day may dawn, and the morning star may rise in your hearts:

1:20 continuously knowing this first, that all prophecy of Scripture is not beginning to be (PI) of private interpretation.

1:21 For no prophecy was ever carried (passive) to the will of man: but by holy men of God spoke continuously being moved (passive) of the Holy Spirit.

2:1 But false prophets also arose in the people, as false teachers will also be in you all, who will smuggle in heresies of destruction, continuously denying even the Master buying them, continuously bringing to themselves swift destruction.

2:2 And many will follow to the destruction, because of whom the way of the truth will be maligned (passive).

2:3 And in covetousness they will exploit you all to deceptive words: to whom the judgment of old is not lingering (PI), and their destruction is not slumbering (PI).

2:4 For if God didn't spare angels sinning, but casting them to Tartarus, to pits of darkness, them having been kept (passive) into judgment;

2:5 and didn't spare the ancient world, but preserved Noah with seven others, a preacher of righteousness, bringing on a flood to the world of the ungodly;

2:6 and reducing to ashes the cities of Sodom and Gomorrah to overthrow (them), condemned them, having set them an example to the ones continuously irreverent, of the ones continuously being about to suffer,

2:7 and delivered righteous Lot, who was continuously being distressed (passive) of the lawless ones in wantonness.

2:8 For to see and to hear, the righteous man continuously dwelling in them, was tormented (in his) righteous soul from day out of day to their lawless deeds:

2:9 the Lord knows to continuously deliver believers out of temptation but to continuously keep the

unrighteous continuously being punished (passive) into the day of judgment;
2:10 but chiefly the ones continuously going after the flesh in the lust of defilement, and continuously despising of authority. Presumptuous men, self-willed, not being afraid (PI), continuously speaking evil of glory;
2:11 whereas angels, continuously being to greater might and to power, not bringing (PI) a railing judgment against them before the Lord.
2:12 But these, as unreasoning creatures, being born (passive) natural animals into capture and destruction, continuously speaking evil in matters in which they are being ignorant (PI), in their destruction will be destroyed (passive),
2:13 they will be receiving the wages of unrighteousness; continuously counting it pleasure in the daytime self-indulgence, spots and blemishes, continuously reveling in their deceit, continuously feasting together with you all;
2:14 continuously having eyes full of adultery, and unable to cease of sin; continuously enticing unsettled souls; having a heart trained to greed; children continuously having of curse;
2:15 forsaking the right way, they were strayed (passive), following out to the way of Balaam of Beor, who loved the wages of wrongdoing;
2:16 but he has had rebuke of his own disobedience. A mute donkey speaking in a man's voice stopped the madness of the prophet.
2:17 These are being (PI) wells without water, clouds continuously being driven (passive) by a storm; to whom the blackness of darkness has been reserved (passive) forever.
2:18 For, continuously uttering great swelling words of emptiness, they are enticing (PI) in the lusts of the flesh, in licentiousness, those who are indeed escaping from those continuously being returned (passive) in error;
2:19 continuously promising them liberty, they themselves continuously being bondservants of corruption; for to whom has been brought into bondage (passive) this one was overcome and has been enslaved (passive).
2:20 For if the ones escaping the defilement of the world in the knowledge of the Lord and Savior Jesus Christ, but to these again being entangled (passive), being overcome (PI), the state has become to them worse than the first.
2:21 For it would have been better to them not to have known the way of righteousness, than after knowing it, to turn back out of holy principle being delivered (passive) to them.

2:22 But it has happened to them of the true proverb, "The dog turning about on his own vomit," and "the sow being washed into wallowing of mire."

3:1 This now, beloved, the second letter that I am writing (PI) to you all; in which I am stirring up (PI) in your sincere minds in remembrance;

3:2 to be reminded (passive) of the words having been spoken before (passive) by the holy prophets, of the apostles of us, and the precept (singular) of the Lord and Savior:

3:3 You all continuously knowing this first, that on the last of the days mockers continuously going according to their own lusts,

3:4 and continuously saying, "Where is being (PI) the promise of His presence? For, from which the fathers were made to sleep (passive), thus all are continuing (PI) from the beginning of the creation."

3:5 For this is eluding (PI) the ones continuously willing, that heavens were from of old, and the earth having stood forth through water, to the word of God;

3:6 through which then the world was, being overflowed (passive) to water, perished.

3:7 But the heavens, and the earth, to the same word are now being (PI) continuously having been stored up (passive) to fire,

into the day of judgment and destruction of the ungodly men.

3:8 But continuously don't forget this one thing, you all beloved, that one day with the Lord (is) as a thousand years, and a thousand years as one day.

3:9 The Lord is not being slow (PI) of the promise, as some are counting (PI) slowness; but is being (PI) patient into us, not continuously wishing any to perish, but that all to come into repentance.

3:10 But the day of the Lord will come as a thief in the night; in which the heavens will pass away with a great noise, also the elements will be dissolved (passive) by being continuously burned, and the earth and the works in her will be burned up (passive).

3:11 Then all of these things continuously being destroyed (passive) like this, what kind of people is it being necessary (PI) you all to continuously be in holy living and holiness,

3:12 continuously hurrying and continuously awaiting with eager desire the coming of the day of God, because of which the heavens continuously being put on fire (passive) shall be dissolved (passive), and the elements will be being melted (PI) (passive), continuously being set on fire (passive).

3:13 But, according to His promise, we being looking (PI) for new heavens and a new earth, in which righteousness is dwelling (PI).

3:14 Therefore, beloved, ones continuously hoping for these things, unspotted, you all be diligent to be found (passive) flawless to Him, to be found (passive) in peace.

3:15 And continuously esteem the longsuffering salvation of our Lord; even as also our beloved brother Paul, according to the wisdom being given to him (passive), wrote to you all;

3:16 as also in all of his letters, continuously speaking in them of these things. In which are being (PI) some things that are hard to understand, which the ignorant and unsettled are twisting (PI), as they also do the other Scriptures, toward their own destruction.

3:17 You all therefore, beloved, continuously knowing this beforehand, continuously beware, that being carried away (passive) with the error of the wicked, you all may not fall of your own steadfastness.

3:18 But continuously grow in the grace and knowledge of our Lord and Savior Jesus Christ. To Him the glory both now and forever. Amen.

Introduction To 1 John

It is interesting that John's epistles were probably the last letters written by one of the original Apostles. The other Epistles by other writers were written before 70 AD, and it is estimated that 1 John was written in the early 90's.

As you may have noticed, 1 John can seem very confusing:

1 John 3:6: "Whoever abides in Him does not sin. Whoever sins has neither seen Him nor known Him."

1 John 1:8: "If we say that we have no sin, we deceive ourselves, and the truth is not in us."

These two verses appear to be saying:
- If we sin, we aren't saved;
- All of us sin;
- Therefore, none of us are saved!

Yet, the Apostle John would never say something so contradictory. Could the English translations be misleading?

My translation of 1 John, going back to the original Greek, eliminates this confusion.

Then you will understand how it can simultaneously be true that: yes, you are saved; and yes, you do sin; and yes, it is also possible for you to not sin. This is because there are places inside us that are indeed inhabited by Jesus. Those "good roots" will produce ONLY "good fruit." However, there are also other places (what Hebrews 12:15 refers to as a "root of bitterness"). Those "bad roots" do cause us to sin. In other words, we have a complexity inside, and are not a single container. Once you understand this, you will be able to see and appreciate the tremendous power of Jesus to take away sin, which is revealed in 1 John.

Verses 2:27 through 3:24 speak over and over of "remaining," which is a translation of the Greek word *meno* (#3306).

It means:

> "To remain, abide, dwell, live . . . to be and remain united with him, one with him" (Zodhiates, page 959-960).

Perhaps surprisingly, here "having been born out of God" cannot be referring to the one-time event of salvation; because when what John is here referring to happens, we are able to not sin. It is true that when we become a child of God, we are filled with His Spirit. But we still sin. All Christians sin, so here he must be speaking of the ongoing process of sanctification, which is the only other option. This is very important to understand, because His remaining in us can only happen as a result of our having been transformed into the image of Jesus. Then Jesus has come into that place in us, and He resides there on an ongoing basis. Then that "good root" of Jesus in us will not produce "bad fruit" (sin).

You will also note that #1785 *entole* appears frequently in this epistle. Translating this as "commandment" is also misleading, because it tends to set us to trying hard to obey with our will power. The meaning here is **exactly the opposite**. It is actually referring to the teaching and precept of Jesus, which is to forgive so we can be forgiven. Then out of our transformation into His image we will spontaneously, effortlessly do these things because of His presence in us.

With this new understanding, you will be able to appreciate the great power in this epistle!

1:1 That which was from the beginning, that which we have heard, that which we have seen to our eyes, that which we saw, and our hands touched, concerning the Word of life
1:2 and the life was revealed (passive), and we have seen, and are testifying (PI), and are declaring (PI) to you all the life, the eternal life, which was towards the Father, and was revealed (passive) to us;
1:3 that which we have seen and heard we are declaring (PI) to you all, that you all also may continuously have fellowship with us, and yet our fellowship is with the Father, and with His Son, Jesus Christ.
1:4 And we are writing (PI) these things to you all, that your joy may continuously be fulfilled (passive).
1:5 And this is being (PI) the message which we have heard from Him and are announcing (PI) to you all, that God is existing (PI) as light, and in Him is being (PI) no darkness at all.
1:6 If we may say that we are having (PI) fellowship with Him and may continuously live our lives in the darkness, we are lying (PI), and are not doing (PI) the truth.
1:7 But if we may continuously live our lives in the light, as He is existing (PI) in the light, we are having (PI) fellowship with one another, and the blood of Jesus Christ, His Son, is cleansing (PI) us from all sin.
1:8 If we may say that we are having (PI) no sin, we are deceiving (PI) ourselves, and the truth is not being (PI) in us.
1:9 If ever we may continuously confess our sins, He is being (PI) worthy of belief and (is) just, that He may forgive us the sins, and may cleanse us from all unrighteousness.
1:10 If we may say that we haven't sinned, we are making (PI) Him a liar, and His word is not being (PI) in us.
2:1 My little children, I am writing (PI) these things to you all so that you all might possibly not sin. And if anyone may sin, we are having (PI) an advocate towards the Father, Jesus Christ, the righteous.
2:2 And He is being (PI) the atoning sacrifice for our sins, and not for ours only, but also for the whole world.
2:3 And in this we are knowing (PI) that we know

Him: if we may continuously keep His precepts.

2:4 The one continuously saying "I have known Him and continue to know Him," and is not continuously maintaining His precepts, is being (PI) a liar, and the truth is not being (PI) in him.

2:5 But whoever may be continuously keeps His word, the love of God has most certainly been perfected (passive) in this one. This is how we are knowing (PI) that we are being (PI) in Him:

2:6 The one continuously saying he is to continuously remain in Him is being fit and proper (PI) himself also to continuously live his life just like He lived His life.

2:7 Brothers, I am writing (PI) no new precept to you all, but an old precept which you all had from the beginning. The old precept is being (PI) the word which you all heard from the beginning.

2:8 Again, I am writing (PI) a new precept to you all, which is being (PI) true in Him and in you all; that the darkness is passing away (PI), and the true light already is shining (PI).

2:9 The one continuously saying he is continuously to be in the light and is continuously hating his brother, is being (PI) in the darkness even until now.

2:10 The one continuously loving his brother is remaining (PI) in the light, and there is being (PI) no cause to stumble in him.

2:11 But the one continuously hating his brother is being (PI) in the darkness, and is living (PI) his life in the darkness, and doesn't know where he is going (PI), because the darkness has blinded his eyes.

2:12 I am writing (PI) to you all, little children, because your sins have been forgiven (passive) you through His name's sake.

2:13 I am writing (PI) to you all, fathers, because you all have known and continue to know Him Who is from the beginning. I am writing (PI) to you all, young men, because you all have overcome the evil one. I am writing (PI) to you, little children, because you all have known and continue to know the Father.

2:14 I have written to you fathers, because you all have known and continue to know Him Who is from the beginning. I have written to you, young men, because you are being (PI) strong, and the word of God is remaining (PI) in you all, and you all have overcome the evil one.

2:15 Don't continuously love the world, neither the things in the world. If anyone may continuously love the world, the love of the Father is not being (PI) in him.

2:16 That all in the world, the lust of the flesh, the lust of the eyes, and the pride of life, is not being (PI) out of the Father, but is being (PI) of the world.

2:17 And the world is passing away (PI) and the lust of him, but the one continuously doing God's will is remaining (PI) into eternity.

2:18 Little children, it is being (PI) the last hour, and as you all heard that the Antichrist is coming (PI), and now many antichrists have arisen. By this we are knowing (PI) that it is being (PI) the last hour.

2:19 They went out of us, but they were not out of us; for if they were out of us, they would have continued with us. But that they might be revealed (passive) that they are not being (PI) of us.

2:20 And you all are having (PI) an anointing from the Holy One, and you all know all.

2:21 I have not written to you all because you all don't know the truth, but because you all know it, and because every lie is not being (PI) out of the truth.

2:22 Who is being (PI) the liar if not the one continuously denying that Jesus is being (PI) the Christ? This is being (PI) the Antichrist, the one continuously denying the Father and the Son.

2:23 Every one continuously denying the Son, is not having (PI) the Father. The one continuously confessing the Son is having (PI) the Father also.

2:24 Therefore, you all, let that continuously remain in you which you all heard from the beginning. If that which you all heard from the beginning may remain in you all, you all also will remain in the Son, and in the Father.

2:25 And this is being (PI) the promise which He promised to us, the eternal life.

2:26 These things I have written to you all concerning those continuously deceiving you all.

2:27 And for you all, the anointing which you all received from Him is remaining (PI) in you all, and you all are not needing (PI) that anyone may continuously teach you all. But as His anointing is teaching (PI) you all concerning of all, and is being (PI) true, and is not being (PI) a lie, and even as it taught you all, you all will remain in Him.

2:28 And now, little children, continuously remain in Him, that when He may be made to appear (passive), we may continuously have boldness, and may not be put to shame (passive) before Him in His presence.

2:29 If you all may know that He is being (PI) righteous, you all are knowing (PI) that each one continuously doing righteousness has been born (passive) out of Him.

3:1 Behold, how great a love the Father has bestowed on us, that we may be being called (passive) children of God! For this cause the world is not knowing (PI) us, because it didn't know Him.

3:2 Beloved, now we are being (PI) children of God, and it is not yet revealed (passive) what we will be. But we know that, if He may be revealed, like to Him we will be, for we will see Him just as He is being (PI).

3:3 And everyone continuously having this hope on Him is purifying (PI) himself, even as He (Jesus) is being (PI) pure.

3:4 Everyone continuously sinning also is committing (PI) lawlessness. And sin is being (PI) lawlessness.

3:5 You all know that He was made apparent (passive) that He may take away our sins, and in Him is being (PI) no sin.

3:6 Any (root) continuously remaining in Him is not sinning (PI). The one (a root) continuously sinning hasn't seen Him, neither has known Him.

3:7 Little children, let no one continuously lead you all astray. (Any root) continuously doing righteousness is being (PI) righteous, even as He (Jesus) is being (PI) righteous.

3:8 (Any root) continuously sinning is being (PI) of the devil, for the devil is (PI) sinning from the beginning. Into this end the Son of God was made to appear (passive), that He may destroy the works of the devil.

3:9 Any (root) having been born (passive) out of God is not sinning (PI), because His seed is remaining (PI) in the root, and (the root) is not being able (PI) to continuously be sinning, because (the root) has been born (passive) of God.

3:10 In this is being (PI) revealed the children of God, and the children of the devil. (Any root) not continuously doing righteousness is not being (PI) out of God, and the one not continuously loving his brother.

3:11 For this is being (PI) the message which you all heard from the beginning, in order that we may continuously love one another;

3:12 unlike Cain, who was of the evil one, and killed his brother. And because of what did he kill him? Because his works were evil, but his brother's righteous.

3:13 Don't continuously be surprised, my brothers, if the world is hating (PI) you all.

3:14 We have perceived that we have passed out of death into life, because we are loving (PI) the brothers. The one not continuously loving his brother is remaining (PI) in death.

3:15 The one continuously hating his brother is being (PI) a murderer, and you all are aware that every murderer is not having (PI) eternal life continuously remaining in Him.

3:16 In this we know the love of God, because He laid down His life for us. And we are needing (PI) to continuously lay down our lives for the brothers.

3:17 But whoever may continuously have the wealth of the world, and may continuously see his brother continuously having need, and may close his heart of compassion from him, how is the love of God remaining (PI) in him?

3:18 My little children, we may not continuously love to word, neither to tongue, but to truth and deed.

3:19 And in this we are knowing (PI) that we are being (PI) out of the truth, and we will persuade our hearts before Him,

3:20 that if our heart may continuously condemn us, God is being (PI) greater than our heart, and is knowing (PI) all things.

3:21 Beloved, if our hearts may not continuously condemn us, we are having (PI) boldness toward God;

3:22 and whatever we may continuously ask, we are receiving (PI) out from Him, that we are keeping (PI) His precepts and are doing (PI)

the things that are pleasing in His sight.

3:23 And this is being (PI) His precept, that we may believe to the name of His Son, Jesus Christ, and may continuously love one another, according as He gave us direction.

3:24 And the one continuously keeping His precepts is remaining (PI) in Him, and He in him. And in this we are knowing (PI) that He is remaining (PI) in us, out of the Spirit which He gave us.

4:1 Beloved, don't continuously believe every spirit, but continuously test the spirits, whether it is being (PI) out of God, because many false prophets have gone out into the world.

4:2 In this you all are knowing (PI) the Spirit of God: every spirit who is confessing (PI) that Jesus Christ having come in the flesh is being (PI) out of God,

4:3 and every spirit which is not confessing (PI) Jesus Christ having come in the flesh is not being (PI) out of God, and this is being (PI) the spirit of the Antichrist, which you all have heard that it is coming (PI). And now it is being (PI) in the world already.

4:4 You all are being (PI) out of God, little children, and you all have overcome them; because greater is being (PI) the One in you all than the one in the world.

4:5 They are being (PI) out of the world. Through this they are speaking (PI) of the world, and the world is hearing (PI) them.

4:6 We are being (PI) out of God. The one continuously knowing God is listening (PI) of us. Who is not being (PI) out of God is not listening (PI) of us. Out of this we are knowing (PI) the Spirit of truth, and the spirit of deception.

4:7 Beloved ones, we may continuously love one another, that love is being (PI) out of God; and the one continuously loving has been (passive) born out of God, and is knowing (PI) God.

4:8 The one continuously not loving doesn't know God, that God is being (PI) love.

4:9 In this the love of God was revealed (passive) in us, that God has sent His one and only Son into the world that we might live through Him.

4:10 In this is being (PI) love, not that we loved God, but that He loved us, and sent His

Son the atoning sacrifice concerning the sins of us.

4:11 Beloved, if God loved us in this way, we also are needing (PI) to continuously love one another.

4:12 No one has ever seen God. If we may continuously love one another, God is remaining (PI) in us, and His love is being (PI) having been perfected (passive) in us.

4:13 In this we are knowing (PI) that we are remaining (PI) in Him and He in us, that He has given to us out of His Spirit.

4:14 And we have seen and are testifying (PI) that the Father has sent the Son Savior of the world.

4:15 Whoever may confess that Jesus is being (PI) the Son of God, God is remaining (PI) in him, and he in God.

4:16 And we have known and have believed the love which God is having (PI) in us. God is being (PI) love, and the one continuously remaining in love is remaining (PI) in God, and God in him.

4:17 In this, love has been made perfect (passive) among us, that we may continuously have boldness in the day of judgment, because even as that One is being (PI), also are we being (PI) in this world.

4:18 There is being (PI) no fear in love; but perfect love is casting (PI) out fear, because fear is having (PI) chastening. But the one continuously fearing has not been made perfect (passive) in love.

4:19 We are loving (PI) Him, because He first loved us.

4:20 If any man may say, "I am loving (PI) God," and may continuously hate his brother, he is being (PI) a liar; for the one not continuously loving his brother whom he has seen, how is he being able (PI) to continuously love God Whom he has not seen?

4:21 And we are having (PI) this precept from Him, that the one continuously loving God may also continuously love his brother.

5:1 Every one continuously believing that Jesus is being (PI) the Christ has been born (passive) out of God. And every one continuously loving the one begetting also is loving (PI) the one having been begotten (passive) out of Him.

5:2 In this we are knowing (PI) that we are loving (PI) the children of God, when we are loving (PI) God and may continuously keep His precepts.

5:3 For this is being (PI) the love of God, that we may continuously keep His precepts. And His precepts are not being (PI) heavy burdens.
5:4 That every one having been born (passive) out of God is conquering (PI) the world. And this conquest is being (PI) our faith conquering the world.
5.5 Who is being (PI) the one continuously conquering the world, if not the one continuously believing that Jesus is being (PI) the Son of God?
5:6 This is being (PI) the One coming through water and blood, Jesus Christ; not in the water only, but in the water and the blood. And it is being (PI) the Spirit the One continuously testifying that the Spirit is being (PI) the truth.
5:7 That there are being (PI) three continuously testifying in heaven, the Father, the Word, and the Holy Spirit, and these three are being (PI) one:
5:8 And there are being (PI) three continuously testifying in the earth, the Spirit and the water and the blood. And the three are being (PI) into one.
5:9 If we are receiving (PI) the witness of men, the witness of God is being (PI) greater; for this is being (PI) God's testimony which He has testified concerning His Son.
5:10 The one continuously believing into the Son of God is having (PI) the testimony in himself. The one continuously not believing God has made Him a liar, because he has not believed into the testimony that God has given concerning His Son.
5:11 And the testimony is being (PI) this, that God gave to us eternal life, and this life is being (PI) in His Son.
5:12 The one continuously having the Son is having (PI) the life. The one not continuously having God's Son is not having (PI) the life.
5:13 These things I wrote to you all, the ones continuously believing into the name of the Son of God, that you all may know that you are having (PI) eternal life, and that you all may continuously believe into the name of the Son of God.
5:14 And this is being (PI) the boldness which we are having (PI) toward Him, that, if we may continuously ask anything according to His will, He is hearing (PI) of us.
5:15 And if we know that He is hearing (PI) of us, whatever we may continuously ask, we

know that we are having (PI) the petitions which we have asked Him.

5:16 If anyone may see his brother continuously sinning a sin not unto death, he shall ask, and it will be given to him life, to the one continuously sinning not unto death. There is being (PI) a sin unto death. I am not saying (PI) that he may make a request concerning that.

5:17 All unrighteousness is being (PI) sin, and there is being (PI) a sin not leading unto death.

5:18 We know that every one (root) having been born (passive) out of God is not sinning (PI), but the one having been born (passive) out of God is keeping (PI) himself, and the evil one is not touching (PI) him.

5:19 We know that we are being (PI) of God, and the whole world is lying (PI) in the evil one.

5:20 But we know that the Son of God is being here (PI), and has given to us an understanding, that we may continuously know the true One, and we are being (PI) in the true One, in His Son Jesus Christ. This One is being (PI) the true God, and eternal life.

5:21 Little Children, keep yourselves from that of idols. Amen.

Introduction To 2 John

It is interesting that John's epistles were probably the last letters written by one of the original Apostles. The other Epistles were written before 70 AD, and it is estimated that 2 John was written in the early 90's.

It is important to keep in mind that those to whom John was writing were Christians. It is clear that John knows that they had been taught the precepts of Jesus Christ (which were to forgive so they would be forgiven). He reminds them of those teachings without here repeating them. Rather than re-teaching them what they had previously been taught, he admonishes them to adhere to those truths with which they were already familiar.

We also know what those teachings are from other parts of the New Testament. Jesus came to save us from our sins. This salvation has two parts. First, there is the one-time event when we made Jesus our Lord. As a part of this, we will then go to heaven when we die. Then second, there is the ongoing process of the forgiveness of our sins, which continues for the rest of our lives. The centerpiece of this transformation is to forgive so we will be forgiven of our sins.

This is the process of "sanctification," which is the process by which we are transformed into the image of Jesus. Then, to the degree that we are like Jesus, we will effortlessly act like Him. And Jesus always behaved in a holy way, never transgressing the laws of God. The laws of God, which are the way the spiritual realm works, never have changed and never will change.

Therefore, clearly, in 2 John, the Apostle is not commanding us to behave properly. He is speaking of the teaching of Jesus about how we can be transformed into His image. The readers were to live their lives by these precepts (Verse 1:6).

It is evident that there were people coming to the church teaching something different. John calls them deceivers, and warns the believers not to participate in those teachings. See Verses 1:10-1:11.

1:1 The elder, to the chosen lady and her children, whom I am loving (PI) in truth; and not I only, but also all the ones having known the truth;
1:2 Through the truth, continuously remaining in us, and it will be with us into eternity:
1:3 Grace, mercy, and peace will be with you all, from God the Father, and from the Lord Jesus Christ, the Son of the Father, in truth and love.
1:4 I rejoice greatly that I have found out your children continuously living their lives in truth, even as we received the precept from the Father.
1:5 Now I am begging (PI) you, dear lady, not as continuously writing to you a new precept, but which we had from the beginning, that we may continuously love one another.
1:6 And this is being (PI) love, that we may continuously live our lives, according to His precepts. This is being (PI) the precept, even as you heard from the beginning, that you may continuously live your life in it.
1:7 That many deceivers have gone out into the world, the ones not continuously confessing Jesus Christ continuously coming in the flesh. This is being (PI) the deceiver and the Antichrist.
1:8 You all continuously look to yourselves, that we may not destroy which we have worked, but that we may receive a full reward.
1:9 Every one continuously transgressing and not continuously remaining in the teaching of Christ, is not having (PI) God. The one continuously remaining in the teaching of Christ, this one is having (PI) the Father and the Son.
1:10 If anyone is coming (PI) to you all, and is not bringing (PI) this teaching, don't continuously receive him into your house, and continuously rejoice, do not continuously speak to him,
1:11 for the one continuously saying to him to continuously be rejoicing is participating (PI) to his evil works.
1:12 Continuously having many things to continuously write to you all, I don't want to through paper and ink, but I am hoping (PI) to come to you all, and to speak face to face, that our joy may continuously

be having been filled (passive).

1:13 The children of your chosen sister are greeting (PI) you. Amen.

Introduction to 3 John

In this epistle John does refer to the evidence of a person having been transformed into the image of Jesus in Verses 1:2-1:4. John knows full well that no one can continuously live their life in truth unless they have Jesus as a "good root" in them. Verse 1:11 also refers to this. Otherwise, the focus of this epistle is primarily on a problem that particular church is having with a man named Diotrephes. This problem is probably the major reason why John wrote to them.

1:1 The elder to Gaius the beloved, whom I am loving (PI) in truth.

1:2 Beloved, I am desiring earnestly (PI) you to continuously be prospered (passive) of all and to continuously be healthy, even as your soul is being prospered (PI) (passive).

1:3 For I was rejoiced greatly, of the continuously coming of brothers and continuously testifying of your truth, even as you are living your life (PI) in truth.

1:4 I am having (PI) no greater joy than this, that I may continuously hear my children continuously living their lives in truth.

1:5 Beloved, you are doing (PI) a faithful work which you may accomplish into the brothers and into the strangers,

1:6 who testified of your love in the presence of the assembly, whom you will do well sending them forward on their journey worthily of God,

1:7 for the sake of His Name they went out, continuously taking nothing from the Gentiles.

1:8 We therefore are needing (PI) to continuously receive such, that we may continuously be fellow workers to the truth.

1:9 I wrote to the assembly, but Diotrephes, the one continuously being fond of being first of them, is not receiving (PI) us.

1:10 Because of this, if I may come, I will remind him of the deeds which he is doing (PI), continuously falsely accusing us to wicked words. And continuously not being satisfied (passive) on these things, neither is he himself receiving (PI) the brothers, and the ones continuously willing, he is forbidding (PI) and throwing out (PI) of the assembly.

1:11 Beloved, don't continuously follow as an example the evil, but the good. The one continuously doing good is being (PI)out of God. But the one continuously doing evil hasn't seen God.

1:12 Demetrius has been witnessed (passive) by all, and by the truth itself; but we also are testifying (PI), and you all know that our testimony is being (PI) true.

1:13 I had many things to continuously write, but I am not being willing (PI) to write to you through ink and pen;

1:14 but I am hoping (PI) to see you soon, and we will speak face to face. Peace be to you. The friends are greeting (PI) you. Continuously greet the friends by name.

Introduction to Jude

The author is Jude, who says he is a brother of James. It is not totally clear which James, but there seems to be agreement that this James is a half-brother of Jesus. This would also make Jude to be a half-brother of Jesus.

There is not very much in this letter regarding sanctification. It is primarily warning the target church to watch out for devious people.

"But this letter is not a systematic setting forth of the faith or some aspect of the faith. Rather, he is calling his readers to consider what follows when people who profess to be followers of Christ deny the faith in teaching and in life. He is taking action in a situation where people with membership in the Christian church live such evil lives that they could be called godless and it could be said of them they 'deny Jesus Christ.'" (Carson, Moo, Morris, page 463).

1:1 Jude, a servant of Jesus Christ, yet brother of James, to the ones in God the Father, having been sanctified (passive) and called, having been kept (passive) to Jesus Christ:

1:2 Mercy to you all and peace and love may be multiplied (passive).

1:3 Beloved, I am continuously giving diligence to continually write to you all about our common salvation, I was constrained to write to you all, continuously exhorting you to continuously contend earnestly to the faith once being delivered (passive) to the saints.

1:4 For some men crept in secretly, those having been written (about) (passive) long ago into this condemnation: ungodly men, continuously turning the grace of our God into indecency, and continuously denying the only Master, God, and Lord of us, Jesus Christ.

1:5 But I am desiring (PI) to remind you all, though you all already having known this, that the Lord, saving a people out of the land of Egypt, again destroyed the ones not believing.

1:6 And angels not keeping their first domain, but deserting their own dwelling place, He has kept in everlasting bonds under darkness into the judgment of the great day.

1:7 As Sodom and Gomorrah, and the cities around them, having in the same way prostituting and coming after strange flesh, are lying before us (PI) as an example, continuously suffering the punishment of eternal fire.

1:8 Indeed, in the same way, these also continuously having vain and empty opinions indeed continuously defiling the flesh, but they are continuously rejecting the lordship (of Christ) but are continuously blaspheming glories.

1:9 But Michael, the archangel, when continuously contending to the devil and argued about the body of Moses, dared not to bring against him an abusive judgment, but said, "May the Lord rebuke you!"

1:10 But these indeed are speaking blasphemy (PI) of whatever things they don't know. But whatever they are understanding (PI) naturally, like the creatures without reason, they are being destroyed (PI) (passive) in these things.

1:11 Woe to them! That they took themselves to the way of Cain, and they were poured out (passive) to the error of the reward of Balaam and to the reproach of Korah's rebellion they perished.

1:12 These are being (PI) hidden rocky reefs in your love feasts continuously feasting with you all, continuously shepherding themselves without fear; clouds without water, continuously being carried along (passive) by winds; autumn trees without fruit, twice dying, being plucked up by the roots (passive);

1:13 wild waves of the sea, continuously foaming out their own shame; wandering stars, to whom the blackness of darkness has been reserved (passive) into forever.

1:14 But to these also Enoch, the seventh from Adam, prophesied, continuously saying, "Behold, the Lord came in ten thousands of His holy ones,

1:15 to execute judgment of all, and to convict fully all the ungodly concerning all their works of ungodliness which they have done in an ungodly way, and concerning all the hard things which ungodly sinners have spoken against Him."

1:16 These are being (PI) murmurers, complainers, continuously walking after their lusts, and their mouth speaking (PI) boastful things, continuously showing respect of persons for the sake of advantage.

1:17 But you all, beloved, be reminded (passive) of the words having been spoken before (passive) by the apostles of our Lord Jesus Christ.

1:18 They said to you all that "In the last time there will be mockers, continuously walking according to the ungodly lusts of themselves."

1:19 These are being (PI) the soulish ones continuously separating themselves, not continuously having the Spirit.

1:20 But you all, beloved, continuously building up yourselves to your most holy faith, continuously praying in the Holy Spirit.

1:21 Keep yourselves in the love of God, continuously looking for the mercy of our Lord Jesus Christ into eternal life.

1:22 And indeed continuously show compassion, to the ones continuously separating themselves,

1:23 But some continuously save, continuously snatching them out of the fire in fear, continuously hating even the clothing having been stained (passive) from the flesh.

1:24 But to the One continuously being able to keep you all from stumbling, and to present you faultless in the presence of His glory in great joy,

1:25 to our only wise God our Savior, glory and majesty, dominion and power, and now and into all the ages. Amen.

Bultmann, Rudolf (1955). <u>Theology of the New Testament, Parts I-II</u>. New York, NY: Charles Scribner's Sons.

Carson, D.A., Moo, Douglas J., and Morris, Leon (1992). <u>An Introduction To The New Testament.</u> Grand Rapids, MI. Zondervan.

Zodhiates, Spiros, ThD. (1992). <u>The Complete Wordstudy Dictionary, New Testament.</u> Chattanooga, TN: AMG Publishers.

Added Resources

If you would like to read my full literal translation, along with commentary that gives details about especially important verses, you can find that in my book, **"Transformation In The Epistles."**

In addition, I have written several other books that address aspects of how we can be set free by Jesus.

I Will Give You Rest. This gives detailed instructions on how to have Jesus take away your sins.

Workbook for I Will Give You Rest. This Workbook is designed to parallel the book itself to help you actually apply it to your life.

Exceedingly Great & Precious Promises. This answers the question of why the very center of Christianity is missing. Here I list the 190 verses in the Epistles that discuss the ongoing process of salvation.

The Mystery Which Has Been Hidden. This is a primer to "I Will Give You Rest." It is much shorter and is meant to open peoples' eyes to the necessity of the ongoing process of salvation.

You Can Read The Greek. The way that Greek is normally taught creates an impossible barrier for most people to read the Greek. There is a very easy way to be able to read it. It is how I do it.

The Whole Truth Will Set You Free. This includes 137 key verses that are typically mis-translated, and which can thus lead you astray. Those key verses are copied from "Transformation In The Epistles," which includes my literal translation of all the Epistles.

Ways To Buy Books:

Online:www.divinelydesigned.com or Amazon.com.

You may email me with any questions or comments you may have regarding this book, or any of my books. My email address is: edkurath@divinelydesigned.com.

www.ingramcontent.com/pod-product-compliance
Lightning Source LLC
Chambersburg PA
CBHW060741050426
42449CB00008B/1281